Sub Chaser

The Story of A Navy VP NFO

A chronicle of the development of anti-submarine techniques by U.S. Naval Aviation Patrol planes in the Atlantic Ocean and Mediterranean Sea, during the Cold War era 1962-1985

Edward M. Brittingham
Captain, U.S. Navy, Retired

ASW Press

ASW Press
Sub Chaser
Copyright © 2008 by Captain Edward M. Brittingham

For further information, contact the author at:

ASW Press
2956 Hathaway Road
Unit 1109
Richmond, VA 23225
804-560-3306
E-mail: captemb@peoplepc.com

Book design by:

ARBOR BOOKS, INC.
19 Spear Road, Suite 301
Ramsey, NJ 07446
www.arborbooks.com

Printed in Canada

Captain Edward M. Brittingham
Sub Chaser

1. Author   2. Title   3. Military   4. Memoir
Library of Congress Control Number: 2003116595
ISBN 10: 0-9727859-2-2
ISBN 13: 978-0-9727859-2-1

TABLE OF CONTENTS

ACKNOWLEDGMENTS

I want to thank Don McKissock, Jim Hagy, and Jim Radigan for their friendship, participation and words of encouragement.

DEDICATION

This book is dedicated to my children, Beth, Anne, and Mike, Jr. Many days and months while I was away protecting our country and occasionally venturing into harms way, you had waited anxiously for me to come home.

As many military offspring do, you were privileged to spend some time in foreign countries. You seemed to enjoy Naples, Italy, Italian culture and language. You have given me great delight and satisfaction in being your father.

PROLOGUE

Submarine technology has been growing since World War II. New steel and, above all, titanium helped put the conventional sub at its peak in the early fifties. The thoughts of many Admirals of both fleets were on building nuclear submarines. The nuclear submarine had yet to be designed and perfected by physicists who were working on this project.

The first efforts to develop a submarine nuclear power plant were made at the Naval Research Laboratory in Washington, D.C. under the direction of Ross Gunn. Beginning in late spring of 1939, Gunn submitted a report which noted that such a power plant did not require oxygen to operate. This provided an excellent military opportunity that would vastly increase the military range and effectiveness of a submarine. All work on nuclear propulsion was stopped, however, as work in this field was directed toward the atomic bomb development. After the war, Gunn and Philip Abelson of the Carnegie Institute resumed work on nuclear power, resulting in a report in the Spring of 1946 calling for a nuclear submarine. The US Navy did not take action in this regard until Captain Hyman G. Rickover was appointed to lead the Navy in a nuclear project at the Oak Ridge, Tennessee research facility. He was an advocate for this type of submarine propulsion. Subsequently, a land-based prototype power plant was constructed, followed by installation of a duplicate plant in the USS Nautilus, the first nuclear submarine.

In 1954, the Navy commissioned the Nautilus. The Nautilus was launched on January 17, 1955, thereafter breaking all records for underwater speed and endurance. In 1958 the Nautilus was the first submarine to sail under the ice at the North Pole. In the late 1950's, the Navy brought into being the first modern ballistic missile submarine. Each submarine of this class carried sixteen missiles in the hull aft of the sail. These missiles carried nuclear weapons that could hit targets up to twelve hundred miles away.

Submarines are ships that can travel underwater. Submarines are adapted for use in war—that is to attack enemy ships or to fire missiles at enemy countries. These submarines vary in length from two hundred feet to more than five hundred feet with about one hundred fifty crewmembers aboard.

In war, a submarine usually attacks from beneath the ocean surface. Conventional types can not stay submerged for long periods and must surface for air for their engines. Conventional submarines are open to attack when they are on the surface or snorkeling. The last conventional U.S. submarine was built in 1959! Today, nuclear submarines can stay underwater for months at a time. Nuclear engines do not need oxygen to operate, and can actually produce oxygen.

A submarine's long cigar-shaped body enables it to move quietly. A pressure hull, made of high tempered steel, or titanium surrounds the ship and keeps it from being crushed by the water pressure. American submarines do not have a second hull.

A tall thin structure called the Sail rises from the middle of the submarine deck. The sail is about twenty feet high and has periscope, radar, and radio antennas. The upper part of the sail acts as a bridge from which the Captain directs the submarine when on the surface. Steel fins are called diving planes that guide the ship to different depths. One or two propellers drive the craft and rudders mounted above and below the propellers steer the boat.

The nuclear submarine engine consists of a nuclear reactor and a steam generator. The reactor uses uranium for fuel and splits uranium atoms in a controlled process called fission.

Pipes carry water from the generator to the reactor, where water is maintained at six hundred degrees fahrenheit or 316 degrees Celsius. This water does not boil. Instead it returns to the steam generator and boils an unpressurized water that turns to steam. This steam spins large turbines, producing power to run the ship.

The USSR maintains the largest and newest submarine fleet in the post World War II era. Their fleet reached a maximum strength of almost five hundred diesel—electric submarines in the early 1960's. The first Soviet nuclear submarines, designated November Class, were completed in 1959 or 1960. These submarines were three hundred sixty feet long and displaced about thirty-five hundred tons of water. November-class submarines run at a speed of twenty-five knots and a submerged speed of twenty-five to thirty knots. Some later and more sophisticated November-class subs were running above thirty knots.

During the 1960's, the Soviets produced large numbers of diesel—electric submarines for specific missions: attack torpedo-armed subs to attack surface ships and other submarines; cruise missile armed submarines to attack enemy surface warships, especially aircraft carriers; and ballistic missile subs armed with long range missiles. By 1971, both the U.S. and Soviet navies had built some ninety nuclear powered undersea craft. The rate of production of the U.S. was just over four nuclear ships per year and twelve to fourteen per year for the Soviet Union (Soviet production of two new classes of nuclear submarines of exceptional size and performance was reported in late 1970).

On the eve of World War II, the US Navy needed a land-based patrol bomber with more range, more armament, higher altitude, and associated characteristics which Lockheed had yet to produce. The first design of the PV-2 Harpoon was stopped and started again with the Neptune prototype being a good performer. Despite receiving orders for more aircraft, these were reduced pending the end of World War II. Lockheed had taken over the lead in more effective patrol aircraft in 1946. Many variations of P-2V aircraft had been developed with add-on equipment variations. The APS-20 radar was installed in a ventral radome in P-2V that was a prototype for an anti-submarine version. The P2V-5 installed a Magnetic Anomaly Detection (MAD) that added a "stinger" extension to the tail. In 1953, Lockheed deviced a power boosting of two Westinghouse J-34 turbojets in wing pods that aided take-off and increased combat speed. The SP-2E, as it was called, finally was outfitted to carry the AQA-3 Jezebel long-range acoustic search and the Julie Explosive echo-sounding recorder.

Quite remarkably, the turboprop engines of the Electra airliner, an excellent ASW aircraft, initially experienced structural and power plant difficulties in 1956 and 1957. Despite being rendered unfit for flight by many of the passengers, it remained in production for four years. Lockheed's technical experts solved the problems, and the Navy found that the Orion was superior for long loitering capability at higher cruising speeds.

The P-3A, also known as the P3V-1 prior to September 1962, was equipped with four 4500 shaft horsepower Allison T-56-A-10's. P-3A was equipped with new gear, such as the dual AN/APS80, the MAD gear, AN/ASQ-10 and the AN/ASN-13 sniffer that had caught a Foxtrot snorkeling east of Cuba. The device called the "sniffer" picked up this submarine and VP-56 did not have anything else functioning in late 1962! The acoustic signal generator was an advancement in this field. The AN/AQA-3 or AQA-4 "Jezebel" put an operator in charge of this system that monitored four traces in very limited modes. The Delayed Time Compression (Deltic) was a major factor in having the P-3A installed on the 110th Orion the AN/AQA-5 system. Another advancement was the installing of the fuselage-mounted APU (Auxiliary Power Unit) forward on the right side of the aircraft just forward of the weapons bay.

Beginning with the 158th Orion, the Lockheed Company began turning out P-3B aircraft. This aircraft corrected all the flaws and made improvement to its engines. The Deltic equipment installed along with a new AN/AQH-1 tape recorder to soothe inflight and post flight acoustic analysis. Much later, the P-3B was modified to carry the Bullpup missile.

The P-3C was next that included the airframe and the powerplant of this P-3B. The P-3C was built intermingled with the P-3B and was first flown on September 18, 1968, designated as the P-3C, 153443. Eventually it was called the A-Nav integrated ASW with the AN/ASQ-114 computer system. Along with many new systems, the AN/AQA-7 system provided DIFAR—(Directional Low Frequency Analysis and Recording) a passive system display and processing. This was the finest airplane made, once the "bugs" were removed.

So the scene is set, 1962, when I am about to start preflight training at US Naval Station Pensacola, Florida. All events during the years of 1962 through 1979 are accurate. The effort of a Naval Aviation Officer in his struggle to become a Naval Flight Officer and to excel in submarine hunting will one day mean accepting command of a VP squadron.

The New Encyclopedia Americana, 1991, by Grolier
The New Encyclopedia Britannica, 1987, Robert P. Gwin, Chicago
The World Book Encyclopedia, 1966 Edition, Chicago.

CHAPTER 1

INTRODUCTION

Why?

My career in the United States Navy has left me with an indelible impression of pride, honor, and a sense of camaraderie that I had the honor of serving in the best Navy this world has ever seen. Since World War II, the Navy has taken over ship building, construction of aircraft carriers and numerous aircraft based on threats to the national security. On the other hand, my motives in joining this expanding organization were somewhat more personal. I had previously joined the United States Air Force ROTC to keep me in good graces with the draft board in college, and during my third year of college, 1957, I was taking two ROTC courses. Also, I had just successfully passed the pilots test. When I impetuously turned my uniform in because the Colonel wanted me to sign active duty enlistment papers immediately rather that wait until the school year ended. I then completed my college work as a non-ROTC student and graduated from the University of Virginia in 1959 unfortunately I was then classified "1-A."

As I think back over the years, I can remember having seen military planes flying around. I had been impressed by a Navy brochure feature write up of the Navy Pilot and Navy Aviation Observer (NAO) programs. The NAO program was divided into five categories; Radar Interceptor Officer, Bombardier-Navigator, Electronic Warfare Officer, Tactical Coordinator, and Navigator. Unsure of my piloting skills, I focused on the opportunities of the NAO program. I had observed that of the two choices of being on the ground, the Tactical Coordinator and the Electronic Warfare Officer Program insufficient for my taste. Let's face it, I wanted excitement and adventure and, therefore, wanted to be flying. If my civilian life plans changed abruptly by a call from my draft board therefore, decided that I would prefer to spend my three and a half years as a Tactical Coordinator chasing submarines.

The Naval Aviation Observer Program was created because the Navy needed more officers to meet its expanding antisubmarine surveillance needs. With the advent of the A-3, F-4 Phantom, A-6 Intruder and specialized antisubmarine other aircraft, the demand for officers was tremendous. Without the NAO Program, non-flying officers would have been required to fill the seats in the antisubmarine aircraft. The Lockheed SP-2E was the first aircraft to be staffed with a NAO Program member trained in antisubmarine warfare. This person was a Navigator specifically instructed to take over the duties of Tactical Coordinator. The NAO personnel were assigned to staff the VP, heavier than air patrol, when all of the operational dirigibles (airships) were phased out in 1961 and 1962. The first NAO to reach any patrol squadron was in 1961 which kicked the third pilots up to the cockpit while the NAO was to take over the two seats behind the pilot in the SP-2E/H aircraft.

The need of the force was being strengthened by the expanded antisubmarine coverage promised during the early 1960's. The patrol aviation community was in a state of frenzy as it built up to meet the threat of Russia in the Cold War. More bases were opened up and different types of equipment were being deployed to cover all avenues of vulnerability that the aggressor might pursue. The Russian four engine turboprop Bear aircraft was designed to sneak up on United States carriers. The elements of a battle group could be completely overwhelmed if the Bear aircraft caught the Carrier Battle Group off guard as it buzzed the carrier at 300 feet! When John F. Kennedy was elected president, my date and I attended his inauguration. He later discussed with the Pentagon that the Navy's antisubmarine forces keep track of the Soviet submarines which were being deployed in all parts of the Atlantic and Pacific Oceans.

How?

In February 1962, I was at the Geological Survey. I was working on my Master's degree. I had decided to finish the geological survey of the Shenandoah Valley around Staunton, Virginia. I had plotted the stream where I would take samples of the water. I had laid out twenty sites where I would get the acid nonacid status of the stream.

In May 1962, I had gone to the stream and made final preparations for the water samples. It took quite a while to go from one site to another. One place was with a herd of cows and another in quite a treacherous spot. Finally, after a day and half of sampling, I was finished. I must say that home looked most inviting compared to what I had been through in the prior days.

The following day I took the samples to the lab; they promised me that I would have all the data within one week. Excellent timing, I thought! Over the next two days I was busy writing my thesis. The lab work would make or break my hypothesis. About eleven o'clock that morning, a call came in for me. I picked up the phone and it said, "Is this Edward Michael Brittingham?" Yes, I replied. "This is the draft board in Fairfax, Virginia. Are you still in a 1 A category?" I was shocked. How in the world did the draft board reach me at the US Geological Survey? I stated that I was 1 A. They responded they were going to give me thirty days to report for active duty as an Army recruit!

That night I went home for supper. I told Mom and Dad about my phone call and asked for their advice about what I should do about the situation. I always loved my folks and they listened and agreed with the conclusions that I had previously arrived at. The next day the lab was on the line to tell me the water samples would not be ready until September! That confirmed in my mind that it was now time to make an appointment at the Navy induction center.

Andrews Air Force Base was a scenic spot. The President's plane was near the hangar and the US Navy Detachment was on the other side of the field. It was 8:00 a.m. when I saw the Navy Chief Petty Officer who knew I was coming. He shook my hand and sat while he gave me instructions on how to complete the test that I was about to take. The Pilot Naval Aviation Observer test was the one that all college graduates take. It took me about one and half hours to finish the test. The Chief graded the test and announced that my score put me in the twilight zone of being a piss poor pilot or a superb Naval Aviation Observer. I thought about it for a moment, but dam; what the hell, three and half years after first considering it, I would become a Naval Aviation Observer. The next hurdle was the doctor's exam. They scheduled me for 8:00 a.m. the following Tuesday.

The doctor's examination was a real sight. All thirty or more recruits lined up and started the long process of the examination. I was on the right and off my shirt came. After giving urine, blood, an eye exam, ear, nose, and throat exam, I was on the left side of the examining room. After freeing myself of all my physical inhibitions, I waited for the doctor's exam.

It took about two hours to get all the men ready to see the doctor. Finally the orderly said to strip, yes go "buck naked," and so be it! The doctors began inspecting the patients en mass. I cannot believe how many men they were examining but it must have been thirty or more! Each doctor checked specific parts of the front of every man. About forty five minutes later, they started on the back of each individual. The rectal exam won the prize! Finally all the men, or so they said, passed the close your eyes one-leg only stand, the final ancient dance of the candidates!

On the 26th of May, 1962, I became inducted in the US Navy. I was supposed to begin Preflight in one month. I asked if I could go to Preflight in September because I have a summer job. I told them that I promised Dad that I would work in the summer for Coca Cola. Both the Officer and the Petty Officer concurred that they would approve this. Two days later I was excited to hear that my Preflight date was September 1962. I would receive my orders in September with my tickets via Delta Airlines to Pensacola, Florida.

CHAPTER 2

TRAINING

Aviation Officer Candidate School

One day in September 1962, I climbed aboard Delta Airlines destined for Pensacola. The plane left after supper and we were full according to the lovely stewardess who kept eyeing me. We landed at Pensacola where I met three friends heading for preflight class.

On Florida's Gulf Coast, just South of the Alabama line, lies the strategically situated and large harbor of Pensacola. This is "The Cradle of Naval Aviation," where the country's first Naval Air Station was established. Comprising 4,218 acres, the site picked has a colorful historical background dating to the 16th Century. In 1910, the first Naval Officers were ordered to learn to fly under the instruction of the Wright Brothers and Mr. Glenn Curtiss.

We got a taxi and spent the night in a beautiful downtown hotel. We had about twelve more hours until we had to report to NAS Pensacola. We spent the time cruising the old town and seeing as many sights that a boy shouldn't see as possible. Well, it was time to check into the arduous place known as "sixteen weeks before becoming an Ensign." Familiar to all flight students reporting for duty was the impressive main gate manned by sentries 24 hours a day at the Naval Air Station Pensacola. The sentries were always alert in keeping the security of the station. We stopped the taxi and we showed our papers to receive directions to the appropriate Preflight Building where we would be put up.

The U.S. Naval School, Pre-Flight is the first step for Aviation Cadets who set out to win their Navy Wings of Gold and a commission

in the Navy or the Marine Corps. In addition, Pre-Flight gives an introduction to aeronautics and related subjects on the way to getting your
wings.

The mission of Pre-Flight is two-fold. First, it serves as an officer
candidate school for the aviation cadets to get them ready for duties as
Officers. It also provides flight students with a thorough mental and
physical background that they will need before flight.

Pre-flight training is divided into three departments—Academic,
Physical Fitness, Survival and Military. The Academic department
provides classroom instruction in aeronautics and Naval subjects.
These subjects include Naval orientation, aerodynamics, study skills,
leadership, engineering, aviation science, and navigation. In addition
to classroom time, work shops and visual aids are also utilized as
learning tools.

In the Physical Fitness Survival program the development of mus-
cular coordination and survival at sea are critical. They are staffed
with trained athletic instructors to develop keen minds and agile bodies that are must's for the aviator.

The Military department is concerned with the administration,
discipline, and military proficiency of each Aviation Cadet. Under the
regimented officers, one learns the manual of arms, sword handling,
and many other techniques before receiving a commission. After sixteen weeks of training, you are ready to proceed in the next step of the
challenge toward the Navy Wings of Gold.

What the handout book said about Preflight training is true, but
what they did not say, will fill volumes. The next morning we were
awakened at 5:00 a.m. sharp, lined up and marched down to the airplanes on the dock. Calisthenics, here they come, so enjoy it. After
spending all summer long selling as many as 350 cases per day of
Coca-Cola, I was sore and needed about a week of unraveling before
I could work out with ease. The challenge encountered is to enter the
mess hall. Standing fully erect, I announce, "Aviation Officer
Candidate Brittingham," orally the quotation should be fortissimo, but
if it was not, you had to go back to the end of the line. After breakfast
we went back and were assigned rooms on the second deck. Then we
marched with the group over to get our clothes. We tried on all types
of clothing that you need to complete your uniform. The next step was
the thirty-second-to-baldness haircut.

Over the next three days we were involved in testing and marching drills. It was during this phase that the doctors would find those not medically able to be in preflight. After ten days you ended up with about forty individuals that would continue with their training. Initially over seventy people had started out and the DOR's (Drop on Request) would be sent home.

Gunnery Sergeant Brennan was the first person to meet us after breakfast on Monday morning in front of Building 633. His oration consisted of how we would have to work to be the best Aviation Officer Class. The Sergeant was 5'2," 125 pounds wringing wet and did push-ups better than any clown who was looking to be the best of the show.

The routine was go to class, exercise, and do it again cause it felt so good. The first class we had was mathematics using a slide rule for the course. History class outlined the Naval aviation since the beginning through present day. This course demanded a great deal of concentrated interest or one may fall asleep. The real problem here was the obstacle course. Each AOC had to run upstairs, peel off his clothes and redress in shorts, tee shirts, sneakers in ten minutes. The obstacle course was about fifteen minutes down the road. This required running five minutes at a time, huffing and puffing when we got there. The course itself was something else. We would start out by twos every ten seconds and proceed through the obstacles. There is one such criterion that my legs refused to go over, in fact many AOC's had trouble getting over this section. The courses lead you to a rope that you needed to walk up a twenty foot wall, step over and down to complete. I flunked the test and was scheduled for remedial training at the obstacle course.

The next physical threat involved the swimming pool. We went in naked and heard a lecture about sharks. Afterwards, we went upstairs, approximately 25 feet, and jumped in. We then moved on to the high diving board and four basic types of swimming. Underwater swimming shows how Navy sailors escape the flames in order to survive. The most interesting aspect of the swimming involved the swimmer blowing air into his shirt and pants that helped him to survive over longer periods of time. Each AOC had to take turns towing an unconscious swimmer using a life jacket. The final test was the Dilbert Dunker. This device permits a single engine fighter to crash in the

ocean. Your objective is to get out. Each man is strapped in with helmet, life jacket, and the straps necessary for flying. The Dilbert
Dunker goes down 45 degrees into the water and flips over. The man
in the cockpit has to unstrap himself, dive down to escape from the
cockpit. This, without a doubt, was an exacerbating experience.

About seven weeks into preflight, I had gotten to know all of my
compadres. John Dougherty was from Arkansas and really talked
about hogs! One weekend we messed around drinking beer at the special club for us and attended church on Sunday. Sunday night was
shower time and time for a hog calling contest. At last back in the
room where I took off my robe, nothing underneath, and there stood
the Preflight Officer of the Day. I called Attention and the Duty
Officer was laughing. He asked my name and for me to quiet down.
When he left, I broke out laughing and soon Dougherty was stopped.
He lived next door and he put his head over the seven foot barrier and
we laughed about the hogs. The next morning after breakfast we
cleaned up our rooms for inspection that we passed. Our next task for
the day was marching with a rifle. All of a sudden, the loudspeaker
was on "Brittingham and Dougherty get down to the Sergeant's office
ASAP." I thought, "Why me?" We ran down the passage way to the
Sergeant's door. I knocked first by hitting the door. The Sergeant
replied, "I cannot hear you!" I tried again and was admitted. "Aviation
Officer Candidate Brittingham reporting as ordered, Sir." Then AOC
Dougherty had his turn. At least two tries, he finally let Dougherty in.
Sgt. Brennan said that he had been informed that we were having a
hog call last night. Was this true? "Yes sir," I responded with fortissimo. He asked what kinds of calls do I do. I went through all the calls
from the rooster to the Caribbean Isle. I must admit I was having fun
as the other two Sergeants were laughing. Dougherty chimed in and
gave his rendition of hog calling and that broke up the group. Brennan
excused us and we went running up the stairs, greeted by cheers from
Class 38. They had all been listening. The walk back to the room was
exhilarating, pats on the back and a lot of hand shaking. The alert was
out on the loudspeaker, so we got our rifles and fell in ranks downstairs. Sergeant Brennan started marching and called for Dougherty to
call the pigs and me to call the roosters. I knew I was going to make
it through preflight.

The final week of preflight was to spot check your skills in all
respects. The second I heard my name I ambled up, saluted, and

picked up my papers. The next stop was Officers' School over at the hanger next to the airfield at NAS Pensacola.

Naval Aviation Officer's School Pensacola became the site of the Navy's latest innovation in aviation officer training school. On July 1, 1960, it accepted its first twenty-two officers and thus became the Naval Aviation Officers to join the fleet.

During the eight week period, the officer-students follow a very specific curriculum, such as: aviation electronics, combat information centers, air intelligence, communications, Navy leadership, jet engines, meteorology, navigation, special weapons and Naval Aviation indoctrination. During the flight phase, we fly in five different types of aircraft: T-34, T-28, TC-45, S2F, and the T2V.

The future NAO's took over as we started our eight week course. We had our share of academics but we were to fly approximately twenty flight hours this period. The first course was aviation electronics, navigation, and flight procedures. The afternoon classes brought us into code work and Morse code. It took a long time before I passed the test. The code and blinker test were easy. The Combat Information course was necessary to all NAO's. We had a recognition slide that contained an airplane that was different to recognize. The next time you saw the slides, they moved according to the speed as which they are set.

The flying familiarization was set up in the smallest airplanes. The airplane performed all of its stuff and when the pilot saw you were comfortable with the flight, you were given the opportunity to fly the airplane. The second fly in the T-28 aircraft was a flight to test your skills as a backseat navigator. I gave the heading to the pilot and we headed in the direction of point two. I recognized the turn point and gave the heading. The third point was a small turn and we made it on time and I gave the heading to the forth point. I recognized the tower about twenty miles ahead so I told the pilot to come five degrees to the starboard to miss the tower. The pilot gave a Bravo Zulu and asked for a heading and estimated time of approach at NAS Pensacola. I gave him the heading and ETA. The flight was very successful and he congratulated me for an excellent "Heads up" I gave him before we ran down the tower.

The only flight that really interested me was a T-1A flight. The T-1A was a training jet that was used at Pensacola. This jet was used in the Korean War. The idea of this flight was to navigate the flight and to make a low-land bombing run on the island. The preflight was good as I had all the information in my bag. We took off and the point to point navigation was fast but right on. The final point was the entry point to the island. The pilot made a dive and pulled up to release the bomb. A pretty site, but I wish I had seen the whole run.

After eight weeks of training, quizzes and flights I headed on to Corpus Christi, Texas to get my navigator wings.

Navigation School

This was the first time I had been to Texas. I got there about the second week of April 1963. I checked in and man they had a wait of six weeks. I flew a couple of flights and I went to a few classes with pilots.

The navigator course was a long and tedious course. This was the process of determining an aircrafts position and directing its' movement. Basic navigation tools included a chart and a compass. An aeronautical chart showed positions of airports and the height of mountains. It also displayed the location of radio transmitters that aid navigators. A nautical chart provided water depth, location of buoys and pertinent danger/warning areas which aircraft were not allowed to enter. The navigator used a magnetic or true compass. A chronometer, an extremely accurate timepiece, determined the speed.

There are four ways in which the plane can be navigated: dead reckoning, electronic navigation, celestial navigation, and satellite navigation. A navigator will become proficient in all depending on such factors as the weather. We were exposed to all types except celestial navigation (simply a method of determining the aircrafts' postion by observing certain celestial bodies). A publication called the Almanac was used which discussed the sun, moon, and all of the stars which may be used in celestial navigation. The navigator became familiar with the sextant and quickly identified the North or Pole Star. Next, he chose the sun in daytime or the stars at night. The individual then estimated an Assumed Position. Then he calculated the time for each star and shot each star. Finally, the following points solve the celestial position or triangle: (1) the Assumed Position, (2) North or South Star, and (3) the geographic position (GP) of the celestial body. The sextant was very interesting and it was a boon to shooting the stars and coming up with a three star celestial fix. Another thing was finding the stars to shoot and which were going to be in the same season as tonight.

Next came the logging of navigation: the times that the navigator should log in (by signing) and the necessary logs for dead reckoning, fixes, and estimated position. Can dead men vote twice at elections? You got it, those are the terms for Compass, Deviation, Magnetic, Variation, true heading, and add East variation that comes from true heading all the way over to compass heading.

The flights were staged so that each navigator had an opportunity to navigate on each flight. The airplanes that we flew in, I got into trouble on, were the T-29, that used to belong to the US Air Force. The third flight was a night flight and the TC 117 D that was an old airplane that is due to retire in June. It came time for me to navigate and I decided I would get a three shot fix. I completed the shot and plotted the shot, the shot did not look good and I went back to check it out and the pilot wanted a vector to Corpus Christi. I gave him a heading and the pilots assumed navigation. I knew I had done something to make what ever happened. The next afternoon I was debriefed and he asked me if I was upset during this flight. I told him I panicked and I could not find out what I had done wrong. He graded me down and said that I would start navigation on the next hop.

Two days later I was back together with myself. The hop was successful and so was the remaining flights. On July 2, 1963, we took off for a remain over night to McCoy Air Force Base in Florida. Just before we broke the ADIZ, we have to report when and at what time we would penetrate the ADIZ. The penetration was right on the money. The last flights were the final flights of the navigation syllabus. The graduation was impressive and the wings were mine. The orders for me were VP-10 Brunswick, Maine. The orders were for me to report to Norfolk, Virginia. There were twenty-one days of leave so I checked out at midnight and headed for home in Annandale, Virginia.

CHAPTER 3

PERSONAL

May 1962 turned out to be a busy month with many things happening chiefly a geological survey and completion of my Master's Degree at George Washington University. I worked part time at the Geological Survey at Arlington Towers, located across the Potomac River, President Abraham Lincoln sits looking up the Mall toward the Washington Monument in the distance. I have been working on various subjects during my part time tenure at the survey. Work began here on April 1960 and I have done several studies involving water wells in several areas in Virginia and North and South Carolina.

I was trying to get a Master's degree in geology. The subjects that I have taken were not what I have hoped to be. Finding oil was my major goal in life but that changed when I heard the depressingly low hiring rate of the master and doctoral candidates. This really woke me up to the fact that I have to do something to retain my career in geology.

In the winter of 1961, Dr. Barnes, an advisor that I was working part time for in the survey, told me of a geochemical evolution that was happening in Virginia. A stream near Staunton, Virginia was depositing calcium carbonates in the bottom of the stream. This factor must be occurring today that was probably the source of this rock (limestone) in the Shenandoah Valley. I am interested in this natural phenomena so I went with Dr. Barnes and three others to check out the area. Well, you guessed it, it started snowing and it was at least four inches when we got there. We camped there in the woods and took samples of the stream. Boy was it cold in the tent!

With some additional work in the survey, I read up on the massive limestone/ dolomite buildup since the Ordovician Period. The thought kept running through my head about the development of massive lime-stone deposits. I briefed Dr. Barnes and set up a system where I would investigate using the Library of Congress and discussing my topic with my sponsor at the George Washington University, Geology Department.

My parents and my sister, Merlyn, were going to Grandmother and Granddad's for Christmas in 1961. I decided that I would call Doug Carr. Doug was an old fraternity brother of mine, whom I had not heard from for two years. Doug was living with his parents. His father was the local judge in Dinwiddie, Virginia. Doug was glad to see me and he promised he would get me a blind date on December 29.

On the December 29, I arrived at Doug's house about 5:30 p.m. Doug sure looked good—red hair and a pot belly, typical Doug Carr. We had two cocktails and had dinner with his parents. They were super. The way they listened and knew when to laugh! I have Dad's '58 Chevrolet, which was a four door sedan with a radio and a bottle of Virginia Gentleman under the front seat!

We stopped and picked up a six pack of beer and we headed out to Blackstone, Virginia to pick up our dates. The jokes were coming out of Doug's mouth as fast as the beer left his lips! It started raining and then we were unfortunately out of beer. We arrived at Blackstone about half an hour before we picked up our dates. We had to urinate something fierce and Doug directed us to a restaurant. Doug and I make our stop at the men's room and Doug bought us a draft plus two six packs. This has the prospects of being a long evening.

The first date we picked up was Page. Page is Doug's fiancee and I had not seen her in quite a while. The next stop was my turn and I must admit, I was well on the way of getting drunk. I knocked on the door, only to respond, "Hi, Mike Brittingham," I said. Jane Ayers Spruill was her name. With the rain and all considered, she was a very attractive individual. As a matter of fiction and fact, she is well endowed. We walked out to the car and then we decided what plan of action we should take for the evening.

We planned to go to a party near Petersburg, so we headed in that direction. I got to know Jane by idle conversation. Eighteen miles later into the trip, "I had to piss like a race horse!" Doug laughed when I told him. So then I said, "Boys on the left and women on the right side of the road!" I stopped the car and opened the door to the cold rain and relived myself. Doug was behind me. We laughed about that until we reached the outskirts of Petersburg.

We stopped at a hillbilly restaurant and bought pizza. Jane helped me pay the bill as Page was hungry! We danced to the band and we had a good time laughing at all the studs at the bar. We left and arrived at the party about two hours later.

On the way home I sat in the back seat with Jane. We talked and we began to kiss. She had something special. She said she was engaged to an Army Helicopter Pilot who was stationed overseas in Germany from whom she had not heard. I told her to reconsider or perhaps to call the whole thing off. Frankly I did not know how to handle the situation; I was falling in love with her.

The next morning when I awoke, Doug handed me two Excedrin to relieve my aching head. We talked and laughed at our actions of last night. Doug wanted to know how I liked my blind date. I told him Jane was a sweet woman and I was definitely interested.

The days went along through the New Year and I could not stop thinking of Jane. I contacted Doug to find out that she had written a letter to her fiancee to send back the ring. I called Jane and told her that I wanted to see her. Two weeks later a cold February Friday night, Doug, Page, and Jane met me in Annandale for a weekend. I kissed Jane and I could not get over the feeling that she was the one!

Jane and I were engaged in August when I bought the ring. I had a month left before I went to Preflight Training and she worked in Richmond at Miller & Rhoades as a sales clerk. I used to ride down to Richmond to see her and her mother, Edna. Edna had moved from Blackstone, Virginia to a two bedroom apartment in Southside Richmond. The apartment complex was new and the renters of the apartments could join a nearby pool. This was nice as Jane and I went swimming several times.

We said good-bye with tears, knowing that Jane would start organizing our wedding and have it on December 29, 1962. We wrote many letters during the months of September through December. We discussed brides' maids, grooms, wedding arrangements and above all, flowers. Next the church was to be the Methodist Church in Blackstone with Rev. Richard Pullen and Rev. Charles Winfree administering. The reception afterwards was to be at Mr. and Mrs. John Koonce's house.

I arrived home on December 15 at Dulles airport. Mom, Dad, and Jane met me in my blue AOC uniform. We spent the whole time ironing out the plans that included ordering seven tuxedos, a blood test, and getting permission to marry Jane due to her age being under twenty-one. The dress rehearsal was a riot and, eventually, we managed to get it right. The after-rehearsal punch was spiked with Sprite and Virginia Gentlemen. The pictures revealed how happy we were and how Jane really mixed with her guests! We said good-bye and kissed for tomorrow, we would be married. Let the bachelor party begin! Jack Bartunek, Basil Delashmatt, Dick Stephenson, Donnie Koonce, Ben Eldridge, Frank Spruill, and John Koonce got me pleasantly bombed. The girl they fixed me up with almost did me in with her french kissing! The next morning three out of all the ushers were without shirts and cumberbunds. John made a call to Richmond so he and I could drive to pick up the paraphernalia. Incidently we drank two six packs on the trip.

Jane looked beautiful that night I married her. The reception brought all of our relatives to see us and many from Northern Virginia, where the weather had turned bad. We left at 10:30 p.m. headed for the Holiday Inn in Chapel Hill. The next day we drove to Georgia where we had dinner and spent the night in an adjoining motel. The next evening we spent the night with Uncle John and his wife Zelda. Uncle Mike, my Dad called him that, showed me around the Warner Robbins Air Force Base. Mike is really a good friend of mine. We celebrated the New Year together.

Jane was my teacher, my leader, and quizzed me when I had a test after I made Ensign. We went through NAO school with flying colors. We left after eight and a half weeks to find a house. The rent was $85 a month. Once again, she quizzed me and again, I passed my navigation syllabus and she was there when the Commanding Officer put on my Navigator Wings.

CHAPTER 4

FIRST OPERATIONAL TOUR

Fleet Airborne Electronics Training Unit, NAS Norfolk, Va

In August of 1963, I entered the Fleet Airborne Electronics Training Unit United States Atlantic Fleet at Naval Air Station, Norfolk, Virginia. The course was designed to teach antisubmarine training to all of its participants. The NAO's were grouped together and discovered whom to report to and what topics would be covered. The first lesson was a course in Jezebel. Jezebel in the Bible was a wicked wife of Ahab, or a shameless, immoral woman. Jezebel on the AQA-4 in the SP-2E aircraft is a recorder. It monitors the sounds coming from a sonobuoy transmitted to the receiver of the aircraft that is fed to the recorder. The operator can listen to these noises by selecting the channel sonobuoy that they are drawing on. The AQA-4 is something that is being drawn or written by the noise the gram picks up. There are four grams (four sonobuoys) it can monitor. The grams are full of background noise, sea state, plant life, and many other things like earthquakes that will make your whole day! Let's take, for example, a merchant ship with a three bladed propeller. It appears in the lower left of the gram and let's give a blade rate of 6.0 Hz for example. The blade rates are scribed every third shaft rate with a darker line. The formulas can be multiplied but let us take 2.0 as the shaft rate times 60 revolutions per minute equals 120 revolutions per minute that merchant is going.

This is the way Jezebel is put to use in solving the ASW problem. Through mathematics the engines, auxiliaries and the gears are worked out. That is called LOFAR, low frequency analysis and recording. We are making grams by the second. Every 15 minutes the operator must sync, synchronization of sound, and calibrate or to adjust the scale so that the four grams will be reading the same frequency from 10 to 200 hertz. CODAR, correlation, detection and recording, is to bring two sonobuoys in a true course and to bring into proper relationship with one another. With one CODAR plant the sound emanated can be fixed as long as the diameter and circumference correlate. The standard length of a CODAR plant is 350 feet. The CODAR scale is laid on the plant and points down the true course line. The Jezebel operator gives the bearings of the plants to the navigator. The rest of the targets particularly, the US submarines, NATO submarines, Russian submarines and other classics require at least a week of studying.

Another course that is taken with pilots is the Julie course. This pattern makes a passive buoy go active! The SSQ-23 sonobuoy is dropped with a charge and the charge explodes at 60 feet. This is a method of finding the range and direction of a submersible in the water by transmitting sounds underwater, timing its speed, measuring the direction of its speed. In the case of SSQ-23 (channel #2), it has a single echo 2000 yards about the buoy. The Julie operator measures this on the Julie recorder. Let us say that another Julie buoy is placed 090 at 4000 yards from this sonobuoy. This gives double echoes on #2 2100 and #3 2100 yards. We now have two fixes. The problem now is to solve which fix is inaccurate.

Another follow on to Julie is the Active Ranging Sonobuoy. The SSQ-15 is normally dropped at a Julie fix. The active ranging buoy can give you criteria to make an attack. The SSQ-15 is usually used in a 2000 yard circle. This technique is a usually viable tactic coupled with the magnetic anomaly detector. The AN/ASQ-8 magnetic recorder in the SP-2E is measuring the change produced by the sub in the earth's magnetic field, located in the aircraft's bow. The MAD is used in all low altitude localization of the aircraft. In daylight the aircraft is at 200 feet when the detection is good down to 800 feet below the water. At night the suggested altitude is 300 feet that may yield to 500 feet when the sea state and wave height are a factor.

The final course in FAETU was the ASA-16 course. This was well worth the time. The ASA-16 has been around a short while, but it really tells how good a Tactical Coordinator is about catching and killing submarines. After going through the system once, he broke the class up and they practiced on the ASA-16. Then we tried out the GTP-4 system and the Drift Compute function. We tried out all functions including the pilot control knob, navigator position, Julie station, and the MAD station. A final examination was given on the ASA-16, I killed the sub, so what is next?

VP-30 NAS Jacksonville, Florida

Before we left for Jacksonville, Florida, we made a call to the folks that we were expecting a baby. Jane said she was sure so we went to the doctor in Norfolk and she was right. We left for Jacksonville to find a place to live. I found a place that was a little steep, but I was willing to try it if we liked it. The second week brought morning sickness. I went to the base housing and got a three bedroom apartment until the third week in December.

The first four weeks of VP-30 was spent in ground school going over previous training. I went to the swimming pool to get my swimming done and I checked perfect. We learned about the particulars of the aircraft, the navigation dry swim, and a super system review.

Smokes, sound underwater signal [SUS], and sonobuoys are an exciting field. Julie is a time consuming smoke and SUS organization which can have you worn out in just two minutes. SP-2E NAO's are mean to the pilots and the ordnance men. They continually bomb the buoys and standby, smoke away, and mark on top!

Light is necessary at night so a MK 58 smoke will illuminate for forty five to fifty five minutes. The short smoke, MK 25, is used to designate the Julie sonobuoys which will keep the pilots stabilized for ten to twenty minutes before the smoke extinguishes. The bang that is provided with Julie is called the MK 64. It usually takes about four seconds if set for 60 feet and longer at the deep setting of eight hundred feet.

We started flying with the day and night navigator flights. The first flight was the morning flight and as it got dark we turned it into a night searchlight run. I met CDR Keith Sharer back at FAETU and he and I headed for VP-10. We fly all the flights and the planes, at least two of them, went down as we aborted two events with Alpha submarines. The two aborted flights ended in trainers where we fixed with CODAR and went into Julie to kill the sub.

The training received at VP-30 was good but I let several things bother me to no end. The disturbing part of VP-30's training was the inflight instructor. The whole purpose of providing an observer is he can teach you the mistakes you have lived with. One, two, or three flights the instructor was asleep and could not be interrupted. The First Class Petty Officer who flew with our crew deserves the credit which might cause nightmares with the Lieutenant instructor. I certainly would like VP-30 to schedule more Alpha sub times. The tactics, procedures and actual monitoring of the ASA-16 would be more beneficial that a weapon system trainer, by and large, I think I am ready for VP-10 and God willing, I am ready to do my best for the Navy.

CHAPTER 5

VP-10

VP-10—Deployment NAS Sigonella, Sicily

When darkness arrived at Sigonella, Sicily I landed by way of the VR 24 Detachment aircraft on the airstrip. It was dismal. Rains and scattered sleet made splashes on the tarmac.

The C 130 taxied up to the operations building and secured its engines. As I came off the airplane, a familiar VP 10 Duty Truck fixed in my eyes and the Duty Officer met me. We make introductions and this petty officer sought my baggage. When they recovered and placed the baggage on the vehicle, we went to the Duty Office where I deposited my orders and itinerary; it was Christmas Eve 1963.

The next stop was at the Bachelor Officer's Quarters where I would make my living quarters until April, when we broke ground and returned home to end the deployment. It took us about thirty minutes to travel the roads, which were treacherously flooded. I could not make out much of the land over which we traveled. We passed a World War II abutment and a thousand ripe orange trees.

NAS Sigonella #2 was the Administration, dispensary facilities, Navy Exchange, commissary, theater, Bachelor Enlisted Petty Officer Quarters, and limited houses were also available. As we passed the gate at NAS #2 Sigonella we showed our identification (I did not have proper identification). One block later we reached the BOQ! I checked in to my second floor room. It was about 1900 hours (7:00 p.m.) and we deserted most of the first floor.

I followed the petty officer upstairs with my bags and trunks. On the right I found my room, knocked and fifteen seconds later, I entered.

Later that evening I met Mike. We talked for about two hours about the squadron, Commanding Officers, and home, Brunswick, Maine. Mike Myers was aircraft commander, in other words, a Patrol Plane Commander. He told of being in the squadron when he had first arrived. He had many good flights and some in which he did not perform as well. He had heard that I would be assigned as the Logs and Records Officer within the Operations Division. I was quite excited about VP 10.

Christmas Day was a sad day as I wondered what Jane looked like. She was just about three and a half months pregnant and spending Christmas at her mother's. I miss her. That morning we had Bloody Marys and I met most of the officers. That night we all went to the C.O.'s, Commander Luka's house for a party. Three young women had come over to Sigonella with their husbands who were officers. They made the whole evening, with their smiles and perfect hospitality. The evening turned cold and immediately it started to rain. I become pleasantly drunk and finally rode back to my quarters with six other drunks!

The bus from NAF #2 left at 7:30 a.m. The ride down to operations was interesting. We arrived at the hangar for muster. We fell in and the Duty Officer called us to attention. It all came back and I suddenly became used to it.

The Operations Office was busy already. I met my petty officer who was a Third Class Petty Officer. I went through the records and started logging information from the maintenance records. That afternoon they gave me a hard hat, two flight suits, a leather flight jacket, and some boots. I was briefed later by a Communication Control Officer who made me sign by clearance badge, and other cryptic devices. Then I checked out a navigation bag. It has many facilities that I have used in VP 30, in Jacksonville, Florida. Some items in the bag I did not know how to use.

Friday I was to report to the Flight Surgeon at 8:00 a.m. Finally at 8:30, we got together and determined that I was "fit for flight." At 9:30 a.m. the dentist saw me to make a new record of my teeth. After I finished, I made a run to the liquor store since they officially declared me the Beer Mess Officer!

Saturday morning was beautiful! Outside the mess hall stood the volcano, Mt. Etna. It is massive when it starts spewing molten lava that flows down the mountain into small towns outside Catania. Catania is the biggest city near this volcano. Often it has erupted and the magma has wreaked havoc as far South as the Sigonella Naval Facility!

Later in the morning, I went to the Exchange and bought some essentials. There were orange trees and trees that I later found were fig trees, all over the place. The next day was New Year's Eve. I found, by chance, that the party was at the Officer's Club, located under me on the first floor of the BOQ! I had quite a shopping list getting the bar ready for all the takers!

At seven o'clock or 1900 hours, we amassed before the bar getting drunk. The band, or so it was called, arrived and begun setting up. The "band" consisted of a drummer, guitarist, bass player, and a piano player. About thirty minutes later the young women began to arrive. Girls defined by Webster means "a young woman." Defined by the squadron and myself, these included spouses of all ages, high school girls, and females through their mid twenties, which men of senior rank accompanied!

The band started playing and the drinks started flowing. I met all my friends at the New Year's Eve party. They kept asking me, "Who is the girl with the short dress on?" I had no idea.

As the hour reached 2200 hours, I had met the Commanding Officer of Sigonella, the XO and the Operations Officer. They were very sympathetic with me and knew that I was thinking about my pregnant wife. That really set me off and I returned to the bar to get totally imbibed. I had been there for half an hour and suddenly I felt someone bump me. I turned and there she was, bent over and yes, in a short skirt. She straightened up and I introduced myself. She responded and said she lost a pack of cigarettes. I offered her a Pall Mall. She was a cute girl, about seventeen, nice breasts popping out of her party dress, and was I enjoying it immeasurably. I asked her if she wanted a drink. She told me she was underage but she would love a Vodka Tonic. One thing lead to another and we began dancing. All the rest of the squadron watched and soon several of my officer friends asked that she dance. I went back to the bar and met another woman. She was the mother of the twin girls. I had drinks with one of the girls earlier. The other girl, her fraternal twin, was at the party also with her collection of men around her. She introduced me to another woman, but she was more attractive. She talked a lot, but she was really eyeing me. We danced and just as I got ready to dance again, her spouse arrived and took her off the floor with a rather snarly look. Oh, well, back to the bar!

It was three minutes to the New Year. We passed out noise makers and various confetti concoctions. Through the noise and shouting we brought in the New Year. I was feeling high and many guys were being kissed. Suddenly the sweetheart of two hours ago found me, "Happy New Year" she said. She grabbed me and kissed me. Boy oh boy, she French kissed me until I really enjoyed it. Suddenly we were broken apart by this boy. He grabbed her and away she went. I watched them knifing through the crowd until they reached the door and disappeared!

I stayed at the party until one thirty. The bar was the mainstay of my existence. The alcohol had reached a certain point in my body that it did not matter what I did to it.

The next afternoon I was checking my beer stock and I filled the refrigerator. After finishing this task I went downstairs to the bar. There were several lads there and when I sat, they asked me how Sigonella was treating me. With a Bloody Mary in my hand, I did not know how to answer this. They opened the secret door of the BOQ. Sigonella #2 was a city of sin, with the officers in a different house, obviously VP 10 and their wives, plus the paternal twins and other children were taking part in frivolous activity.

The first week of January 1964 was busy. Crew Two had the Ready Duty. I went down with the four officers Lt. Wally Courtney, Plane Commander, Lt. Marty Merrick Co pilot, LT Chuck Veith Tactical Coordinator and myself as Patrol Plane Navigator. The plane was on the taxiway. This recalled the World War II days of when the airfield was under attack the P 2V's or the other aircraft had a tough time getting hit. After checking the maintenance records of the aircraft, we put all of our gear on a four wheeler and drove down to the plane. The plane was covered with fog and wet spots. An aviation gas truck was adding gas that amounted to eight hours of flying. This was enough to get the aircraft out to an oustation while they called Ready Two topped off with fuel, to relieve us.

We entered the aircraft and finally I saw my seat in the aircraft. I opened my Navigators bag and with NATOP's in hand to preflight. All the sudden, it had become cold. The attendant removed the overhead dome as a flight attendant was out on the wing checking the fuel. After preflighting the aircraft, we had two hours of squadron instruction. We had survival training, mining training and numerous instructions that updated our training at best, once a year. Being deployed, we were constantly being drilled with photos about Soviet submarines, Elint identification, and combat ships. The combat ships are all over the Mediterranean Sea. This covers a vast area. Look for Elint collectors around the US battle groups. We are constantly told that, "loose lips may sink ships!."

On January 11, 1964, I flew my first flight on a shipping surveillance flight. We took off from Sigonella, Sicily heading due East and set up a surface track suitable for the SP 2E. The preflight was cumbersome but when we were airborne, Chuck Veith set Condition Three. I checked my systems and found everything working as planned. The PT 396A Dead Reckoning Trace was working and this wind in the windface (ASA 13A) was the preflight wind that I had set in earlier. The APN 122 Doppler passed the preflight with flying colors, but was stuck in memory for the remainder of the flight!

As we continued our track checking each surface ship, we made our way Southward. The B-5 driftmeter really helped me finding the drift and ground speed; plus the wind. We came across several Soviet trawlers in the area. We rigged them both and took the necessary photographs of the trawlers. After about nine hours of flight on the surveillance mission we were 300 miles south of Sigonella. I used the navigation system to my advantage. When I needed a fix I went to radar or I used a celestial fix, or just about any thing I could think of!

I asked the Co Pilot (Marty) to tune in the Sigonella ADF. The ADF is displayed on the number 1 needle at the navigation station. Finally the ADF or the "bird dog" had a lock on and I gave it to the pilot. The PPC then took up the magnetic bearing of the #1 needle and radar took it to Sigonella within two minutes.

On 12 January Chuck and I began preflighting a trip to Athens, Greece. The purpose of the flight was to detect important emitters along the Albanian and Bosnian coast enroute to Athens. The flight went east to the heel of Italy and next it turned north and flew up to Avianio, Italy, the Air Force Base. Then back down the side of Italy and once in Greece, cross over the mountain and land in Athens.

The morning of the flight, we were briefed by the squadron ANTI-SUBMARINE CLASSIFCATION AND ANALYSIS CENTER [ASCAC]. We were given all sorts of radars including low pulse search radar, medium pulse radar, and finally high scan rates which could mean lock on or watch your six o'clock position!

The Direction Finder (AN/APA 69C) is quite a system for the SP

2E aircraft. The Electronic Counter Measure operator is the primary operator. The AN/APA 69C is the mint of the ECM (electronic counter measures) and it monitors three frequencies: low, medium and high. The ECM/Radio Operator was at the briefing and got all the particulars that we might meet with during the flight.

Preflight went by quickly. Soon we took off and we reached our station about an hour and half inflight. Chuck set Condition Two and the ECM was turned on. At first the signals were overbearing, Tacan, VOR's and ADF's blinded the ECM band if we were searching in the low spectrum. The ECM operator quickly guessed that these signals would be a predominant signal in the low frequency spectrum. We finally got a signal of interest. I acknowledged the first bearing and plotted it. I asked for an additional bearing on each three minute interval. After thirty minutes I had the site located and fixed by three or more ECM bearings.

Suddenly we were turning 180 degrees to retravel the track to try to regain or detect new signals. We detected a strange intercept in the lower spectrum. The radar was a low frequency signal, but it disappeared after three rotations. I told the ECM operators to check the medium range and sure enough, the emitter had shifted operation to a medium frequency. This correlated with the initial frequency for about six sweeps and then she was lost. I quickly contacted ECM to shift to the high band. You never guessed it, but the scan rate was there in sector scan locked on to launch a weapon at us!

The tape recorder is vitally important on this mission. The ECM operator is loading the UNH 6 recorder that is a dual track magnetic record that is installed behind the navigator's station. This recorder is a record only and the four operators involved have been assigned the following priority: Pilot, Julie, ECM, and the Jezebel operator. The pilot can override despite the four operator priority systems.

The ECM was turned off when we reached the northern border of Greece. The pilot's contacted the Air Traffic Control [ATC] and filed to Athens, Greece. The only problem was climbing over the mountains that was down right chilly. After 8.7 hours we landed in Athens. We carried our gear to the Air Force Communications Center and stored it. We took an Air Force bus to a hotel downtown. It is a beautiful city near the water. The crew was happy to get to Athens and see the sights. Incerlik Air Force Base in Turkey is the next part of the ECM mission. This flight takes off in Athens and heads straight South before breaking ground on Africa. We must turn left twenty-five miles before land.

Many bad things have happened close to the borders of Libya, Egypt and the territorial coast owners. We had a pouch of information included in our pack that LT Veith briefed us on the radars in the area.

We arrived at our station late in the afternoon. The radars were keeping me busy. At last we were flying and the Plane Commander noticed someone was following us. He reported the plane was coming up along side of us. He said he was watching his "peas and ques," but he could not tell what nationality it was. I saw the plane was to the left of the aircraft. It remained there for half an hour and then disappeared! After 6.2 hours of ECM and a threatening episode of a jet escort, the beer in Incerlik, Turkey sure tasted good.

The next morning in Incerlik, I was tired and short on sleep. We had been put up with sixteen other officers who had also arrived last night. After breakfast, we headed to the Air Terminal. With our flight bags in hand, we began preflighting back to Athens. There was some trouble with the plane and we ended up waiting for a part. Incerlik did not look like much, in fact it is a desolate area. I do not know the Air Force policy, but I did not want my spouse or spouses here in this Turkish bath of sand! Our trip back to Athens was uneventful. We stayed one night in a hotel and were flying the next day. Everyone was glad to be back in Sigonella when we finally arrived.

In the morning, our charts of navigation logs, and records were reviewed at the squadron OPCON. The information that we had gained on emitters that last five days was lost by improper debriefing. Many things that my crew had experienced were lost and the necessary value of the encounters of the signals were never really explained to us. The ECM portion of the flight attracted a great deal of attention. Several of the ECM fixes were right on track and the information obtained provided additional intelligence on the radars intercepted. The intelligence obtained near the Libyan and Egyptian border caused great concern and was reported through the proper channels. I was happy with the navigation procedures until I was approached by an ECM Officer. This Lieutenant chose to chew my ass out because the radar bearings were not plotted. I took objection to this and we went back to verify this information. Everything was there but I had not made the ECM particularly clear by not replotting the intercept without the rudiments of navigation. In other words, "Let's fix it so it's right" said the ECM Officer. So then again, why fix it after a series of four flights?

During the twenty-five minute ride back to the BOQ, I was able to relax and lower my blood pressure. With new DRT's, I started plotting my estimated Line of Bearings that lead to a fix. Once finished, I was congratulated for a job well done. I was so pissed off from this experience that I decided to make my job the highest order of excellence in VP-10 and become the best Patrol Plane Navigator.

The squadron organization of the Operations Department has many changes when aircrews are away. I found this out when LT Austin Rehfield, the Flight Officer, was the only officer in the Operations Office. I was made the temporary Schedule's Officer. I first had to see who was going to be there tomorrow, who is down (unable to fly), and who is on Ready Duty. I looked at the number of hours we had flown this month compared to how many we had left. Looking at the commitments laid out over the month, I wondered if the projected total will equal the amount of hours scheduled? I decided to work on a 25.0 hour schedule and submit it to Austin for enroute for a final check. I went down the schedule and noticed Pilot Training. Two Pilots were rapidly approaching there PPC checks. I scheduled them for PPC flights and we have only one patrol. By 1300 hours I had a rough cut and gave it to LT Rehfield. He agreed that the Ready Duty was correct. I had made an error because one PPC that I had a training flight scheduled for tomorrow was down, and who wrote note #3 on the flight schedule? I went back and straightened it out and gave it back to Austin. Next I passed the yeoman, the flight schedule and had it typed thirty minutes later, read, reviewed and corrected. This then left the Operations Department and travels to the Maintenance Department for aircraft. By the time the Maintenance Department reviews the plane assignments, the schedule goes to the Executive and Commanding Officer for signatures. This did not take any time right? I got the schedule back signed and mimeographed it for the squadron on the base and back at the BOQ, where it would be posted.

One other story that I may as well divulge happened when I was writing the flight schedule and there was at least four aircraft away on other operations. Lieutenant Commander Redmond, the Operations Officer, LT Rehfield the Flight Officer and LT Mike Myers Schedules Officer were tied up with the four crews. I started out with the Ready Duty and of course I did not go back to the BOQ at 1300. I did not pass an hour without two or three Pilots wanting to know what is happening tomorrow. Finally I had the schedule put together by 1330. There was a Maintenance chop, but the Executive Officer was gone and the Commanding Officer , Commander Don E. Gately was due back at 1500. I waited for his return and presented the flight schedule. He became infuriated and began to chew me out from head to toe. After five minutes of unmitigated lecturing about scheduling and why we needed twenty-five flight hours a day, I excused myself. I was so red in the face the my assistant asked if I was all right! I called Maintenance to tell them I needed another airplane. They said yes, so I penciled in a pilot trainer. I went back and clearly knocked on his door. CDR Gately laughed and said he was sorry for blowing up at me. He signed the schedule and the yeoman made all the copies. Never again will I present this schedule unless I have questioned all specifics pertaining to increasing the flight hours.

The junior officers of VP-10 were to assume the duties of Duty Officer. A Duty Officer is in charge of the squadron after working hours. He is supposed to report to the Command Duty Officer for guidance. The Duty Officer has a list of instructions that are squadron generated for NAF Sigonella instructions and Commander Fleet Air Facilities Mediterranean. He is also in charge of the Ready Duty crews. My first time instruction for this duty was to read all the instructions and ask the Duty Officer about specifics to be ready for my first job as Squadron Duty Officer.

February and March were spent with NATO exercises. These flights were flown at night all night long. We provided protective operations where most of our hops where ahead of the carriers providing various air plans that would drop sonobuoys to detect submarines, then spent the whole night chasing down surface contacts for a destroyer.

One of the NATO exercises was a mine laying exercise. The mining exercise was very important as it was used in wartime if we were called to employ mines in a real time situation. We spent a lot of time preflighting for this mission. We were told where the field was, position and storing of mines, and how many to drop. We had many ways to fix our position before going on the final heading on which the mines were dropped. This was a very interesting facet of being on a SP-2E and conducting a successful mining operation. On the other hand, the SP-2E and the SP-2H were assigned the mining mission which can be a pitfall leading to the loss of aircraft. An unnoticed airplane can sow many mines, but anti-aircraft fire can respond to eliminate many of the remaining aircraft.

On March 24, 1964 we went on a navigation flight to Naval Station

Rota. We landed and checked in to the BOQ. The main reason we went to Rota was to get qualifications' signed off. This is a series of things that must be completed for a crew to be an Alfa (A) crew. The exercises include: Light EX, Rocket/Bomb EX, Mine EX, Sniffer EX, ECM exercise, Radar EX, Jezebel exercises, Julie exercises, MAD exercises, MK-44 torpedo drop, Special weapon exercises, and three exercises with an actual submarine. This is a Commander Wings Atlantic manual and is used to gain overall combat proficiency or Alfa status.

The next day we ran several exercises and we had an observer from the squadron based with us. We were trying to find a surface ship moored in the water but there was none. At debrief the Lieutenant criticized me because I did not handle my plotter correctly, no ground tracker used, and more superfluous techniques that must be used. That did not set right with me nor any other officer of the crew.

We left Rota about 1630 (4:30 p.m) the next day and went to Sigonella. I preflighted the trip and it would count as a night navigation flight. Weather was clear, but as we headed East we were expecting to run into thunderstorms. The flight was going smoothly, the sextant and the stars indicated we were right on course. Just before we passed Sardinia, we entered the clouds. I had gotten my celestial shots in and had already given the Pilot the estimated time of arrival at Sigonella. There were thunder flashes in the distance, nothing that would be unusually distressing. Suddenly without my seat belt on, I went straight up, head first, in the top of the cabin. Chuck was there also and we fell back into our seats. Fighting the yoke, the Pilots in the front section of the aircraft were trying to keep the SP-2E out of the water. Chuck announced Condition One and I had already turned my seat to the AFT position! We were battered around for almost thirty minutes. The Pilots were on nav-aids that helped, because the air facility was below minimums! They vectored us to the South of the airfield for ten minutes. Finally the field was back up to 300 feet, one mile visibility. We made the pavement and boy were we glad to be on terra firma!

My calendar said April and my it is now time to begin packing up and heading West for home in Maine. We were scheduled to leave Sigonella on April 4. Our squadron equipment was packed and the gear was split into two bags that we carried on the plane. The remainder of the equipment went back with the four engine transports. The crews were just about the same but Chuck Veith had to stop as our TACCO, LT Ed Soberiay came along with us. We preflighted the whole track including the trip from Sigonella to Rota, Rota to Lajes Air Force Base, and from Lajes to Argentia, Newfoundland Navy Station. There was not need to put the preflight wind in since it would probably be five days until we will fly.

Before we left, there was a squadron party attended by all. CDR Gately and the XO were at the bar with all the Department heads. Now is the time to get all officers to pay the Beer Mess dues for the deployment. I spent the evening chasing around the officers for money. I woke up with my clothes on and $350 dollars in my pockets! Yes, the beer must have gotten all their money, but it's amazing that I was tipped so much!! Immediately I went to the bathroom and urinated profusely while throwing down two Excedrin. After washing up and changing clothes, I headed down to the beer machine only to find it was empty! I took the money and deposited it leaving me enough to buy three cases of beer. I went downstairs and several officers were waking up drinking Bloody Marys so that they could think clearly.

It was miserable loading the P-2. Bags upon bags were loaded. We computed a weight and balance, which Pilots love to watch the NAO's complete. All VP-10 Plane Captains used to provide these, but believe it or not, ours was right on the money! We completed all the flight checks and we started taxing toward the runway. After completing the warmups, LT Courtney said that we would fly over the runway. We started taking off and with us took an additional 1500 feet of runway due to the loaded condition of the bomb bay and all the other storage space throughout the aircraft. The Pilot climbed the SP-2E to 1000 feet and requested a low approach over the airfield. He was cleared and what a low approach! We cleared the squadron hangar with jets running at 99%, 325 knots, and clearing at 100 feet. I am sure the officer who drank a cup of coffee when we flew over, sure had coffee spilt on his pants, shirt or both!

The deployment to Sigonella was difficult to adjust to, particularly when you are in a strange environment. The setting being in the Mediterranean Sea promotes undersea activity. For my part this was only one submarine and it was friendly! The most time consuming activity of this deployment was rigging and photographing ships. This task, I guess, was very rewarding if the tracks of the ships were documented. Nevertheless, I was trained to find submarines. What happens now? Do I become trained again?

Flying time to Rota was 7.3 hours. Ed and I were making sun

shots and keeping track of where we are. Once we landed we took out a bag which was designed for the trips to Brunswick, Maine. We showered and reported to the Officer's Club. We drank and then had dinner. The next morning we took out the preflight and followed the Pilots to get the predicted weather. The weather was plugged into the system and we were all set. We caught a ride back to the aircraft and finished preflight.

Lajes on the ASA-16 was a pretty sight. It looks like a volcano that came up from the surface of the ocean. It is part of the chain of volcanic islands that start with Iceland and wind their way South splitting the Atlantic Ocean. The base was chosen long ago as a strategic station as most aircraft of World War II could not transverse the Atlantic. The Air Force built quite a facility and in 1964 even C-141's landed with supplies. We landed and checked in at the BOQ. Portuguese is the language of the military base with many planes and a special hangar. We went to the Officer's Club and there was already a crowd there. You can do anything there—slot machines, barber shop, billiards, and of course, drinking. We ate dinner and enjoyed the sights. In the morning, we took off and Ed had the navigation. The wind was from the Northwest at 15 knots. Our driftmeter confirmed this and what should my waiting eyes find, but the Doppler actually working. We tracked outbound on the TACAN and the off flag fell at 192 miles. That was the last fix for quite a while. At two and one half hours, I assumed the navigation duties. We were overcast and just about to become undercast as the fog was moving in. I used the driftmeter and expected to get something from the Doppler, but the memory light was still on! There is nothing like a dead reckoning position. The sextant was my favorite buddy. I looked and strained through the periscope but to no avail. I asked the PPC if he saw the sun and to let me know so I can take a spot shoot of it. LORAN was horrible and I could only get one line that did give me an estimated position (E.P.).

It is now coming up on four hours and I am beginning to hurt for a fix. The PPC called and said the sun will be over us in three minutes. I used the air almanac to plug in our latitude and went to the sextant. I looked extra hard and the sun was there but not clear. Suddenly the sun was out and I was shooting the sun. Quickly I sat down to finish my E.P. A loud bang came from the cockpit. The PPC came on the loudspeaker and wanted the Ordnance man to look at the starboard engine. He reported that all looks normal on the engine. Power was pulled back by the Plane Captain, checked the points, and set the engine back to its original power setting. The PPC called the plane a head of us and told him what had happened. Again we had another loud bang and the power was reduced.

I finally had an E.P. that was perpendicular to course line and west of my DR. I quickly computed the ground speed and we were closer to Argentia than Lajes. I gave the position to the Co-Pilot and an estimate for a touchdown at the base. We have two and half more hours till we reach Argentia. Back to the sextant, nothing at all. LORAN yielded only one line and It was an E.P. of course, but it looked good on the navigator's log.

The starboard engine was still putting out the horsepower. At six hours into the flight, the APS-20 saved the day as land appeared on the scope. The land was identified as Newfoundland. The fix was given to the Pilot and the ADIZ penetration was given to the Co-Pilot.

Landing was successful at Argentia, but the weather was touchy. At the end of the runway, LT Courtney called Ground Control for an aborted take off and it was authorized. He made a simulated takeoff to an abort. Everything pulled smoothly and we shutdown. The next day the oil was changed including the strainers. Several metal slivers were found inside the engine, unfortunately the slivers were below the standard measurement needed to require changing the engine.

Argentia was a busy airbase that handled many barrier flights between here and Iceland. There is one "Willy Victor" on station around the clock either from this base or from Iceland. The VAW squadrons that are based here are VAW-11 and 15 manned by twenty or more flight crews each. They do just that, they keep their radar on in hopes of detecting Bears and other Soviet aircraft so we know the approximate position before they break the ADIZ penetration rules. This of course launches the USAF Fighters who keep track of the violators of the ADIZ. We are stuck here until the rest of VP-10 reaches us. We have heard that one plane landed in Lajes with an engine change. Meanwhile back in Argentia, we spend our time bowling, going to the movies, and drinking at night. Finally enough crews arrive on April 8 that it looked as we may finally see Brunswick, Maine. We climbed aboard and the Pilots admitted they would need navigation for about an hour. Pilots and the aircrew were concerned about the starboard engine, at least maintenance control gave it a thumbs up. Eight aircraft taxied left, but one aircrew did not take off.

This crew went back to the line and drained out the oil and found small splinters of steel too small to call for an engine change. This crew missed the flyover of Brunswick by half an hour.

VP-10 Naval Air Station, Brunswick, Maine

The people at Brunswick were amazing. They ran and kissed us with love. One was a two year old girl who was crying at her mother's feet while her mother was kissing her five and half months-back-from deployment husband. I missed Jane and her well developed stomach which was coming due in June. She was in Norfolk waiting for me with some friends in VR-1. I called her three hours later and a tear fell. I had arranged to catch a bus from Brunswick to Boston National Airport. I was pointed to a plane that I did not need a ticket. Shortly after the stewardesses welcomed all the passengers aboard, we were airborne. Our Captain announced that we were released from our seatbelts and would arrive in New York in one hour. Oh Boy, now who can tell me why I got on this flight to Washington! When the flight attendant came back collecting money for the flight, I found out I could land in New York and be on the way to Washington in fifteen minutes.

I landed in Washington, D.C. and went straight to the airline that handles Norfolk. All flights were full because General Douglas MacArthur was being buried tomorrow. This was the first news that I had heard of the General's passing away. I called Jane and told her the news. She said she was coming to get me from Norfolk. I resisted but I wanted Jane. I agreed and told her to be careful. The trip will take her at least three hours maybe three and a half. I wandered back to my seat to wait the long three hours. I eventually got up and went to the bathroom to clean up. I went out outside and the Washington Airport was busier than hell. Out of the distance I saw a white Chevy II convertible, Jane had come to the rescue!!

I held her and kissed her while the rain was dripping down my raincoat. She looked great pregnant! I loaded my gear on board and we left National Airport for Richmond. We stopped to get something to eat and spoke of everything; her friends, mother, and the trip to Brunswick from Sigonella. The car was running well and the knack for driving was coming back.

Richmond was the same as we reached the outskirts. We started looking for a motel. Finally we found one and checked in. After the bags were unloaded into the room, I found a surprise bottle of champagne! We talked and finally got into the bubbly! We hugged and kissed and I felt the baby move from side to side. Jane was shy but as I undressed her she knew me as I was. I caressed her and carried her to the bed, she knowing at last that I would not hurt her. We made love and for me it was very quick for reaching orgasm.

Morning finally arrived and I was awakened by her kissing my ear. That started my day and dam it felt much better than masturbating yourself! We left the motel and headed back toward Richmond. We had breakfast and we bought a paper. The front page was filled with articles about General MacArthur's funeral. At one o'clock in the afternoon, we reached Edna's apartment, Jane's mother. Edna was a wonderful person, who lost her first spouse by massive heart attack. Frank was particularly fond of Jane and his sudden departure almost broke her up.

We spent two and half days with Edna. We said our good-byes and headed north for my parent's home in Annandale. Dad is the Production Plant Manager of the Coca-Cola Bottling Plant in Alexandria, Virginia. As my Dad said, he gives Coke, Sprite, and grape drink out of his fingers when the doctors ask for blood samples! Mother still works as a cafeteria worker at Fairfax High School serving the kids a hot lunch each day. Merlyn, my sister, was going to school in Alexandria. Dad was home early when we arrived and we went out to dinner. We went to a wonderful restaurant in McLean. Our time over the next few days was passed shopping for maternity clothes and other things needed when the baby arrives. We met Dad at the Coke plant one day to meet Mr. William Mays, the Plant Manager. The Plant had won many awards of the Richmond Crass Organization in Richmond, Va. My Dad won all the awards and was instrumental in making the Alexandria Bottling Company one of the highest honored facilities. I also got together with some of my old friends there when I was a route salesman during the summers of 1956 through 1962.

Driving back to Maine was an arduous task with the Chevy II loaded down. We had Jane's clothes, household items, and many things we kept with us rather than pack it away. The first night we stayed in a motel in Connecticut. It was a Howard Johnson's restaurant made into a motel. I am glad I planned on an extra day.

After breakfast, we headed for Maine. This is the first time I had driven from Portland. The town of Brunswick was beautiful and scenic with its shoe factories on the water. We drove on to the base while I was scrambling for my identification card and trying to find the BOQ to get a placard for twenty-four hours. The BOQ was quite large. We checked in and our room was on the top (third) floor. I hauled three loads of stuff and had to sit down with a Virginia Gentleman and water. We had many plans tomorrow, but renting a house was primary.

I checked into the squadron on Monday found my spot in Operations. I went by the housing office to find our position for base housing was number twenty-two on the list. It would be July before officer base housing would be available.

Jane met with a Realtor on Tuesday and viewed several homes. The house that interested me was on Merrymeeting Drive. The Realtor wanted $12,000 dollars to buy the house but only $110 dollars a month to rent. We finally agreed and signed the lease. We made all the necessary utility connections but did not have any furniture. A good friend of Jane's told us of a place in Bath, Maine where we could buy North Carolina furniture. After work we went to Bath and found the place. All the sudden we had a pine bedroom set, a dining room table, living room sofa, a chair, and mirror (and that's close enough for government work)!

Things were hot and heavy for the upcoming squadron operations. There was a great deal of turnover's and many new faces at work. Jim Hagy was one new guy that I took a liking to, mainly because he was bald or nearly bald on the top of his head. He and his wife Judy, had attended Duke University and she had just given birth to a little girl named Alison.

VP-10 was reunited! We met in the squadron officers meeting CDR Gately welcomed us back, but then briefed us on upcoming events:

1.) Mining Exercise
2.) Administrative Inspection of the Squadron
3.) Operational Readiness Inspection

This information scared me, I did not know who did what or when. The dates were set, homework started, and we began to prepare for the worst! The Mining Exercise was my first experience since I had been promoted. A new crew list came out and interestingly enough I was listed as a Tactical Coordinator for the crew. The manuals were unclear how the actual mine exercise was going to run. This left to the crew qualification and certification mining runs which sharpened my skills as Tactical Coordinator.

The NATOPS (Naval Air Training and Operating Procedures Standardization) officer gave the tests for the Pilot and the Naval Aviation Observer. I was scheduled one day to go and be questioned about the systems in the SP-2E aircraft. He began by running over the systems for the navigator. Questions were firing about all of the systems. We moved on to the ASA-16, whereby I turned on the gear. Then he asked me about the three major buttons on the "Chinese Televison Set." I explained the features of button or cursor three which can be used as a range and bearing to some distant point or detach marker three and put it on a point of land or on a contact which the plane must get to by placing the marker on the BDHI. Then we covered the Julie system, the Loran, and finally the Jezebel recorder. We covered the number of sonobuoys we can cover and the number of CODAR plants we can monitor. Next, we went to the Magnetic Anomaly Detection in the aircraft. The MAD system was fairly easy to go over. He asks me how I could tell that I had a MAD contact. I explained that a light comes on above the MAD indicator. To get the button to display on the ASA-16, I turned on the marker which has selected the MAD signal. The NATOPS instructor threw me for a loop, when he asked if the MAD operator contact could be displayed in the cockpit? I wasn't thinking when I said no but when I said it, I wish I hadn't!

Up on the flight deck, he told me to sit down at the nav station. I put on a ASW-1 chart and he told me he was going to the cockpit and will start the first problem on a drop 4000 yards short of datum. What he really meant is a five buoy pattern with sonobuoys at each cardinal heading and one buoy at datum. The buoys were away [simulated] and a SUS went with it. Twenty seconds later he said no echoes on the first drop. Forty seconds later the datum buoy when in. A single echo on buoy two, 2000 yards. The sub could be anywhere but maybe I'll luck out. The third buoy goes out with SUS a I told the pilot to roll out to the left and to fly the BDHI. There were no echoes on channel three, the north buoy. Forty seconds later four were away and the instructor had the buoy in sight. No echoes on buoy four and I was waiting for results. Charge away, and, "mark ontop buoy 1," said the instructor. Buoy 5 was ready to go; buoy and charge away. I briefed the pilot to go ahead and charge three. Echos on sonobuoy 5, 2000 yards. Standby for a charge on 3, charge away, and mark on three. Well, I had to change patterns, so I told the pilot to fly the BDHI and datum which is

2 and make buoy 5 datum. But no, I changed that and I wanted him to ontop 5 and standby for a new datum buoy six. Six away, charge away, and no echos 6 or 5. Standby for buoy 9 and a deep charge; buoy away and I told him to fly his BDHI. No echos on 9 or 6 and standby for buoy 7. Buoy 7 and a deep charge and standby for a mark on 5. The original 4000 yard pattern was pretty reliable but the instructor said he has the buoy in sight. Echo on 7, 2000 yards, but I had to do something drastic, so I told the instructor to mark on 6 and outbound 045 degrees true for another buoy drop. Mark on 6 and outbound to lay 8. Away went buoy 8 with a charge and wanted double echos so bad I could taste it. Double echoes and I told the pilot to make a port turn and fly up to the northeast where the fixes were. When you have two fixes, the submarine could be at one fix or the other. The first fix did not yeild a MADMAN, so I continued dropping ten and a deep charge. I got a single echo of 500 yards on buoy 10. I selected a pinger or a SSQ-15 sonobuoy. The instructor dropped the SSQ-15 [commonly called a pinger] and we got a MAD signal! I finally killed the sub which was going 12 knots.

Finally the instructor came back and sat down and told me it was a good exercise. He warned me of keeping ahead of the problem, and for God sakes lets keep the drift or the electronic fluctuation out of the ASA-13. He asked me if I had any questions. Well, I had a few but I was rusty and I needed that workout. We had box lunches so we talked more about parameters of using various types of localization patterns.

With lunch finished, he brought me into the cockpit and explained what they were going through on patrol. What an eyesight he painted on those gauges and dials of the two Wright compound engines driving Hamilton Standard Hydromatic full feathering propellers. He asked me if I had started an engine before. No, I said. He then took out the Check List, put me in the pilots' seat, and went step by step throught the check list until I started the port engine. I continued the Check List and he started the starboard engine. What an experience! The instructor showed me the dials, including the fuel pressure, oil pressure and many gauges which were very important when the engines are turning. We went through the engine shutoff by reading the Secure Checklist and we secured the aircraft. What a interesting five hour period where I had a great and challenging part of my life answering questions about where I worked and if I wanted the challenge of transfering my reserve wings into a regular Navy Officer.

The Small Point mining range is located South of the Brunswick

Airfield. This range was controlled by radios which would clear the aircraft on the range when we commenced our runs. The bombs we used are called "water sand fills" (WSF). Just before we released them from the bomb bay, the WSF's had a tendency to hang a split second after the bomb release solenoid had released them.

The reason that the water sand fill hangs in the bomb bay is because water has leaked out of the practice bomb and it floats upon release and waits one second to fall from the bombay. A five hundred pound mine when released from the bombay will fall as planned! The visual or radar run must compute the following factors: along the true course of the bombing line marks the drop of the bomb. Actually in a squadron Minex there are four mines (bombs) dropped. Each bomb has a box in which it must be placed. This gets pretty tricky when the wind is blowing perpendicular to the airplane.

The mine, when it is dropped, falls according to its weight and speed of the aircraft in relation to the altitude it is dropped. Depending on the drift of the wind, the drop points are plotted and the drop times are a function of maintaining proper ground speed and course formation. The major force of the SP-2E completing this minelaying exercise is strictly amazing! I use that term as bullshit, but admit I worked my ass off to get all my mines in the box. The first couple of flights I became certified but then came the radar controlled flights. The major part of calling the drops was left to the navigator. I did not like that! A navigator did much work preflighting the trip, but depended on the nomograph that he maintained on the final bomb release run.

The Minex bleed down to the final brief, given by the Minex Officer. Fleet Air Wing 3 Staff was at the brief. The flight was a low level mission that did not include LORAN. Our route of flight went down below Massachusetts offshore about four hundred miles then back up to the North. The route took us back to the east of Portland, Maine and then about ten miles North of it. We then would turn east to the mine field. The interesting thing was we laid the mines with jets turning 100% at 300 knots.

At preflight we conducted checks of our gear and we made sure the radar was performing. (Incidentally, the radar was down twice during preliminary mining flight. We returned and had the radar repaired. The major cause of the radar failure is unknown, but the range error of one half mile too short of a mine will ruin your whole minex grade!). The brief was conducted by the PPC who introduced the Wing

Observer. All facets of this flight were covered including dog tags and personal identification of each member of the crew.

The crew then jumped aboard and started the engines. We were number five for take off. It became time for us to take off, but the plane ahead of us had left the take position to go back to the squadron, apparently it has a malfunction. It was a pretty day and we took sun lines up the gumstump. About five hours inflight we turned back to Brunswick and gave our estimated time of arrival at the ADIZ, the Air Defensive Identification Zone.

After penetrating the ADIZ, we turned to the Northwest. I brought up the APS 20 radar. Land was appearing on the 60 mile scale. By comparing it with the local map we were right on course. I picked up Portland and then I put the turn point on the end of my number three cursor that was fixed to the origin of the APS-20. I told the PPC the range and bearing. Five miles from altering heading the PPC comes on the loudspeaker—"Set Condition One," altered heading and the count down had begun. The APS 20 pulse repetition frequency was in the 300 pulses per second. I selected sector scan about the true course line. I picked up the range and moved my number three cursor from the origin to the radar point on the mining range. I moved the drop distance from the radar point and selected the high mode of 900 PPS with sector scan.

I started with twelve miles as an entry point on the nomograph. LT Courtney had already had the jets started and we are at 300 knots inbound to the first mine drop. Ten, nine, and eight mile limits were what the nomograph needed and the navigator called the number seconds to the first drop. Bomb bay doors were opened and the necessary adjustments to the power setting were made to continue the 300 knot speed. I did a good job on the scope (APS-20) as I only had a two degree correction on the six mile range to correct for drift. The first mine was away, the second, third and then final mine left the aircraft. The bomb bay doors were closed. We simulated taking a hit and declared a bail out drill. They checked us for our hard hats, parachutes, and other items they ask of us.

We landed on a ground approach radar to the runway. Everyone was tired, unfortunately we did not know whether we hit the bullseye or not! Our debriefing was methodical—all navigation charts and sun charts were reviewed, checked, and analyzed, as well as the ADIZ estimate. The Executive Officer, CDR. Keith Sharer, told me I had gotten three out of four in the box. This apparently was the best result of all the other flights. We obtained our satisfactory rating on the Mining Exercise from Fleet Air Wing Three. I went over to the ASCAC and looked at the mining range plot. The last mine was on the line, but they did not count this and I did not know why.

Jane had really gotten big in her final month of pregnancy. Our furniture had been delivered the day after we moved in. The house was old but it was well kept. Jane's doctor was located in Brunswick Hospital. He told us in the second week of June that the baby would come anytime. We had many friends come by and meet Jane. She had many friends invite her to play Bridge or just drop by and visit in the afternoons.

I applied for leave so that I could paint our bedroom when Jane was in the hospital. June 22 at 11:45 p.m., Jane was having labor pains and ready to go the hospital. The nurse informed us at midnight that Jane was only three centimeters dilated. She was given some medicine to relax her. It was going to be a very long night. At 3:00 a.m., nothing had changed with the baby. When 6:00 a.m. came around, things were beginning to happen. The doctor asks me at 6:45 a.m. if I wanted to see the baby being born, I did, and in rolls Jane, on the table, in pain and giving birth to a baby girl—Mary Elizabeth. She was 6 3/4 pounds. Jane was tired. I was dead tired and went home after Jane fell asleep.

We bought Mary Elizabeth home three days later. Jane was happy and had started breast feeding. Her mother and my parents were coming next weekend. We had all the basic necessities for the baby when she came home. Beth, that's what we called her, was a great baby. She became colicky two weeks later and the doctor tells us, she is unhappy about something. We switched formulas, one that consisted of soybeans, hoping this would remedy her unhappiness. Jane was becoming a zombie, but fortunately things began to settle down.

The aircraft qualifications kept me moving. The A-1 Litex and the searchlight qualification were of interest to me. We finally got blocks of aircraft time near Cape Cod. There is a ship that can be made out of the final run. The searchlight qualification is the AN/AVQ-2 that is mounted on the starboard end of the starboard wing. The searchlight is a high intensity carbon arc light that reaches 70,000,000 candle power. This is carried in the right wing tip nacelle. The Co-Pilot is provided with a hand control with by which he can maneuver or handle the aircraft. The arc of the searchlight is fixed by a trigger switch. Illumination is created by the vaporization of positive and negative carbons. The hand control permits elevation movements to plus five degrees and minus forty-five degrees. Azimuth limits movement to 27 1/2 degrees left and right of center.

The Sniffer device is an unusual sensor. It sniffs or smells the scent of smoke equal to a snorkeling submarine. It's opening is just a tube of air aft of the Pilot's station. It works by allowing the ambient air or wind flow into aircraft. The water that is put into the device activates the alarm. Diesel smoke in a submarine can provide you with quite a drawer of foul air.

We had no luck with the Sniffer. On a training flight we decided that the wind blowing smoke into the sea was from several chimneys in Portland. The westerly wind was drifting out to sea so we went out fifteen miles to determine if we could detect it. The proper way to use the device is to position the aircraft downwind and to fly perpendicular to the wind for initial contact. Well, kiss-my-ass, I got a loud noise from the Sniffer and both the navigator and myself marked it on the ASA16/PT 396. The band was relatively short so I turned left for five miles and left again to become perpendicular to the wind. We gained contact again; it looked as if we might have something this time. The third attempt, I gained contact and did a 360 degree turn to home in on the bearing. The trail narrowed down to a left/right turns of five miles, to a sighting of smoke coming from tall chimneys. Hurray at last!

The Administrative Inspection of the squadron brought the Wing Three inspectors over to check our records. I was in charge of the Flight Log Book, aviation orders, officers and crewmembers aboard, and those that are grounded. I was thoroughly questioned and got an excellent report from the inspector. The Wing representative wanted the Schedules' Officer, but he was flying at the time. I was next in command and went through the scheduling process with him. He wanted to see the Schedules' Officer tomorrow as soon as possible.

The Operational Readiness Inspection is an inspection of nuclear weapon loads, drills, and an antisubmarine exercise involving the entire squadron. I flew with the crew and it did not happen on our flight. We went out and announced on station. We went to datum and dropped a seven buoy Jezebel pattern and we were looking for a snorkeling US submarine. We searched the LOFAR grams for five hours and left without making contact. Three or four crews had LOFAR contact and connected to a kill. The final result of finding a snorkel in the ORI was a passing grade. CDR. Gately expressed his opinion that we had done good work in all of the simulated drills and the

Nuclear, Biological, & Chemical (NBC) attack. He then presented us news from earlier that morning. Task Group Charley, Delta Squadron (VP-56) stationed at the Naval Air Station in Norfolk, would receive four planes and assists from us in their Task Group Operations on August 10. Then he shared the bad news with us. Beginning in September, we would have four planes at NAS Key West, Florida. I thought when you were home you fly, and more importantly you were with your spouse and child. I did not say anything. I went home I played with Beth, fed her, and rocked her to sleep.

On August 10, 1964, we left Brunswick and flew to Norfolk. The airfield was packed with planes. Many of the big transport planes were headed West to Vietnam. After checking in at the BOQ, we attended a brief regarding the air plans, the task force commander, and the Office of Tactical Command to whom we would report. Afterwards, the Detachment met to make the schedule. I was given the position of Squadron Duty Officer the first night. I was a busy camper. I finished the flight schedule complete with signature, ordered chow for the flights, and stayed up all night. It was a smart thing, I did take time to read up on the orders and I now know what goes into a report to an OTC asking to take your safety of flight.

On the 11th of August, I slept. I was relieved at 0800 and awoke about 1500. I cleaned up and attended happy hour with the XO and most of the two crews. I was lucky; I did not end up paying for a round!

At 0700 we reported to ASCAC for a brief of our flight. The weather was rough. We went out to the airplane and began checking the gear. We had already done some preflight before hand that had prepared PT396 charts or ASW-1 charts that were 16:1 charts. The charts we use go to on station and then to change to another chart that is bigger in scale (i.e. an 8:1 or a 4:1 chart showed the type of work asked for by the OTC).

Upon arriving on station, we contacted the OTC with the initial report. He then sent the Air Plan we were to initiate. The TACCO's bag was a mess, eventually we knew what was happening. The Air Plan was to search ahead of the group of destroyers' fifty to one hundred mile sector using intermittent radar with visual sighting. The weather was rotten. We flew for two and half hours calling the OTC every one half hour. Four hours into the mission we were called back by the OTC because he thought he had sonar contact. We sent an estimated time of arrival and arrived within ten miles of his position. Then we started magnetic vectors or an attempt for us to gain magnetic airborne detection (MAD) of a submerged submarine. This was continued for three hours. It was so rough and turbulent in the sea and in the air that the P-2 made me sick as a dog! At three hours we gave our off station report, checked the altitude and headed back to Norfolk. The XO appeared tired after trying so many attempts to get a valid MAD contact during the debriefing. With great zeal and a deep thirst, we headed back to our rooms to clean up and head for the Officer's Club for many drinks. Our final flight went entirely different. The extra Tactical Coordinator on board was undecided on whether or not he wanted to stay in the Navy. Bunky Mauer is a Boston, Ma. sailor. As a Tactical Coordinator he could not hack it. He was a bachelor, drinker, piano player, and a general goof off. I ran the ASA-16 out to onstation. Bunky took over for me as I sat back and watched. The OTC has some instructions for us to coordinate our search plans. After one hour onstation the TACCO brought up the APS-20 radar to see if any small radar contacts were present. The radar looked clear because the wind was 7-10 nautical miles an hour. I was watching the radar when I noticed a small return ten miles away. The TACCO had already reported no contacts, but was about to shut off the radar. I interrupted him and pointed out the contact. He directed the plane to the heading of the small contact. Almost immediately the acting Plane Commander announced it is a snorkel. Condition One was set and the TACCO was preparing to drop a sonobuoy near or on top of the snorkel. The plane appeared to bomb the snorkel with four MK-54 bombs that would straddle the submarine. "MAD Man" shouted the sensor operator as we marked on top of the snorkel. The SSQ-15, the active pinging buoy did not go out. The P-2 was going into a MAD hunting circle. I jumped over the wing into the radio station and ran to the ordnance station. The SSQ-15 buoy was jammed in the chutes. Standby was the PPC call and I grabbed a smoke, reset the smoke to arm, and out goes the smoke. I used one side of the airplane and the Ordnance man dropped the sonobuoys out the port side of the aircraft. Eventually, we drove the submarine to the surface and I was pretty tired throwing out all those smokes.

Well, the long and short of it all, Combat Air Crew 2 killed the only submarine in the whole exercise by bombing the United States FM-10 conventional submarine and receiving three successive MAD men forcing him to surface to acknowledge the attack.

The XO CDR. Sharer was waiting when we shut down the

engines. He was excited and shook our hands. The Task Group Monthly Newspaper had a short article that had a synopsis of VP-10's CAC-2 investigation of a snorkel and simulated killing of the only submarine in the exercise.

I finally returned home on August 15 before summer had departed. We had a very warm and cloudy period in August. I spent time with Beth. Jane and I toured all over Booth Bay Harbor and many sites near Brunswick. I met many people in the neighborhood including a VP-10'er named Al Manson, his wife Priscilla. We spent a lot of time with this couple socially. I told Jane, but she already knew I would be leaving for Key West Florida September 2.

VP-10 Detachment NAS Key West, Fl

The flight to NAS Key West was uneventful. Key West is the final stop in Florida before going onto Cuba. The Naval base there is a site for sore eyes. There is a Replacement Airgroup set up of F-4's who get their Pilots and Naval Aviation Officers ready for the fleet. The station also uses F-4's as a ready alert for possible Mig flyovers, Cuban revolt, that is, missile launches or protection for the SP-2E's!

The SP-2E's were all lined up with the engine propeller at the North and the South level perpendicular with the taxiway. The barracks were at least twenty years old and there were two people to a room. The showers were a mess, but they will do!

The squadron hanger was a far cry from Brunswick, Maine. The maintenance detachment had to pull the plane just inside the hangar to do any work on the engine that left half of the plane outside on the taxiway. The squadron duty officer had a desk on the first deck of a building next to the hangar and upstairs was allotted to the briefing/debriefing spaces for officers. The Air Intelligence Officer, normally a Lieutenant junior grade, was assigned as a permanent detachment officer. He attended our briefings that told them certain things to look for and specifics on using some of the gear.

The next morning and afternoon, we went to briefings by the AIO. The officers there were from the Air Force and Army giving us the lay of the land. Cuba is a big island. Remember, while I was in Aviation Officer Preflight in October 1962, a blockade of American Navy ships was set up trying to keep out all the missiles that the Soviet Union was sending down by ship. President John F. Kennedy won by forcing the

Soviet Premier to return those missiles back to Russia. The briefer could not over emphasize that there was a chance we would be chased by a Cuban aircraft. Certain procedures were to be used when we needed assistance. Normally, the F-4 ready alert would be at our disposal. The KAC-130, that decodes our messages, is our bible of communication. We also have an Air Force radar plane onstation anytime we are out there. We can monitor this frequency and we can guess what airplane the Air Force (or Willy Victor) is flying.

AIO gave us our cameras, a KB-10 and a normal big camera. Cameras are the keynote of surveillance whether you are on a mission, test flight, or a pilot trainer.

That afternoon, by the pool, we discussed all the things that were not included in the mission brief. The XO made some good points and indicated that all the crew be briefed including emergency procedures. The roaring F-4's keep us from talking as a flight of five was making' touch and goes' on the runway.

In the morning, we ate with the crew at a local chow hall. We, the full crew and I, followed a track that went East out through the Straits of Florida and back through the straits heading West. The track heads West and coming within five miles of Cuba. We continued on that track until we reach Havana. Then we would do a 360-degree turn and head East over the same track. We took off on time and sent our take off time and onstation report. My God, look at those ships! That's the way it was. Rig that ship, it is a type 2, no it is a raised one and four. Mind boggling isn't it! It took four hours to reach all the ships before we checked out Cuba. We radioed ahead that we would be giving our position every fifteen minutes. We finished the western time without any problems. We turned and had about six and half hours of flight remaining. We landed with 9.0 hours in the flight and 75 ships photographed.

Because there was no flight scheduled on the fourth day, the Pilot's had a pilot trainer. I went to the Navy Exchange to get some toothpaste and assorted items. At 2:00 p.m. the mighty LD-2 was doing touch and goes. I watched only for a minute before the F-4's invaded. There was so much noise and thrust expelled it is amazing how I can still stand here. After about fifteen minutes more, the F-4's landed. When this plane lands, a drag chute is released from the tail to slow the plane down. What an excellent idea, because the runway cannot stop a dangling hook, but a drag chute fits the bill.

The duty in Key West was simple—fly, fly, ready duty, and an occasional day off. The flight schedule was my duty so the crew got to know what they are going to do days before they are scheduled. I wrote a flight schedule a week at a time. The operations yeoman handled many things, but one of them was the flight schedule. Clearly, the yeoman always took the schedule to the Squadron Duty Officer to be signed, copied, and distributed twenty-five copies to the officers and enlisted barracks.

My second week in Key West means just as much as anything. The XO did not fly with us. I got in the bow of the airplane and made my position reports using a mike and a WAC chart. Right behind the navigator there is a sextant mount and three feet behind this is an opening to the air. I disconnected the sextant mount and it made cool air flow as if the door to the nose wheel was opened slightly. One day the ordnance man motioned me to come see him. I leaped over the wing and he showed me a carbon copy of the F-4 drag chute marked VP-10. He was just laughing but I was roaring! He told me that he and the radio man were going to stream it out of the opening in the bottom of the aircraft at the ordnance station. When we were coming in over G.C.A. (ground control approach), I had already warned the Pilots! At touch down, the ordnance man announced—'Drag chute deployed'. The Pilots had to laugh. They could not see the chute, but the two F-4's that we caught taxing thought the chute was funny and gave a thumb up for effort!

We flew various missions North of Cuba but never south of the island. The briefing offered many ways to treat the Cuban Air Defensive. If we ever suspected that we were being followed, we were to call out for help and the F-4's will come with their afterburners on. The mission also required any freighters or submarine activity be reported immediately.

We took off and headed South to our track entry point, turned and headed West. The PPC rigged several ships, but there are several of major significance lying at anchor within five miles of land. I was occupied giving my position every fifteen minutes. In three minutes, we passed the Western border and we altered the heading to 180 degrees true. We traveled around the back side of Cuba and rigged several tankers, but nothing else.

We had been airborne for seven hours ready to turn to 090 on the Western side of Cuba, when the ordnance man announces, 'PPC from Ordnance there is a Mig following us!' The Pilot questioned him and set Condition One. The Co-Pilot was starting the jets. I checked the UHF switch and the PPC is sending a flash message to get help to us

ASAP. The PPC came on the air and stated we were going down to 350 knots at an altitude of 300 feet. I guess I was scared but what the hell, I will ride it out! Ten minutes later, at 300 feet, the Cuban aircraft was still closing. All the sudden, two F-4's appeared about 30 nautical miles in front of us. The two F-4's reported to us but the PPC alerted them to the Cuban aircraft that was behind us at ten miles. The F-4's continued past us and five minutes later they were right beside us giving us a well done on UHF. The F-4's saw the Cuban aircraft that turned inward or 180 degrees within five miles from shore. The PPC asked them if they would meet us in the bar. That's affirm as they hit the afterburners and headed back to Key West.

We settled back, secured the jets, and took a leisurely trip back to Key West. We took a GCA and landed. I undid the hatch over the wing, with my hard-hat on, jumped into the Julie seat and climbed acting as a plane guard for the PPC. I could not believe the crowds that had gathered at the airfield. Representatives from the F-4 squadron and possibly three crews of people were walking as LD-2 ambled on to its parking spot. Once the engines were secured by the pilot, the crew was mobbed by the other crews. The Master Chief came forward with a case of beer. God, Budweiser never tasted so good. The XO and other officers were there including the two F-4 crews. We decided that we would meet in the BOQ bar.

That night I got drunk for a special purpose. I was alive only because the Co-Pilot had sense enough to get the crew out of Dodge City. I can not remember any more incidents when VP-10 was jumped by a jet and chased the way we were. After an hour we sung the famous VP-10 song. Not many of the jetjocks knew too many songs. The VP-10 song was my favorite and between the officers, we really lambasted our song to kingdom come. My last waking thought was that possibly my two Excedrin will ease my head tomorrow.

One day during the middle of the week I was the Squadron Duty Officer. I got up and ate and reported to the Duty Office. This was a hectic day, because we had a full schedule, Crew 2, my crew, had maintenance day, we had another crew scheduled for a ten hour patrol, we had a Naval Reserve submarine for the third crew that was supposed to take off at 1000, and the Ready Duty crew. I effected the turnover and properly relived the off-going duty officer. The petty officer who monitored the phone was there with me. He was in charge of the Duty Driver that was on a run to get chow for the crew that takes off at 0900. The crew finally got their food and the Duty Driver (that is what he is called) was to go to the mess hall to get the chow for the ten o'clock flight. The 0900 flight was off on time and then, the XO showed up and wanted to know what was happening. I briefed him and told him we were about to go to a brief at the Air Force OPCON. Anyway he left, as the petty officer had all the numbers to reach the Executive Officer.

It was time for the second airplane to launch and it just started its engines. I decided to walk around the squadron spaces. The maintenance chief was directing a walkdown of the taxiway. This walkdown is principally a lookout for nails, pieces of wire, or anything metallic in nature that sucks up into the engines of the SP-2E or heaven forbid the F-4 aircraft. In other words, if a nail or wire gets into an engine or jet, it is an engine change!

It's 1200 and boy I am famished. I let the petty officer go to chow. The Duty Driver went to pick up a hot dog and soda for me. The phone rang shortly after 1300 and I answered it. The caller was from OPCON, a Major in the Air Force. He had received a Situation Report from Communications and was sending it by Duty Driver. He advised that I send it by driver to NAS Key West Communications to get an operational immediate message. I hung up and had the driver moving post haste to the communication center. The Duty Driver was okay, as he stopped his car with a grinding halt, and ran with the message to me. I read the message and had the petty officer call the OPCON immediately to report that we were in receipt of the message. I also had him contact the Ready Duty Patrol Plane Commander. While he was trying to get the PPC, I called the XO. The Executive Officer answered the phone and I explained to him that it appeared we would have to launch the Ready Alert. He commended me for my good work and instructed me to get the Ready Duty crew. What a 'Katie Bar The Door' situation this was turning into.

At ten minutes after calling the "powers to be," the Ready Duty crew arrived, I told them to get the airplane and make sure they had enough fuel for eight hours of flight. The XO and the Ready Duty Officers came with the Air Force Major right behind them. According to the Major's brief a tanker was leaving the Gulf of Mexico and had reported a snorkel. This was picked up by a communication network and was given to the OPCON wherein we are going to launch into the area to see if the snorkel is friend or enemy. Forty minutes after the call was received at the duty office, the driver had delivered the chow, the crew received their charts, and the plane had taken off.

Now, we look over the crossed out flight schedule and holy cow, I have started out as the Maintenance Crew, the Squadron Duty Officer, and at 1400 I will be assigned the Ready Duty Tactical Coordinator! My crew arrived appropriately dressed in flight suits. We went upstairs to get the Ready Duty brief. I went to get a Coke after the brief. I desperately needed another and went to get it in Maintenance Control where I splashed my tropical khaki shirt.

At 5:00 p.m. the first patrol landed. The crew was hot and tired for the debriefing. The TACCO said there were many ships below the Florida Straits and a lot of activity Northeast of Havana. The airplane took pictures of a freighter moving East towards the Florida Straits. The nationality was overlooked but it appears to be Russian. Just behind the suspected ship, is a Cuban Navy Frigate. This ship seems to be guarding the freighter as it clears the Florida Straits. I cannot help wondering what is within the holds of this ship? After the debriefing, the photos were sent to the lab for processing ASAP. At 6:00 p.m., they were ready and I was to pick them up. The Duty Officer picked up the photos that were being examined by the Air Intelligence Officer. The name of the ship was clearly Russian. The ship was headed out of the Gulf of Mexico—back to Russia—with an unknown cargo. The Cuban Frigate was guarding her until she turned left beyond the Straits toward Russia. Our AIO called the OPCON and gave his own perception of the photos and was instructed to bring them to OPCON. I left the duty office to get some chow. I had finished eating by 6:45 p.m. when the AIO called me to get my flight suit on for the launching of Ready Duty! I had to run a block; hustle upstairs to my room so that could get out of my uniform and into my flight suit, boots, and piss cutter (my fore and aft) cap; and run back to the Duty Office. The Air Intelligence Officer was just about to begin his brief when I walked in. He started to apologize for interrupting dinner. The flight was going to be launched to find and locate the Cuban Frigate. The Soviet ship should be alongside the frigate. The searchlight is authorized for use in obtaining the exact location of the Cuban Navy vessel. A number of questions regarding the course and speed, firepower, and the location of the two ships currently came up. I only have one question, do we take cameras? A representative from OPCON said no, all they wanted is to know the position of the two ships with their course and speed, and to return to base. We were to report their position by KAC 130 over the assigned communication frequencies. Our crew was preparing the searchlight if needed to identify the targets.

At 2000, we were launched. Marty Merrick was PPC, Dick Petrucci was the Co-Pilot, and I was the NAV/TACCO running the radar. I had plotted the earlier position of the two ships using a speed of twelve knots and a course using a speed of ten knots. We began searching thirty minutes into our flight. I built in a course + or - ten miles on either side of the course line. Immediately the radio operator had a message for me. I decoded the message using KAC 130, only to find out the OPCON wanted to know what was happening! I responded to them that no contact had been made at the present time. It was starting to become dark outside and a hazy layer was forming just above the ships in the water. Marty indicated that we would use the searchlight if necessary.

Back at the ASA-16 were marker one and two, displayed so that the bearing were pointing representing the course. There were several ships remaining in the areas to be searched. The fog had worsened and the shipping lanes were beginning to get hazardous. We came upon two contacts close together. Marty had a bet on these two ships. Dick, the Co-Pilot, wanted to use the searchlight. It was not the culprit. I continued to give OPCON contact information and again, the radioman had a message for me from them. I knew what this was all about, they wanted a position report. I sent a message back giving the position moving northeast and continuing the radar search for the Cuban frigate. We were approximately two hours onstation when they think they have the contacts in the Co-Pilot's BDHI. I soon gave them a fly to point that they put on the Bearing, Distance Heading, Indicator that would pass along side the contacts. Dick set the searchlight to standby, so that when the PPC announces, "Light the searchlight," the 70,000,000 candle power comes online! The wide beam picks up the Cuban frigate and also the aft guns located on ships trailing the searchlight! The searchlight was brought down and boy was Dick a happy camper! I marked the target and obtained a Tacan range and bearing from Homestead AFB. The freighter was sighted right along side of the frigate. I began to KAC-130 my message, with the course and speed, that would be the contact report that OPCON was waiting for. I showed it to the PPC, he sent the message and the radio operator confirmed receipt of the message. Fifteen minutes later, they requested a position report and we should do the following: take pictures, send positions of the frigate and the freighter, and to remain onstation. An aircraft will meet us at first light to refuel. Well, I tell you I was pissed off beyond belief. I walked up to the cockpit and briefed the PPC about what the OPCON wanted. Marty broke up and laughed. He also remembers my question about the cameras and our instructions to only identify the ships and return. The PPC and Co-Pilot were discussing how much fuel we have on board while I returned to reply to the message. I got the TACAN fix for the targets and said something to the effect that we will remain onstation until 0500 and return to base. The PPC concurred and the radio operator sent the message.

Dick Petrucci had the radio set to a certain station that played local songs. It brightened me up as 2300 passed and the radio man had another message for me. This on was to remain onstation, take pictures, and we will send you a relief onstation. I guess I had to tell them that our camera was broken. The radio man did not quite understand what the message said, but sent the message anyway.

We passed out the chow that consisted of bologna and cheese sandwiches, milk, etc. It suddenly got quiet in the cockpit. The aircraft was on autopilot and the jive booming on the ADF station. This called for a definite plan of action. I went back and lifted up the door to the nose section and released it with a bang. All hell broke loose in the cockpit. Once they realized who made all the ruckus, they were able to laugh. I asked for a position and they knew they had lost the contacts. I gave them a BDHI insert that was the last position we were orbiting. Bingo, we found they targets of interest. The course and speed were the same as I had last reported.

By the time it was 0430, the clouds were opening up to light from the East. I was monitoring the HF 1 & 2 toggle switches to detect the airplane that is coming to relieve us. We can see the ships below us, but not the Cuban frigate. I fed them the dead reckoning position and there they were. By monitoring the UHF, VHF and all the radios, the PPC was able to gain contact with the airplane. It was 0500, time to leave station. The Plane Captain said we had enough fuel until 0530. I have slept about two hours on and off and boy I could sleep all day. About twenty minutes later, the pilots tallyhoed the aircraft and we sent our off station report. We landed at Key West exhausted. When we arrived to the debriefing, the Air Intelligence Officer apologized for the camera foul up. The searchlight saved the patrol but without it, we were shit out of luck. I got back to my room at 0900 and I slept until 3:00 p.m.. I set my clock so I could wake up and join my compadres for a swim. There is nothing like a swim being drowned out by a F-4's making touch and go landings!

VP-10 NAS Brunswick, ME

After spending seven beautiful days in Key West, Florida, we returned to Bruswick. Jane and Beth were waiting for me. Beth had grown and she was standing up but not quite enough to walk. Jane noticed that one of Beth's legs was not straight. The leg and foot were bent in toward the other leg. I suggested that we should talk to her doctor at her next appointment. The weather was brisk outside, but I wanted to be with my wife and daughter, so I ended up going downtown shopping!

October was Change of Command time for Commander Gately. He was to move on to Norfolk, Virginia and Commander Keith Sharer was to assume Command of VP-10. The Change of Command was exciting. We had several parties before and after the change of command we had a party to welcome the CO. I was proud of CDR. Sharer. I was impressed with his ability to motivate young junior officers to analyze a situation and come up with the best solution to get the job done. This not only means military tasks that we have learned, but flying antisubmarine tactics that you changed just a little to make the evolution run more smoothly. We moved up the ladder to Crew One. CDR. Russ Roberts moved up to the Executive Oficer and took over Crew Two.

The skipper made some interesting moves as the Commanding Officer . He decided to take his crew back to Key West, Florida during the Christmas holiday. We were to leave December 20 and return January 6, 1965. We planned on doing some early shopping at the mall in Portland. We bought presents for our parents and some goodies for Beth. The house was another item. Jane had done some looking around and bought a lot of Christmas decorations. It was getting time to pack the bags, but I still had not bought a tree. We looked at the Navy Exchange. These trees were priced way to high. I went home discouraged. My Christmas was torn apart. Where would I get a tree so that Jane and Beth would not feel embarrassed without having one? The next door neighbor came over for a couple of drinks that afternoon. I asked him where I could get a tree. He finished the drink and with an ax, boots, gloves, and hats, we left on foot. Two blocks down the street was a small group of pine trees. It was just about dark so we had to look quickly. We chopped a six and a half foot pine that looked great. It was quite cold when the north wind found its way down your back. It was dark when we hauled the tree into the front of the house. It fit perfectly in the living room. We wanted to trim the tree immediately, but first, it was time for another eggnog!

We left on December 20 for Key West. The men on board did not have much to say. Halfway into the flight we laughed and said, "well we should be thankful for this Christmas, we will be here next year!" When we landed we were escorted via taxi to our parking spot. Our rooms were the same as our last trip down here. We headed for the squadron to get a brief of what has been going on since we left.

The patrols were basically the same with many merchant ships that had to be rigged. The detachment was planning a Christmas Eve party and the Ready Duty was being released at 1800 for the party. The OPCON threw the party and we celebrated without our loved ones.

The Commanding Officer had a thought. "What about searchlight qualifications in Key West?" After discussing the idea, we were scheduled to go and check out the target. It was a winner as we had multiple PPC, TACCO and Co-Pilots on board to getting their qualifications. The second flight, on the next evening, resulted in two additional searchlight qualifications.

When the detachment was ended on January 6, 1965, we flew back to Brunswick, "lock, stock, and barrel." The weather in Brunswick was terrible, snow, ice, and an unbearably cold wind. The first All Officers meeting was held on Monday. The Commanding Officer thanked everyone for the work they had done at Key West. He was expecting messages with numerous accolades citing the awards bestowed on the aircrews. The topic quickly changed when he announced that Operation Springboard was in full force. Six crews would be participating next month. Springboard is an exercise that emphasizes all elements of the Navy and is held in NAS Roosevelt Roads, Puerto Rico. That afternoon everyone met with the CO, Operations Officer, Training Officer, Flight Crew Training Officer, and myself, the Schedules Officer. The Commanding Officer stressed we needed to get some qualifications and soon before the transition to the P-3 aircraft. We had a week to present to the Commanding Officer the six crews that we had decided to send to Springboard. LT. Austin Rehfield was my sidekick. We checked the schedule to see what crews were available. I talked with the qualifications man and we decided on six crews of which Crew One was one of the most unfortunate to go!!

A week later we met and the six crews were discussed. All efforts

would be concentrated on obtaining the non-essential submarine qualifications in Brunswick, any additional sub time will be used as Alfa
time for the submarine. I had a list of qualifications needed by each of
the six crews. Additionally, a block of submarine time (conventional
or nuclear) was being sent to us at Brunswick. We finally got a message with open mining slots, rockets and depth bombs, and submarine
time available. The next monumental task that lay before would be to
schedule the needs of the six aircrews over a two week period. We
worked on this until we were blue in the face. We eventually were
ready to submit this to the Operations Officer and he bought the whole
thing! In fact two days later, the Commanding Officer liked it and only
two changes made. We got into some what-if and buts; however clearly it's a sellable program.

A week before we left for Springboard, I stood up and briefed the
six aircrews. I started out with the qualification exercises that were
necessary. Many of the crews had been reformed and had a minimum
number of qualifications that were still necessary. I went over the two
week schedule that Austin and I had created for them. The submarines
would be thirty minutes to onstation. I started to sum up the brief by
showing them a slide illustrating the readiness increase to an Alfa,
Bravo, or Charlie crew. I ended the brief by passing on some rules that
as members of VP-10 we would have to follow. First, there was no
ASCAC at NAS Roosevelt Roads. We had to copy logs and make
immaculate DRT sheets. This meant correct symbols on the charts for
fix changes, Julie fixes, and attack or kill of a submarine. Once again
I stated that we cannot brief you, but maybe the TACCO can get
together with the essential crew members and go over the flight. I sat
down and Austin was left for the question and answer session. Many
of the questions were related to the qualifications exercise manuals. I
stood up again and suggested that someone from each crew should
find out who has or does not have the qualifications for Springboard
and this person make an extreme effort to get the necessary qualifications for those without them.

VP-10 Operation Springboard 1965

February 12, 1965, we left for Roosevelt Roads, Puerto Rico. Our flight
took off around 0900 and I helped the navigator get a qualification on
the flight. The flight went over Bermuda. This was my first time seeing

the island from the air. It is beautiful with all those cabin cruisers tied up beside the pier. LT. Dallas Lassiter was my trusted navigator. He could not get along with the P-2 as he had his personalized bag which had container bags for barf. They shot several sun lines, a latitude shot that confirmed our line of latitude. The land fall to Puerto Rico was spectacular with the mountains in the background. The US Naval Station is quite picturesque nestled in warehouses holding many of the parts for the ships, submarines, and aircraft it services.

We brought all of our gear to a hangar where it is stowed. The ride to the BOQ was long. The facility was at the other end of the field. It took us about twenty-five minutes that was faster due to the time being after work and a Saturday. The BOQ was a nice facility, even if the shower only worked at half power, it was still hot.

On Sunday after church services were held, all the crews met down at the squadron spaces. Officers from NAS briefed us on the base, the sun and weather, and the major areas that we would be working in. The last important action was the most recent changes to the planned evolutions. Great balls of fire, I had to do some more work. The schedule we had planned for Monday and Tuesday was still good, but standby for the rest of the week. Once the briefing was over, I started rearranging the flight schedule. After an hour of reassigning crews, the Commanding Officer wanted to know how it was going. The Commanding Officer was gratified, we rode back to the BOQ in his car and headed for the bar.

The brief case that I owned held a particular interest for me and the adventure of the qualifications. I started studying the layout of the whole evolution. I wanted things to happen at the right time and place for a kill. Monday's flight was laid out in my notes on the bed. There were three exercises we should get. The primary exercise is known as the Jezebel which begins with the aircraft not knowing where the submarine is. We start with 'Comex, Comex, Comex' followed by an order for the Jezebel pattern and commencement of dropping sonobuoys. Once the buoys begin drawing on the grams, the Jezebel operator announces contact and the necessary command is 'Set Condition TWO for Localization.' TACCO then drops two CODAR plants that will coordinate which bearing is the submarine. Two additional CODAR plants are dropped and hopefully the operator fixes the submarine. The TACCO fixes the submarine and will follow the bearing from the CODAR plants to mark on top the submarine.

I held the brief on Monday. We talked about everything under the sun, including staffing the lookout at all times. We should leave earlier if we could and proceed into our operation area. We got onstation and began to call our submarine. An hour later, the Commanding Officer was mad. Here we were with no submarine. I realized that the submarine moving spot was near the northwest position of the area. We flew up in that area and finally, God Bless the lookouts, spotted it about ten miles away. The Co-Pilot made contact with the submarine and said he would take another hour before he can snorkel. I suggested we started to make radar run-ins. Well, what a way to ruin an airline. We started making radar run-ins and the radar caught fire. I turned off all switches to the TACCO station, and the navigator's station while the crew members investigated the APS-20. The report from the technicians was bad ; the radar was short circuited and the plane smelled like burning rubber. The Commanding Officer left station and thirty minutes later we landed. What a hell of a mess we had!

Another airplane was available, so we tried again to complete our mission. The PPC had made arrangements to check in with the submarine before we checked into the area. The submarine was still available, so I read him the Julie exercise. We acknowledged the exercise and decided to meet at the Comex (the start of the exercise) on the hour. After comex the submarine is marked on top, the aircraft proceeds outbound for three minutes and returns inbound to mark on top the old datum at six+00 minutes time late. The Co-Pilot radioed to the submarine, 'Comex, Comex, Comex.' I gave the PPC a heading to fly and a new heading to datum. I put marker #3 on datum, marker #1 on the 4000 buoy short of datum, and also on the BDHI. Buoy one and a charge was dropped at 4000 yards short of datum and the drift computer was cut on. The BDHI was switched to the datum buoy. Evidently no charge was dropped on the first buoy. Single echo, range 1800 reported the Julie datum buoy and a charge was dropped. I rogered that and the Co-Pilot announced buoy away and a charge to Northern buoy. The Western buoy was placed on the BDHI, Julie reported no echoes on the North buoy. Western buoy smoke and charge away and buoy in sight for a mark on top and a charge reported to the PPC. The drift computer was ready, 'standby for a MOT'; I selected two mile scale corrected the cursor by GPI N-S, E-W controls until mark on top was announced. Simultaneously I hit the green light so the drift computer can be calculated. Buoy one had a range on it of 2700 single echo and buoy five with all its charge and smoke went out.

The ranges yield double echoes fixing the target still within the 4000 yard circle. I placed the BDHI on the fixed position about where I thought it might be. We marked on datum, headed outbound for the drop, 'Madman, Madman, Madman' was heard; the Julie buoy and the smoke and charge was dropped. The P-2 was in a turn to arrive on the mad marker. I told the PPC I had a rough course of 089 true. Range on buoy five 800 single echo yards the Julie operator announced 'standby for Mad.' Madman again was the call and the PPC called the Ordnance man to have the appropriate setting for the attack signal. One minute and fifty-eight seconds later we got another madman and Ordnance delivered the attack.

We stood easy and climbed up to 1000 feet. I was bushed. There was another plane in the area, late for onstation, that our PPC spoke to. The submarine was not snorkeling as yet as I figured the exercise lasted sixty minutes. My best calculation was twenty-three minutes from first buoy drop till the final simulated torpedo was dropped by charges. One hour and fifteen minutes later, the submarine gave me the Alfa Bravo Charlie report. This gave the course, speed, and depth of the sub, a rundown of the mixed layer depth, and an estimate of the attack. The attack was given as 'close aboard'. The Co-Pilot rogered the report and turned him over to the on-coming plane.

The on-coming plane wanted the same exercise. They bounced around and they began forty-five minutes later. By this time, we were not doing very much good for the cause. It was night now and the moon was just coming up over the horizon. It sure looked pretty, but I knew the PPC would head back now. Finally the PPC called the airplane to say we had enough and were going home after a long tedious day.

I slept like a log and found it hard to wake up in the morning. I showered and headed for the hangar. The Duty Officer was busy working on the maintenance side of the house. I took the flight schedule that the duty officer had and went to finish it in the operations office. The yeoman who worked with us at home was busy running tables and chairs to this room. I noticed he had put a large chart that showed each crew's objectives day by day. The changes to the operations' messages last week had come in. I started checking these messages and found that only two crews were effected by the changes added on later in the week. On the right of the two week schedule is a list of qualifications that corresponded with their schedule periods. An hour later, skipper called to see how things were going. I told him that I was finished with the rough copy of the schedule and the changes were a bit of a problem, but it will work out.

The schedule moved along smoothly the next two days. Crew One had to fire the rocket exercise in which a high velocity aerial rocket which is fired at a surfaced or partially surfaced diving sub. The parameters for the five inch rockets and the MK-54 depth bombs, are used to get maximum advantage over the escaping culprit. The rocket starts at 1500 feet perpendicular to the submarine. A sight is used in the cockpit to maximum advantage. The PPC noses over, dives at fifteen degrees, fires a rocket, and pulls up no later than 800 feet; then the MK-54 depth bomb comes in the nick of time. The depth bombs are dropped four at a time, five degrees either side of the course dropping the first four at the start and using the intervalometer for the three remaining drops.

We went out to the airplane and witnessed the loading of the rockets. The MK-54 depth bombs were old World War II bombs. They loaded in the bomb bay and we got on the P-2 to conduct a quick preflight. The plane was started and we headed to the run-up position. Off to the side there was an ordnance truck. The men got out of the truck, plugged in their headsets to the plane, monitored the final checklist, and armed the rockets. When the checklist was complete, the pilot announced the appropriate condition for takeoff.

LD-1 lumbered down the runway for take off and soaring into the blue, we switched from the tower to the range facility. We began checking in with a boat that was designed to cover the area in case of any weapons going astray. We dropped two smokes about 100 yards apart. These were dropped to ensure that it was the same size submarine. The PPC turned, headed out two miles, and performed a one eighty turn heading back towards the smokes. The rocket checklist was brought out. We had progressed down the checklist to the hitting the arm button. The PPC rolled over fifteen degrees, descended toward the target, and WHOOSH goes one of the HVAR's as it is launched. The PPC starts bringing the plane to 1500 altitude. We see the rockets penetrate the water about in the middle of the two smokes. The PPC turn to the right dropping down to 200 feet. The checklist is brought out with two more steps, 'bomb bay doors open and pickle'.

The first MK-54 was just short of the first smoke, but the rest were kicked out by the intervelometer. It was a pretty sight. There were three out of four actual MK-54's that went off!

The Jezebel exercise was one of the qualifications that I had to get.

We were scheduled to get this one today. I went over the qualifications and spoke with the Jezebel operator if he needed my help to call me. The AQA-4 is certainly a mystery. I have been in a VP-10 airplane and can remember four times where we have really used the system. A meticulous preflight is important. I believe the Jezebel operator understands the system, but isn't a better system available for LOFAR?

We got to our area and right away we gained contact with the target. We read the exercise instructions and set a comex time. The PPC told me that the submarine was an FM-10, this information I passed onto the Jezebel operator. He and I briefed one another on the fixing rated that we would be looking for.

With comex announced, I laid a buoy pattern that kept us inside our area. Talk about sound in the water, we had merchants, trawlers, and I swear it looked as we had fishing boats out there too! Thirty minutes later, the submarine started snorkeling. I would not have noticed but I sighted it and asked, 'what in the hell is that?' The Jezebel operator reported it to me. The LOFAR contact of the submarine was of medium quality on the eastern buoy and it was printing of a lesser quality on the southern buoy. I set Condition Two for localization. I selected two buoys and set up the intervelometer for 350 feet. This was called plant Alpha. The buoys and smoke went, the PPC started turning the plane so the Plant Bravo will be 90 degrees or perpendicular to Alfa. Bravo was away and I turned on my drift computer to keep the aircraft stabilized with the CODAR plants. Jezebel acknowledged that all the buoys were up. The CODAR plants were turning into a mess. I said we were to get long ranges on sonobuoys today, welcome to LD-1. I got up to pass the bearing to the navigator. With the APS-20 radar on before comex I could explain the ships but I still could not figure out the real plot before me. I finally decided the bearing was 210 so I told the PPC to mark on top plants A and B outbound 240 degrees true. The mark on top showed that my drift was perfect.

We dropped Plant Charlie and Delta and waited for this one and only bearing. It never came, so I stood up and helped the Jezebel operator. We synched and calibrated, finally beginning to see the bearing we had saw on the other plants. We had thirty minutes left, so I asked for a bearing from Charlie, Delta, Alfa, and Bravo. The bearing looked like 210 degrees at four knots. I called the PPC to give him the course that I wanted him to fly over Charlie/Delta and the fix is on the BDHI. The PPC came over the loudspeaker and announced Condition One.

He marked on top the CODAR plants and inbound to datum. In this exercise, we had to be within five nautical miles of his position. The Co-Pilot saw the snorkel and it appeared about one o'clock on the aircraft's nose. Our BDHI was on three miles to go. That looks like a winner to me. The actual distance was a mile and the sub was 180 degrees going on a bearing of 205 degrees. The sub acknowledged the Finex report and in about fifteen minutes, he gave the ABC report. Another airplane was waiting to get onstation, so the PPC thanked the sub for his services and we left station. He reminded me that he would be waiting in the bar to buy me a drink. I believe I am ready for a drink. I am puzzled as to how I pulled that one out. The modern miracles of 1965 can afford a chance to be lucky, but what about being scientific and factual in all instances. There is something coming down the pike that will clarify the whole dam situation; we transition to the P-3A in four months.

The weekend in Roosevelt Roads was not a good place to have fun, clearly I had fun figuring out how each crew stood in their qualification scenario. Six crews were doing quite well, however, only two crews have mastered a Bravo status. This is assuming all crews have done their homework and each dead reckoning sheet has been redone, who knows if they have passed or not! February 23 is the last time we are scheduled for subtime. Each crew has at least one sub, or possibly two sub periods if they radically stump their toes!

That afternoon the navigator and I went over the logs and records of our subtime. We had new DRT charts and naturally, brand-spanking-new log sheets. I was interested in the UNH-6 tape recorder, the qualification was a bust. The tape recording system is a dual track magnetic recorder that is installed at the Navigator's station. It is a recorder only and the four major operators involved have been assigned the following priority: Pilot, Julie, ECM, and Jezebel. The other tapes or logs which must accompany the packet are logs of Jezebel operator, including the grams and the preflight of the AQA-4; the Julie tape and preflight logs; the mad operator with a mad tape and preflight; the ordnance man with the number of sonobuoys, SUS's, and smoke drops; and the Tactical Coordinator who fills out the members of the crew that participated in the event.

February 23, 1965, we went onstation like gangbusters. We hurried through two qualifications and finally the skipper said, "let's give the A-36 a try." The A-36 as best as I can remember, is a qualification that starts with Jezebel, CODAR, and into some sort of close-in tactics to a kill. This was the masterpiece of Antisubmarine warfare. If we achieve this we will be an Alfa crew! The instructions were relayed to the sub as we left datum to start the exercise. At comex, we have an hour to go before we left station. The first sonobuoy drop was an SSQ-28 set for one hour. After five minutes the Jezebel operator reported no contact. The PPC questioned this. I decided to lend a hand. The Jezebel operator knew in a heart beat what the signature will be. Finally I noted that he was printing and we were immediately laying CODAR plants. Well you guessed it, the plants each had multiple targets. I selected a similar bearing back to the datum area. We jumped the gun and added power to go into this area for our final two plants. The PPC jumped on the headset, he had a snorkel. Mad was alerted. The ordnance man loaded pingers and smokes. 'Mad Man, Mad Man, Mad Man' announced the MAD operator along with a pinger and a smoke. We made two more passes with Mad and we killed the sub with three PPC's on board!! I looked at my watch and the onstation time was over. It was time to rerun this exercise back in the hangar before the ASCAC can see it!

The next day all of the charts and records were analyzed and we substituted logs and DRT charts that made an artifact from the living dead. For the life of me, I was uncertain of the fact that we really had LOFAR contact. I would have let this signature run while we were laying the CODAR patterns. But for now, we have a perfect qualification or qualifications to turn in. It is back to Happy Hour and being hammered when we return to Brunswick.

VP-10 NAS Brunswick, ME

Our skipper was beside himself as he was called to the FAW-3 ASCAC on Wednesday afternoon. After four days back from Roosevelt Roads, the Commander from ASCAC told him that A-36 (the final qualification for Alfa Crew) was rejected because the Jezebel operator did not have enough signature to classify it as a submarine. The Commanding Officer looks at the gram and saw the one quarter inch of gram he knew it was a US sub. He called the squadron and wanted the Crew One Jezebel operator in ASCAC ASAP! The Jezebel operator arrived at ASCAC and was given the gram. He was asked what the signature on the gram was. The Jezebel operator said it was too early to tell what the signature is. Remember I told you, keep that LOFAR printing on the gram until you switched to CODAR! The final result of the achieving session—no qualifications. Where was I, frankly I was in a trainer!

Spring in Brunswick was non-existent until May if it ever happens at all. Jane, Beth, and I drove down to the Portsmouth Naval Hospital. The doctor had reviewed Beth's leg problem and he was considering breaking her leg in order to reset it to correct her walk habit. Jane went with Beth to the doctor. I waited outside in a waiting room and read old magazines. I got a Coke and flitted around. Jane came back from the doctor's to tell me that he did not break the leg but she has toe-ing in of the feet. Beth would be ready to leave in a few hours. We had a hurried lunch and went back to check on Beth.

At 4:00 p.m., Beth was ready to go home. God bless her heart, I knew that her leg was hurting. The doctors saw me earlier and addressed the leg and how it should be strapped or positioned at night-time. She had a device that corrected the feet when she went to bed. We opened the door to go over to our car, but winter is not done with Maine yet, there was four inches of snow already on the ground and it was still falling! We got all buckled up and started back to Brunswick. Interstate 95 was covered with snow. As few minutes went by, and the saints preserve us, a snowplow was coming. This man was obviously a native of Maine. He was driving the plow at fifty miles an hour and I loved it! I had one occasion that totally frightened me. A car passed me doing sixty miles an hour that threw slush all over my car. Needless to say, it scared the shit out of Jane too!

The P-3A has gotten into my vocabulary. I am reading all the pamphlets Lockheed sends us. Many of the officers have received orders to the training command. We are surprised that there are so many LCDR's ordered into the squadron. As a matter of fact, with the Commanding Officer and XO having crews, all twelve crews will be PPCs' with the remainder as LCDR'S .

The last exercise before we disestablish the P-2's was held off the coast of Massachusetts. We were planting sonobuoys in a transit area. We were plastered with merchants and no contacts. A second flight in the area yielded a surfaced US sub. The Commanding Officer reported a visual and attacked. Two weeks later we got a Bravo Zulu (Well Done) for getting an excellent kill on the sub. I cannot remember if this series of flights invalidated this exercise or not. One evening as we were flying south of Nantucket, a loud bang come from the starboard engine. The plane Captain feathered the engine. We were only two hours out and had to abort the flight. The jets were turned on and we flew back to Brunswick.

Since August of 1963 I have been involved in Lockheed's SP-2E Neptune aircraft to fly and operate the Tactical Coordination equipment. This trail of endeavor led me to all facets of patrol aviation such as surveillance, mining, searchlight, electronic illumination, countermeasures patrol, and rocket/depth bomb exercises. After my first deployment, I forgot why I was training so diligently. Antisubmarine warfare is, and even now these years later, is becoming a masterful plan of plotting, directing, and carrying out the demise of a submarine. The answers are in this aircraft to develop, refine and produce a P-3 airplane which can produce effective submarine prosecutions. The SP-2E has the guts which will make its successor a significate achiever with respect to magnetic anomaly detection, impaired radar, Jezebel AQA-5 system, and a better inertial navigation system synched to the real world. With my world in disarray, excepting the Navy Flight Officer designation, I would try for trading in my reserve status for a regular Navy status.

Before I left to VP-30 to begin P3A training, I noticed in the Navy Times the reorganization and redesignation of the 135X category of Naval Aviation Observer. More recently the Bureau of Personnel Notice 1212 of May 13, 1965, redesignated the Naval Aviation Observer as Naval Flight Officer, 132X. CDR Sharer called me into his office an explained why the change was made. The way had been paved for a Naval Flight Officer to assume Command of a VP squadron or command of a Naval Air Station, carrier, or Chief of Naval Operation. The recent BUPERS notice explains this new procedure. He congratulated me and gave me a piece of paper to sign that I was now a NFO. I signed the papers that went back to BUPERS and received my copy of the designation. This meant a lot to me and I wanted to apply for regular rather than reserve. The letter was sent to the Chief of Naval Personnel requesting transfer to the regular Navy!

VP-10 Detachment, VP-30 NAS Patuxent River, MD

It was the month of July, we were heading South to begin transitioning to the P-3 Orion. I drove down to my parents house in Annandale, Virginia. Beth was happy to see Nana and Pop Pops! We spent more of the weekend with them. At lunch Sunday, Jane and I went to the Paxtuxent River Naval Air Development Center. We checked into the VP-30 Duty Officer and learned that we had classes at 0800 the next day. I checked into the BOQ and saw all my navigators and tactical coordinators. We emptied the car and said our goodbyes. Jane was supposed to meet me on Friday afternoon. After Jane left, I had a few beers and ran into the VP-10 pilots. The skipper told us there was a lot to learn, so we had better be ready.

The first week of training at VP-30 concentrated on the airplane and basic knowledge of it's systems. Of significance is the four turbo-prop engines installed on the P-3. These are Allison T56-A-10W constant speed, axial flow single spool gas turbines. The turbine engine provides thrust principally by driving a propeller. An auxiliary power unit (APU) is installed to provide power (pneumatic and electrical power) necessary to make the airplane self-sufficient.

The primary mission of the P-3A is antisubmarine warfare. Each crew member plays a vital role in this mission, as well as performing other tasks. Generally, the P-3 crews find themselves flying surveillance missions, patrols, special patrols, and training flights involving the many jobs the P-3 crew is asked to do. The major difference is the P-3 Orion is the ASN-42 inertial navigator system as display set as well as other ASW systems. The ASN-42 provides the P-3 aircraft with inertially derived navigation data. This set operates in two modes Navigator or Pilot. The Pilot mode consists of three submodes: Slave, Free, and Compass. In the Nav mode, the inertial provides position data (latitude and longitude), ground velocity, distance travelled, stabilized magnetic heading, magnetic variation, true heading, turn rate, and roll information.

The first thing that you do to align the system is to start the system by activating the lever from I-D to Fast Erect and back to I-D at the co-pilot station in the cockpit. There is a latitude set knob that you will have to set. Back at the Nav station you have to set in the magnetic variation and set in the position on the indicator. This sets up the inertial. The navigator must continue his preflight. The inertial is taken just before engines are started.

One of the things that amazes me is the platform of the inertial. The North-South orientation is constant and the East-West accelerometers keep that of pulls and altitude changes that the aircraft (inertial) senses. The shuler cycle system of the inertial is based on a 42 minute cycle. The system in the airplane is trying to keep within the bounds of this system, but when it fails, or the inertial has a problem, then the platform or computer light comes on. The only way you should turn, is either try the system in slave or compass mode.

The Air Mass Computer, ASA-47, located at the navigator's station represents the P-3A's attempt to put the system right in the hands of experts. The Air Mass Computer acts as an information center that breaks down the navigation systems into three distinct modes. The first system is the I/D mode or inertial/Doppler mode. In this mode there are two positions, AM/LN2C. Both modes one and mode two give true heading to the major components of the ASW equipment located around the Tactical Coordinator. This equipment consists of the ASA-16/ASA-47 air mass computer, the four BDHI, radar compass and the search radar, cockpit plotter, the ground track plotter, ASW maneuver monitor (MAD), and lastly, the direction finder—the ALD-2B. The magnetic heading drives two horizontal situation indicators (HSI) when inertial reference is selected. Therefore the Pilot's HSI with the heading reference in inertial provide him with VOR1 and VOR2, TACAN, ARN-21 or ARN-52, search radar and PB-20, and autopilot. The variation is supplied to the ASA-47. The pitch and roll are also key in this category. The Co-Pilot's MM-4 altitude indicator, the doppler, the APN-153, maneuver monitor, and the search radar (APS-80) receive pitch and roll inputs.

The two most important components of the I/D and AM/LN2C modes are North-South and East-West velocity and distance traveled. The velocity is passed through the Integrated Display System, the ASA-16, and the Bearing Data Converter—ASA-50. The distance traveled goes through the ASA-16, ground position indicator for the APA-125, ground track plotter, PT-396, and the cockpit plotter, OA-1768.

New in the P-3A Lockheed aircraft is in APN-153 Doppler radar navigator. The doppler navigation system computes and simultaneously displays aircraft ground speed and drift angle. The antennae system transmits two pairs in the left forward and right aft; then in the right forward and left aft. The switching rate is once per second. The limits of the APN 153 is +/- 25 degrees pitch and +/- 60 degrees of roll. This is a reliable mode of doppler radar. I look forward to the success it advertises!

As we are discussing all avenues of navigation, let's switch to tactical navigation. The drift computer on the ASA-16 of the P3A is a godsend! When in a low level search, 4000 or 8000 yard Julie pattern or active pattern expecting MAD, you get good plot stabilization with the drift computer. The drift computer course comes on when you punch out a buoy and right away hit the green button. Two minutes later the green button comes on indicating that it is ready to accept a drift computer. The PPC sights the buoy we want to mark on top and calls a ten second standby. The TACCO grabs the ground position indicator correct knobs labeled North-South, East-West and centers the cursor on the assigned marker of the buoy. 'Mark on top' said the Pilot and the Tactical Coordinator hits the compute button. This computer measures the range and distance displayed. You can select the correct drift or BDHI after you hit the green button. The AQA-5 is a significant improvement in our passive sonobuoy system. The LOFAR grams arc wider and they can monitor eight buoys at a time. The sonobuoys used are the SSQ-28 and soon we will get the SSQ-41. The SSQ-23 is on the way out for Julie. The SSQ-47 is coming but we will have to wait for its arrival. There are certain advantages to using the AQA-5. The Jezebel operator thought is was 'neat and sweet'. Along with the AQA-5 is its AQH-1 tape recorder. This is a fourteen channel recorder that records LOFAR channels as well as active buoy and Julie sonobuoys. The recorder is located near the galley section of the aircraft. The recorder is keyed to the various ICS audio systems in the aircraft. The ASW audio permits the TACCO and other members in the aft bulkhead to record when they turn on the mike to communicate. One of the systems that must be attended to was the OA-1768 Plotter System. The OA-1768 consists of the pilots ground track plotter board and plotter control monitor; a GTP center control panel; and a tactical coordinator's plotters control panel. The plotter's displays the relative positions of the aircraft and any inserted marks. The plotter marks any search stores released from the aircraft. The aircraft display consists of a crab that is illuminated and the aircraft is depicted as an arrow. The crab is positioned by the N-S and E-W components of ground track from the navigation system selected by the NAV system mode switch on the air mass plotter. The pilot has limited control of the plotter operation with the plotter control on the center control stand. The tactical coordinator may control the plotter with the panel located at the tactical coordinators station.

The pilot's cockpit plotter, on his instrument panel, consists of a transparent bezel glass with etched compass points and range reference markings, a cable driven crab, controlled by servomechanisms, travels beneath the plotting film in accordance to the N-S E-W components of ground track information. The rotatable illuminated arrow is to represent the aircraft displaying true heading that the aircraft is flying. This is really interesting because the pilot centered the GTP-4 himself but the OA system never works in the SP-2E aircraft. The P3A finally has a helper when Lockheed built this airframe and make this plotter really work. Unfortunately, the tactical coordinator must guide the pilot into an 8000 or 4000 yard pattern with the OA-1768 plotter. The pilot really needs this device at night when its twenty-five plus knots or the water is gusting to forty knots. Believe me, its harry flying a bucking bronco in darkness knowing that one false mistake can ruin your whole day. The airplane had some 'holes' back aft, but the student load was tremendous with the Vietnam crisis building up. One squadron had already been picked up from Patuxent River to participate in the deployment to the Philippines. This squadron was flying around the mainland looking for junks, camouflaged as a fishing vessel that could knock you out of the air with a self-propelling launched missile! The P3A's had bomb bays filled with MK-54's on all flights.

The squadron was fast moving on in its change of aircraft to the P3A. Many pilots and NAO's said that they wanted orders or reassigned. The visits to VP-30 were on a four crew detachment. I was part of the first detachment and I did not know it at the time, but I worked and trained along with the pilots. We had August 1965 through January 1966 to get ready, and we would deploy at that time. Where, when, what time, but not now, we have to train and that is what we are going to do!

VP-10 NAS Brunswick, ME

The onset of P3A training was begun with the first flight made on August 3. The skipper said we would make all the flights as a crew. We would take our Navy Air Training and Operating Procedures Standardization manuals and read everything and preform all the drills. The flights started out with four crews and two airplanes. The flight crews split the days and flew the aircrew twice in one day. The navigator was new on the crew, LT Carl Baumann. He was a great guy and we got good together as we learned the new system. We even were good up front in the cockpit as it was called. We were asked to sit up in the co-pilot seat and to make radio transmissions relative to safety of flight and where the airplane is at all times. The syllabus that we adopted in VP-10 was the same source of instruction that VP-30 endorsed. For the pilot, it had three or four training flights that trained the pilots in rudiments of flights to the more advanced characteristics of engine failure, two engines out, and various emergencies that would occur during flights. The plan of scheduling was broken apart by two more planes that were ready in beautiful downtown Burbank, California. The skipper called WINGSLANT and miraculously took 152169, our plane, three crews of pilots, and me to Burbank to get the two planes. What a chinese fire drill it was to go get the airplanes. I went along, without orders, but I needed time for the rough road ahead with flights coming and going.

During the many flights we started from the beginning of the qual manual. We did the all the basic qualifications that were prescribed in the manual. We then did a lot of Julie, active patterns, and MAD hunting circles. We loaded a mine, a special weapon, and a MK-44 dummy torpedo. I was loading officer and each team member knew at all times what he was supposed to do. VP-10 made arrangements to visit VP-30 and to take the NATOPS evaluators and his team for a standard check flight. Lieutenant Commander Gene Bernard was the head evaluator and I gave him the tactical brief. We asked for questions and he said this brief covered it all. When we got to the aircraft, we preflighted our gear and we answered many questions from the NATOPS team.

Upon takeoff from NAS Pax River, we were into emergency drills, one engine out, and Carl, my navigator, could not get the ASA-47 working. After two minutes, the evaluator in charge of Julie showed him a switch on the front of the ASA-47 that was in the 'off' position! Carl apparently did not know about this switch, presto changeo, the

ASA-47 works again.

Meanwhile, back at the ASA-16, the PPC announced onstation. I started laying a pattern and it was a modified five buoy Jezebel pattern. We got contact and the Jezebel operator called it a foxtrot submarine. I went right into CODAR. Plants Alpha and Bravo entered the water. We got plants of bearings and we threw them majority out. The second set of plants went out and I changed drift compute points. The bearings were pretty good, we had a fix and according to my book we were going into an 8000 yard Julie pattern. I set up the pattern and inserted the pattern on the pilots GTP-4 buoy, a charge and smoke out, sonobuoy two, a charge and a smoke, datum buoy, a charge and a smoke; and them the PPC came forth and said something is wrong, because there is an echo on the second buoy. I did not know at the time, but I had forgotten to select SUS on my armament panel. I selected it and Gene reared up a laugh and we proceeded to make a kill on the laborious submarine. Then we had two more drills including the bailout and the world famous fire drill. When we landed at the airfield, Gene Bernard said we passed and a letter should follow within a week. I think I caught a nap on the way back to Brunswick. The skipper said I did well, but please don't screw up the 8000 yard Julie pattern.

The second half of the pilots and NFO's were back in Brunswick and ready to fly. I was extremely busy keeping all the records of who was flying FAM-3 or who was flying ASW-2 (antisubmarine warfare flying exercise). Most of the pilots in the first four crews had finished their syllabus. The pilots were up for PPC and now they were getting the chance to succeed in this endeavor. The chance for submarine time was few and far between. The diesel submarine was on it's deathbed. The submarine forces in Washington had just about closed the lid on many new conventional submarines.

Crew One went down to Norfolk to pick up the skippers PPC. My mind has drawn a blank but this man, I believe was responsible for many techniques that were about to break in ASW. The flight went very well and a dreamt up an ASW problem was an exercise in the fundamental tactical problem solving of the PPC. We ran the LOFAR sonobuoy to a contact, and then we employed CODAR. The CODAR plants are simulated and can develop a fix into a 8000 yard pattern. With the kill being made with simulated torpedoes and climbing to 5000 feet, headed back to Brunswick to let the crew off. We lined up for a TACAN approach and suddenly we had a two engine out approach. Now those two engines were not out but were at 100% idle. As the plane drops final flaps, the plane started to falter, the tenacity and vigor of the Flight Engineer showed when he announced, "wave off horsepower setting 2000!" The skipper took control and the guest PPC notified NAS Brunswick that we were taking a waveoff.

The last tale that I must tell about Commander Keith Sharer has to do with which submarine is which? One night, Crew Eight and myself, led by LCDR Erive Goschke went out to work both submarines. We got onstation and located the submarines. The skipper talked to the submarines and decided to do a Jezebel exercise and the other submarine will qualify for searchlight qual. The events went well for the first hour as we performed all necessary radar, electronic countermeasures, and searchlight qual. The second, actually it took about thirty minutes to get started, but we commenced laying sonobuoys. The Jezebel operator reported contact and we went into CODAR. Alpha and Bravo plants were a little shaky, but after ten minutes the bearing stabilized and a quick mark on top, we were off to lay Charlie and Delta CODAR plants. The bearings were slow to mature and when I got a fix, I inserted one on the GTP-4 and ordered the PPC to mark on C/D outbound to the fix. Well let me tell you, the skipper saw his other aircraft light off the submarine that he was working. He turned to this submarine and I was so irritated that I got up, off from my TACCO seat, threw my headset, and went aft to the galley to get a cup of coffee! Carl Baumann, my navigator came and got me a cup of coffee and asked if the BDHI was the fix of the submarine. Of course it was and I went back to the TACCO's station. We passed within one mile of snorkeling submarine, that undoubtedly would have been a qualification.

We got back to Brunswick and I was still pissed off. My TACCO bag was slammed into the locker, off came my boots, and into my uniform. Finally I closed the locker door, and what should appear before my eyes but the skipper. He said to me, "Mike, I will never do that again, I am sorry!" He shook my hand and that brought a smile to my face.

In November of 1965, there was a Change of Command for CDR Keith Sharer. He was relieved by CDR Russ Roberts. He came up through the chain of command and specialized in the maintenance field. He has written several documents that were needed in the field of Naval thinking. CDR Karl Bernstein was the next Executive Officer. The commander was from the Senate House Armed Services where he acted as a briefer, researcher, and mister-fixit officer. His wife Jane was certainly a wonderful addition to VP-10. Commander Sharer said in his farewell address, that we should be proud of the Lockheed P-3A and should achieve new antisubmarine tactics with this aircraft. The reception for him was packed and I said my goodbyes with Jane in hand, to CDR Sharer who had orders to Washington, D.C.

CDR Bernstein was to be my Patrol Plane Commander and was busy as a bee trying to get his PPC check and learn the squadron. It finally came before in the end of November. We had a brief in Fleet Air Wing 3 briefing area.

With the brief finished, all questions and answers provided, we marched to the aircraft to begin preflight. An hour and a half later, CDR Bernstein briefed the crew and assigned different crew members to inspect and report during Condition Four. The last thing that he did was he told me that I was responsible for the Co-pilot's aft. Now that earned my respect for the man and surely I was willing to do just as he requested. It was a black, hideous, rock and roll night. The submarine finally communicated with us and we conducted a Julie exercise with them. The Julie Exercise went well but the crew in the back got sick. Carl almost blew his lunch, and I must confess so did I. The Julie ranges were 1800-200 yards that made it extremely hard to get a fix. I had different technique to employ and we bombed each Julie fix until we got double echoes. We killed the sub in one exercise, but the second exercise the plot in the cockpit did not work, I had him, but the range just became a 1000 yard range or less.

When we arrived back at Brunswick, I was worn out. CDR Bernstein sought me out and thanked me for doing an excellent job. He mentions that he lost the pattern several times due to high seas and of course the GPT-4 pattern freezing up in the cockpit. That was one for the books. The P3A was capable, but not stable or strong to resist rough water, or gusting high winds flying at extremely low altitudes at night! Incidentally, we have a new PPC! Word was out that VP-10 will be enjoying two fun-filled weeks at Roosevelt Roads! COMFAIR-WINGSLANT message announces that Springboard would be scheduled for the first two weeks of January 1966 and then deploying on January 25 or 26 to either Keflavik, Iceland or Argentia, Newfoundland. Undoubtedly this required a massive planning evolution and some have just finished their four weeks of training before Springboard. LCDR Craig Gilchrist, the training officer, and a number of us planned what to do next. Twelve crews were without many of the submarine qualifications. These were primary in allocating these times equally. The next meeting was scheduled a week later.

The meeting was different, we all had slides. There were slides of training verses, nonqualifications, increased subtime, and on and on. I, too, have two panels of graphs. I have all the crews with most of the crews blank with absence of qualifications. I have the number of MK-54's available per crew; the number of 5" HVAR rockets on hand and the number of SSQ-23-41's, PDC (practice depth charge), and the number of smokes per aircrew. Finally, I showed the qualifications that each crew had to get. That pretty well told the story about why VP-10 drastically needed Springboard. The XO sat in on the discussion that followed. We decided to prepare a brief for all the aircrews depending on when the Springboard Operations schedule arrived. You might have guessed, the operations schedule arrived the next day. The schedule was difficult to figure out, I in turn stayed until 2000 hours unravelling all periods assigned to VP-10. The next morning I started filling in the blanks. By 5:00 p.m. I was through with the schedule. I was through, finished, and off to the Officer's Club for Happy Hour.

The morning of the brief on Springboard 1966 was packed. The skipper stood up and talked at the upcoming evolution. He spoke and challenged each officer to get as many qualifications as they can. He then passed the gavel to me. I went by crew what each individual needed. I showed the master schedule for the two weeks in January 1966. There were very few question for me to answer. Next the Commanding Officer asked an interesting question, "who will lead the maintenance team down to Roosevelt Roads and who is the Officer in charge of the VP-10 Detachment?" Well I guess I was the lucky one. The XO was the only one coming on the crew. I had him flying with other members getting the piddley exercises out of the way. Right now my crew was a Charlie status and I had hoped we might get and additional subtime that could increase our readiness.

Christmas was so much fun that I used to take Beth and Jane shopping. We went to many stores in the mall on the outskirts of Brunswick. Beth was walking and when we were shopping she road in a stroller. We decided to stay home for Christmas and the coming deployment. Believe it or not, I went shopping for a Christmas tree. We set it up and we decorated it with Beth's help. Incidentally, Beth's right foot is not right but it's turned in more that it should be, I hope she will break the habit and walk right.

There were many parties during this time of the year. The Commanding Officer and his wife were coming to a squadron party. The party was hosted outside and it was called a calling party. I guess about forty or fifty people showed up. The weather was ice cold; snow was six inches deep, and the Wassail punch kept the body warm. We sang at all the Wing 3 houses and we all went to our skipper's house. We knocked at the door and CDR Roberts came outside. He invited us all, yes, all of us in! We left for other parties at 10:30 p.m.

Christmas Day was beautiful. We opened presents, drank coffee, and watched Beth play with her brand spanking new doll. We had guests over for Christmas and luckily enough, I carved the turkey. I ate enough turkey for two; sweet potatoes, mashed potatoes, Waldorf salad, and at least three glasses of wine. I was fat and mellow.

We celebrated the New Year and danced until one o'clock. We skipped out of the club and made it home to release the baby sitter. The noon hour come fast enough and I, by my leave, was catering a group of forty VP-10 sailors who were as drunk as all get out! At 1300 hours the planes started arriving at Brunswick. I went out to see the inside of the planes, but guess what I saw? A nail, I can not speculate what penny the nail qualifies at, but it was sticking out the left tire about two inches. This was a C-130 I believe from Norfolk and it was down until the tire was replaced. The acting pilot called from the duty office and reported his demise!

Four hours later, a second plane landed and we began to load the airplane. The back of the airplane was used for spare parts, maintenance records, and supplies that we were sure they had them ready for issue in Roosevelt Roads. In the meantime, we had the men back over at the Enlisted Club drinking beer.

VP-10 Springboard 1966

We took off about 1800 hours and had six hours until we reached Puerto Rico. The muster had four Chief Petty Officers, a dozen First Class Petty Officers, and the rest were Second Class to Second Airman. That was a sick gang of humanity! Several guys vomited in the lunch bags and slept on the way down. We landed at Roosevelt Roads after midnight. We unloaded the airplane and we had problems finding the keys to the spaces. The Chief called the head of the maintenance division and the keys were held by another First Class Petty officer who will be there at first light. The Chief assigned two seaman to stand guard and this has been worked out with the shore patrol. I spoke with the second class shore patrol and he agreed, that he would bring rations to the two seamen standing watch. Just about that time a great big truck arrived that had a tremendous back end that could haul our men. The men loaded up and the Chief said he would be at the hangar at 0600. He noted that all the gear was not ready and he had to be ready for the VP-10 aircraft by 0800 in the morning. The Duty Officer lend me his duty driver to go to the BOQ. It was twenty minutes from the airfield and that ride sure made me sleepy. I checked in and when I found my room, I went right to sleep.

Five o'clock did not seem as it was, I was flat worn out but needed to get 'turning and burning.' I arrived at the air field dressed in khakis with my new pisscutter! The Chief was there and had organized the crew into a mass of collective ants that were busy laying out chains for the nose-wheels, carts for the APU's and numerous other details. I checked out the Commanding Officer and XO spaces, operations, training and administrative spaces. They were well assigned but once again there were no desks and chairs but for three people. The duty officer spaces seemed dirty so I got a seaman and he cleaned up the duty office. It was 7:45 am. and the skipper was due to be in at 0800 sharp. I called the tower and the planes were at Puerto Rico and they were twenty-five miles from landing. I ran down stairs and told the Chief that they were about fifteen minutes from landing. We had the CO's plane positioned in front of the hangar while the rest of the eight aircraft parked in a line facing the hangar.

At 0800 the skipper touched down and the Chief was standing beside me with a lineman at the ready. VP-10 looked beautiful in the P-3A with it's new shaft! CDR Roberts under the lineman guidance parked right in front of the hangar. With the engines shutdown the truck stopped about one hundred feet from the airplane. Roosevelt Roads dignitaries begun to arrive, which included the operations officer, the Springboard coordinating officer, and the master chief from weather. The other planes were being tended to and it looked like everything was planned according to Hoyle.

I saluted CDR Roberts and he asked how things were going. I told him that we had very few problems and that a brief was going to be held at 1300 covering everything about the air station. The skipper rogered that and the officers stored their flight bags and took a van to check in at the BOQ. I met the XO and asked him about the flight. I told him about the brief and he said he was going up to the BOQ and take a shower. I was sweating like hell!

The brief this afternoon was well covered and the coordinations office gave us a new copy of the operation message which changed the schedule somewhat. I worked on the change and updated the board that made it to Roosey unscratched. I put together the flight schedule for tomorrow. It was published and like it or not the hangar spaces looked like Roosevelt Roads Detachment VP-10. The flight schedule was carried to the BOQ and the seaman in operations took copies to the BEQ.

VP-10 started the deployment running hot and on the first day at Puerto Rico. Rockets and depth bombs made up the first day of operations and many hours of subtime. The squadron had some trouble with the subtime, but boy the skipper had words with the PPC's and everything was made alright! I went on a rocket and bombex with CDR Berstein. It was an eye opener. At altitude of 3000 feet, we saw the island and the many acres of sugarcane that Puerto Rico was harvesting. Standby for the rum, there are two or three manufacturers of rum here on the island.

On Friday I went over to the other side of the runway. Here they were VP-11 SP-2H and the skipper wanted an observer to watch him fire rockets and drop depth bombs. I arrived about 1100 and watched the crew load the rockets and MK-54s. There was a problem with one of the engines. When the engine was fixed the brief was held under the wing and I can tell my face is getting red from the sun. Finally we took off and the crew put me in the TACCO's position. I looked at the displays and, yes, was I ever glad that I had transitioned out of an airplane older than this. Once onstation, the PPC dropped two smokes in the water. He fired two of his four rockets and then dropped his four MK-54s. Viewed from the bow section of the aircraft, it was a successful exercise.

I got back to the BOQ and a cold beer really tasted good. All of the officers were going to the officers' club for happy hour. Carl Baumann and others were trying to bring me along, so what the hell, I joined them on the bus. The club was packed and I know why; rum was free until 1800. I tried a rum and Coke and it tasted good, "like a cigarette should." I was a smoker then and I smoked from one and a half packs of Pall Mall or the same with Marlboro each day. The drinks came more frequently and soon Happy Hour was over. Finally,

I got up and went to the restroom and as I was washing my hands, I looked up and saw my face in the mirror. My face was totally red along with part of my neck. My pisscutter showed that my bald head was unaffected. Soon it became 1900 and we ordered hamburgers, fries, and beer. The waitress brought our chow and I nearly ate the whole burger. I was pleasantly full and I had a slight buzz on.

The Kingston Trio was supposed to perform that evening at the club. By God they did perform and we cheered when they finished playing there first song. Everybody stood and applauded and the group acknowledged by bowing and this crowd brought a new life to the trio. The songs like "Hang Down Your Head Tom Dooley" rang well into the evening. I am sure that Jane was in my thoughts as we sang along with them. Suddenly we stood up after a song, and sang "drink a highball," the old VP-10 song. The band listened and started clapping their hands!

The next day was miserable to be waking up. All precautions were taken ahead of time to prevent headaches. Even with sunglasses and all other medications the head still hurt. Today was my day off. I went to the golf course and played nine holes. The rental clubs were very old but the warm humid day sweated the alcohol right out of my body. The rest of the day was spent watching movies and shooting the shit with the rest of the officers. Sunday I went down to the hangar to catch up on qualifications and to prepare a flight schedule for the next few days. About an hour later, things were looking good except the qualifications in the last crew that transaudient. I expected that so I planned the flight schedule accordingly. That left the last two days free, unless we had to do those qualifications over. That night I suffered a major relapse when they told me that Chuck Osier had broken his ankle at the swimming pool. Well, guess who will be filling in for him.

The flights were fast and I remember not getting out of my flight suit. I flew the XO one flight and spent the next four days helping Lieutenant Commander Charles Prindle. Charlie was the Administration Officer and was a very likable individual. He believed you, but you had better be right, or 'Katie bar the door!' He was very articulate and polite around officers and enlisted personnel. I flew with LCDR Prindle and got qualifications in the MADEX, Julie, and Jezebel. Bravo status was awarded to Combat Air Crew Five. You might remember Dallas Lassiter, a former navigator who went from my crew to another back in the days of the SP-2E world. Dallas was having trouble with the Julie pattern. I went out with him early one morning to get his vernacular straight. I helped him get two Julie qualifications. The crew thanked me, including the PPC who was all smiles. I told him that I had an hour and a half to go flying again. The next happy hour I would approach him and ask him for my free beer!

Back home again and it's ready to go on deployment. We are going to Argentia, Newfoundland. Five crews were going there and the Commanding Officer was taking seven crews to Keflavik, Iceland. All the maintenance men were starting to divide the parts and supplies to go to various sites. A great amount of headwork was involved in coordinating the movement of so many parts and supplies for this operation. I had to figure out what I would need and to pack according to the requirements specified.

Jane did not want me to go on deployment. It seems as if I was on a hobby horse since I have been in VP-10. Downstairs in the basement of the house, I brought up a trunk that I had not used since I went overseas to Sigonella. Beth was helping me pack my clothes and shirts. Following the shirts came the sweaters and my God, better get the pants into the trunk. We had a going away party, but it was a drag. The party was a mistake but I guess you have to have one anyway. January 20, 1966, was cold and great accumulations of snow was falling. It started snowing and it did not stop. The big four engine airplanes arrived and start packing up the squadron gear. The first plane load took off for Keflavik, Iceland. The next group packed up all the gear that I was planning to use for the next six months. Jane was blue and not talkative, but what to do, let's count the hours until January 28. Jane and Beth were with me at the plane and it was blistering cold and snowy. There was at least three or more feet of snow on the ground. The Chevy II was moving well and I did not have a problem with Jane driving it. We said good-bye and after hugging Beth, and hearing her say, "airbus, airbus," and I knew she was trying to say airplane.

CDR. Bernstein lead the way as he took off in the snow, followed by the other three planes in the detachment. We climbed up above the snowstorm and headed Northeast for Argentia. The radio kept the XO advised of the weather at Argentia and the original forecast was for blowing snow. The ground control radar was down (inoperative). I talked with the XO and he decided that if the field was zero-zero, the GCA Radar was down, then back to Brunswick go our planes. I have alerted the planes what we are going to do. At about 75 nautical miles from Argentia the XO communicated with GCA. The wind was howling, snow was drifting, and the dam radar was still down. The XO said, "Will see you tomorrow." I alerted the three aircraft and they did a one eighty and back to Brunswick, Maine.

At 1900 or thereabouts, we had landed again at NAS Brunswick, Maine. Snow was still falling and we, the crew, had decided to wear our flight gear home. I called Jane who was staying the night with Mott Atherholt, the wife of LT. Bill Atherholt. Bill and Mott went on vacation after Springboard and were skiing. Mott broke her leg and a week later her husband goes on deployment. An hour later Jane and Beth came to get us, Bill and me, to get back to Bill's house. We laughed and drank over the incident. Bill worked in the administrative office and was the assistant administrator. We talked and laughed until eleven o'clock. Jane drove home and I carried Beth inside. Morning arrived and it was cold as the wind started blowing. We arrived at the airplane about nine thirty in the morning. CDR. Karl Bernstein met us and he said Argentia had fixed their radar. After hugs and a big kiss from Jane and Beth, I climbed aboard LD-7 and took off again for Argentia.

VP-10 Detachment NS Argentia, Newfoundland

We landed about three hours later. The wind was just beginning to blow and the sky was almost clear. Argentia Hilton was the code name of the vaunted BOQ that were housed on top of the facility ten stories high. Among the many conveniences that it has included a bowling alley, cleaning pickup, pool tables, a bar, television, stereo, mess facilities, movies, and at last BOQ spaces for the men and women. Retired officers and their wives were set aside on the eight deck, whereas distinguished officers were placed on the top floors. Overlooking this giant building is Placentia Bay which bounded the massive base of Argentia. VP-10 came back to this base a little over a year and a half ago. Argentia is located on the Southwestern Newfoundland on the west coast of the Avalon Peninsula on Placentia Bay, sixty-five miles west southwest of ST. Johns. Here is one large United States base, obtained on a 99 year lease in 1940 from Great Britain. In August 1941, the Atlantic Charter was signed by President Roosevelt and Winston Churchill aboard ships off shore. Although the base was not as busy as in 1964, it lost the two VAW squadrons. Now there are a lot of empty spaces around including the hangar. Miami Hangar is the only facility that we will occupy. It consists of three hangar bays that we can do a hell of a lot of work inside. The rest of the facility is used to store parts, engines, and food that come in airplanes from the United States. There is a harbor that lumber arrives in and various materials for construction.

Looking out of the window in my bedroom of the BOQ it was wintry scene. Fir trees, or whatever they are called are covered with snow. The wind has picked up and you can hear and see it blowing across the snow-covered road. The officers are all put on two floors. LT. or whatever you derive you are assigned a room that is available. Each man gets two rooms, one for sleeping and one for studying. Of course, the way each officer uses his second room is his secret!

Officer working spaces were set up in upper deck of the Miami Hangar. The duty office, the Communications Office, and the Operations/ Training Office were set up. Another office was reserved for the ready crew to conduct training and for the all officers meeting. We found out that VP-8, the squadron that we relived, had trouble returning from deployment. Snow was the reason and they had planes that landed at Norfolk because they could not land at Patuxent River, Maryland. In fact, one plane was relieved and finally they decided that would launch and land at NAS Norfolk. Incidentally there was twenty-eight inches of snow in beautiful Patuxent River City! The second day we had a brief at the OPCON. Many officers had left when the barrier patrol squadrons departed. Antisubmarine Warfare was similar to Barrier Patrol! The ASW sector of Argentia consists of a vast portion of the North Atlantic Ocean. This span of water covers NE and Eastward to the Lajes, Azores Chain. There were times in the coming Spring months when we would be flying Ice Patrols up to Sonderstrum, Greenland and all the way north to Thule. But, by and large, they spent most of their time on rigging and photographing the Russian fishing fleets. Many questions were not answered such as, 'where do we drop sonobuoys?' The answer to that one, were we will be given a spot to 'water sample.' I almost barfed! Can you believe this the OPCON officers had never heard of a FAIRWINGSLANT Tactics Manual! A pack of Tactical Coordinators (five in all) agreed that the TC's would do what they could about this problem! They all met at the bar at the BOQ and we got smashed.

Happy Hour at the BOQ bar started at 1600 hours. We all showed up and the dice started rolling. We started playing darts, but that's not all, there were slot machines in the bar. I am not a professional gambler, but I threw in my change and if I won some change I would play until I lost all my nickels and then quit! I got into an interesting conversation with the XO about the totally inept briefing that we had received this afternoon. He agreed with my conclusion, but on the whole, that is against the way we are supposed to operate. CDR. Bernstein was going to talk to the facility to see if we could join their network and fly in support of their operations on a weekly basis.

On the February 2 we took off to Lajes AFB. It was on a track flight east and north of Newfoundland. The northern border is close to Greenland. We bumped and finally the XO called back and asked if we could fly about 1000 feet higher. I rogered that and believe me, it was getting back aft. As far as you can see to the port side of the aircraft, all you saw was ice and glacial foundations. About four hours had passed, Carl decided to take a fix. He plotted the fix and shook his head. I finally checked it out. LORAN was on, but we were making forty and fifty knots ground speed! I asked the Co-pilot to tune in the Lajes Radio Beacon. It pointed 180 degrees. I suggested that we might turn to 180 and enter the shipping lanes to rig some ships. I went forward and found the XO alseep and so I told the pilot what to do. We must have rigged thirty ships and since Lajes was South, we entered a more gentle sea state, more comfortable to fly in.

The trip to Rota, Spain was more work for everybody. We rigged and rigged some more. Dam we were tired when we got to Rota. The next day we rented a taxi and went to the sherry bottlers in Jerez. We sampled sherry at the distillery and bought some wine also. It was a long day, but the results made it seem wonderful.

After takeoff from Rota the airfield at Lajes was closed due to the high wind conditions. We proceeded cautiously and when it came time to make a decision, Lajes was still closed. The next day we made it to Lajes, because it was point to point navigation. The next day we took off for Argentia. We encountered very few ships and landed in Argentia. We brought back wine, sherry, and just about anything your heart desired. Because CDR. Bernstein made contact with the Navy Facility Argentia we routinely flew with them once a week. The communication system has two high frequency communication networks. The Navy facility uses systems like this for their communications. If the message requires KAC-130 then it must be sent on voice. For now, I was high time leader in the race for the same number of contacts that are held by the facility. LCDR. Goschke was the Operations officer and he was a great guy. I used to plan my flights by making schedules on paper in case something happened. I had the ready duty and he was available so he was the ready duty PPC. We went for the ready duty brief as nothing was happening. I set about writing the schedule and then, Carl said they were launching the ready duty. I put on my coat, hat and I ran down the steps to get in the truck to go to the OPCON. The officers were getting in the truck, and I saw the Flight Engineer and told him to set the inertial. I drove like hell on fire over to the OPCON. The briefing officer advises us that he had a position on a U.S. nuclear attack submarine that was headed home. The position of the submarine was in a radius of one hundred miles. I did not ask about it, but I knew it was too good to be true. The submarine was headed home at eighteen knots on a course of 240 true. I asked but no answer was given about the signature characteristics of the submarine. We asked if we were to track the guy or if we gain attack criteria, should we attack? Yes, the briefing officer said followed by the standard communication frequencies I ran down the steps and the crew followed me. We headed to the aircraft that was inside the hangar with the big steel doors open to let the aircraft out. Up the ladder, a quick brief, I aligned the ASW-42 inertial and right away we started engine number four. I spent a few minutes with the ordnance man who told me what I have in regards to sonobuoys, PPC's smokes and their were eight MK-44 simulated on board. "Set Condition Five," the PPC announced. I did a complete check of the aircraft and strapping into my slot I mentioned the Condition Five was set. Finally, the aircraft turned one hundred and eighty degrees and you guess it, we started down the runway. When we lifted off the ground we set Condition Four. About a minute later, Condition Three was set and we began to get out of our hard-hats and do our quick assessment of the ASW gear. I inserted the last latitude and longitude of the fix and put it on the BDHI. Carl was busy setting up the ASW charts on the DRT. We were only two hours away from datum so right away LCDR Goschke was checking with the Flight Engineer what would be the fastest horsepower setting to fly. Condition Three was set throughout the aircraft. A cup of coffee really tasted good and before I took off my headset, the immediate message came over the airways. The radio operator copied it. I used the KAC-130 and it was a new position, which I informed the PPC and reentered the datum on the BDHI. I look at the Doppler and we were flying at 398 knots. Carl said we would make it in an hour. The weather was not bad with broken clouds to the surface of the water. I figured the range was in the order of ten nautical miles. I briefed the copilot on the type of Jezebel pattern planned to use.

When we were twenty minutes away from the first drop I briefed the Ordnance man. He knew what I wanted and he said, "Can we kill him, I mean simulated?" Yes, I will give the word when.

Sonobuoy one was dropped and the GTP-4 was in run and headed for the next drop. Jezebel reported maypole is up and no contact. The datum was dropped and there we started a eight buoy on the perimeter with one buoy datum. We dropped five sonobuoys and suddenly Jezebel has a contact. The AQA-5 printed a classic gram but showing the contact must be further out than the original pattern. For the hell of it we dropped another buoy. It had contact on the sub but it has the same number of lines. "Set Condition Two," I responded. Plants A & B are sent to the GTP-4 and the airplane goes down to 1000 feet and we go about fifteen miles to drop the plants. The sonobuoy launch system is lowered and Alpha plant is dropped and at the same time the Drift Computer is cut on and the reset knob is pushed. Plant Alpha is up and just as he said that, Bravo plant goes in. I told the nav that I was looking for a bearing that was moving down the sub true course. Jezebel had the bearing we wanted and the marked on top Alpha and headed to the next Charlie and Delta drop. The drift computer looks good on the mark on top and I briefed the PPC to turn to one five zero true before dropping the buoys. One minute to drop, the PPC turned to the right and was steady on 150. Charlie away and I hit the reset button. Delta plant was away and I told the pilot to head inbound 240 for a mark on top. Five minutes went by and finally the only bearing he had was a broadside bearing from plant Charlie. Of all the bickering on arguing about the CODAR pointing between the PPC and me were ended when the bearing come through for the Delta plant. The bearing put all the money on broadside and the bearing from plants A & B computed a course of 235 at eighteen knots. Ordnance was way ahead of me, by switching Q-15's instead of SSQ-41's. He announces when he was ready and the retro was loaded. The retro is the automatic device that loads itself and the ordnance keeps filling with smokes. GTP-4 responds with a Target Center (TGT CTR) which I positioned the aircraft to where I wanted it to go. The datum or center of the pilot's plotter is the fix position of the sub. Mark on top plant Charlie and we were inbound to datum. Buoy two was already selected as the first drop of a 4000 yard pattern. Pinger two is away and I hit the reset knob on the drift computer. Four away and believe it or not, "range 1400 down Doppler," said the Jezebel operator. I was getting set to go back to the first buoy when pinger four reports 2500 yards up Doppler. I listened to pinger four and it is inundated with noise form the propeller. "Return to pinger four course 235 degrees true and bomb the buoy," I said. The PPC acknowledged and the master arm checklist was being read, and the torpedoes were MK-44 and bomb bay status light was selected. The bomb bay doors were coming open range 1000 yards up Doppler and we were fifteen seconds away from the drop. The drop was mine and I had warned MAD and then about five seconds later he announced," MADMAN MADMAN MADMAN," and I dropped the simulated weapon. What a sight and what a proud feeling that we had accomplished. Range 300 yards up Doppler and two minutes later he was 1000 yards down Doppler out of range for the torpedo. We sent a contact report and said we have placed an attack on the sub and request instructions. We tried to get an additional MAD contact but the sub was moving smartly! The response was to return to base. LCDR Goschke was happy with that call as the flight engineer indicated that we had three hours of fuel on board. The weather was all right at Argentia so we raised the sonobuoy package and emptied the smoke ejector or retro and we climbed to 20000 feet and headed back to base.

I had a cup of coffee and I shook hands with every member of the back of the aircraft. Then we met in the back of the plane and got all the ASW records for the flight assembled. Carl has the Nav and Tactical logs, Radar and MAD logs, Julie and ECM logs, Jezebel logs, the GTP-4 paper log, and finally the ordnance logs. The last items of interest were the UNH-1 tape as well as the radio communicator's logs that are finished with the flight.

After landing at Argentia the plane pulls in front of the hangar where many of the officers were waiting for us. The Executive office finally walked out of the hangar and awaiting shutdown of the engines. The ladder was put down by two crew members and the XO came aboard. He saw me and he approached me as if he was going to shake my hand. "Congratulations Mike," he said "you really did a superior job in catching our own nuclear submarine." Thank you was a really great occasion as all of my friends wanted to shake my hand.

The OPCON was alive as I walked in and they began reviewing all the charts and records that I brought with me. The senior officer asked me if I had a tape of the flight. "Yes sir," I said and I showed them the UNH-6 tape. Naturally they did not have a recorder that could reproduce the flight. Regretfully, I knew who could play the tape. After a phone call, a bus came by and we went as a crew plus the XO to the Navy Facility so we all can hear the tape. After fifteen minutes of driving, the bus stopped at the facility. The tape was laid on a machine and there I was giving orders. The OPCON office wanted to hear the SSQ-15 sonobuoys and to hear the active ranges. The tape started with the first buoy drop. From there on it was wait and watch what happens. The Naval Facility had two Ensigns listen and they reacting most favorably and went to get the Commanding Officer. The crew was excused and we were forced outside the room that had the recorder. The Commanding Officer came outside and he came to me and shook my hand "Mike you are in fact a indicator of the superior work that the Tactical Coordinator can do, Well done," said the CO.

The flying at Argentia was getting to be old hat. The crews were restless and kept wanting a trip home. The four engine plane which went to Quonset Point was bound to have some fun for VP-10 personnel. I made up a package which lowered our crew availability by one crew that went on leave for a week. It was dependent on this airplane because if they missed the returning flight, we had a problem. The XO went to the Commanding Officer to ask if we could capture nine seats on the airplane. The Commanding Officer wanted to know more about the flight. CDR Bernstein presented the proposal and the Commanding Officer bought it!

Starting in two weeks the crew would take leaves. Which crew will go on leave? I did not think that was fair. I suggested the crews by planning ahead their schedules in advance. I showed the crews and by damn, LCDR Goschke bought it. We were third on the totem pole.

When I landed in Quonset Point the R4D taxied to the parking spot. I got off the plane and walked into the lobby. There was Beth running towards me. I grabbed her and held her. She looked like a million dollars and Jane was there beside her. I kissed her and told her I still loved her. In the Navy overcoat that I had on, I pulled a small doll that Beth hugged and them kissed the doll. As we drove home, Jane told me about switching houses. I listened as closely as I could while watching Beth.

The new house was a Navy house that Jane had found out about.

She started moving in March and it was a beautiful house. We did many things when I was home for six days. We talked about who, why, and what was going on. I told Jane that I had decided to go regular Navy. Jane asked me if I am sure about it. I told her that I am happy about what I am doing, but wait until the offer comes to fruition.

On Sunday afternoon, we were bored sitting around. Bill Atherholt, Carl, and several others had a dart game in the Officers' bar. The establishment opened at 1300 and we grabbed a beer and played darts. The record player had a lot of our favorites, but quite a few songs had been changed. One of the favorites, Nancy Sinatra's "These boots are made for walking" was still there on the record player.

On May 28, an unannounced meeting was held. The message flow was beginning to bring our detachment as part of the information addees. The handwriting was on the wall, because it looks like we are moving to a different site at anytime. That night the plans looked like it was going to happen. VP-10 was going to be rejoined by May 30 with the detachment bringing them to a full squadron. The flying there is unbearable and so everyone begins to pack up. VP-44 intends to depart from Patuxent River, Maryland with a four plane detachment to cover Argentia until we come back. On May 30 we said good-bye to 'Argie Bird' and off to Keflavik to help our squadron.

VP-10 Naval Station Keflavik, Iceland

The Commanding Officer was there to meet us and so was the beer. The buses were there, so we went to the BOQ. Keflavik is located on the Southwestern part of Iceland, on the Northwestern shore of Reykjaves Peninsula on Faka Bay, known only as a fishing port. This site was built during World War II. It is a big complex with an Air Force squadron and an adjoining NATO hat. The NATO hat culminated in one massive exercise including the English, Norwegian, German, and US countries during the year.

The brief today was to prepare us for our flights. The main reason for our being here was a cable layer. Increased cable laying would make sure even more knowledge was gained of the topography. The work has little help for those who sought details of underseas mountain ridges, hills, slopes, and trenches. Knowledge of these are strategically important in matters as diverse as the employment and transit of nuclear submarines. Along with the cable layer, there are several

US Diesel submarines. These submarines are not to be reported and are to protect the cable ship. Our part in this is to conduct surveillance of the ice around Greenland and to keep clear all fishing banks and to look out and report Soviet ships, either trawlers or Elints.

The next day the flight schedule was full, ninety-one hours! We took off from Keflavik and headed Northwest. We took a radar plot of the area and sighted the ice extending from Greenland. We went all around half of Iceland checking to see if any trawlers were block, i.e. Russian. The other half of the mission is to locate the cable layer. The first thing was to shut down the APS-80 radar. We then turned left and we sort of disappeared but travelled to the new area where suddenly about ten miles ahead was the ship with a submarine snorkeling near-by. I dropped a SSQ-41 and it was an FM-10. To complete the mission, we had to make a pass to see if he wanted to pass us a message. He did and we made another pass to acknowledge receipt by rolling the wings from side to side. I told the Jezebel operator to keep quiet about the US submarine.

We landed at Keflavik and went to the debrief. Right away I was asked a question. Greenland, the eastern edge, was reported that the edge of the ice flow was X miles, this I reported was the mileage of the ice flow. What could be the problem with this information? The debriefing officer was about to come unglued! After an hour and a half we left the most disorganized debrief since elephants' walked.

For about eleven days things seem to slack off as VP-10 rested. The planes were worn out as well as the maintenance gang. We were given a Andoya, Norway flight that we accepted with great joy. The trip over did not cause us any problems. We dropped several sonobuoys and got negative results. We landed and were met by several Norwegian officers. They escorted us to the debrief and then to the BOQ.

The next day involved a trip into town. There was not much to do but we had great fun playing with their youngsters. Back at the base, there was a drill going on where a fighter was firing at a dummy with a 50 caliber gun.

On June 16 we were tasked to head North of Andoya and head East to twenty five degrees East. We were to locate everything with photographs. If we saw a submarine, report it and track if possible. It was a beautiful day for flying, but it was cloudy and with a visibility of twenty-five miles. After rigging several trawlers I dropped several buoys. Jezebel reported a contact but it looked more like a trawler than anything else. We finally arrived at our Eastern end of the track and we headed back toward Iceland. I noticed something significant during our mission. The AQA-5 was holding the same contact about thirty-five miles away from the trawler. This was amazing to me because I had heard VP-10's TACCO's talking about convergence zones. If the proper definition of an event occurring thirty-two to thirty-five miles away, I just saw a definite convergence zone.

VP-10 Detachment NS Argentia, Newfoundland

Finally the squadron got the word to send us back to Argentia. We left Keflavik on July 2, 1966 to finish our deployment and be back in Brunswick on July 21. Carl Baumann could not fly with us, but he said I had better do a good preflight of the NAV station. I climbed on board 152180, the skipper's plane, to do a quick preflight. I checked everything except the LORAN. We had an uneventful takeoff and two hours out I thought I had better get a fix. The LORAN looked funny. Half of the switches were screwed up so I did a quick NATOPS preflight and Carl had really put an unexpected flaw or imperfection in the LORAN system. Naval Station Argentia was ready for us when we landed. The crowd was there when we shut down the engines. The CO, XO, and all the department heads with their wives met the VP-10 sailors. There must be something here that smells of frivolity so let's hug and shake their hands.

The next two weeks were busy. I scheduled all Pilot trainers and two Rota and Lajes, Azores trips. The last weekend, we were all there, CDR Bernstein was asked to go fishing. The Commanding Officer asked if the XO had someone else to invite. CDR Bernstein asked me and I accepted. Saturday morning the CDR and I went shopping for a steak. We bought several items including a bottle of Canadian Club and ever popular bug spray. At noon we met at Air Operations. We had dressed alike and took extra care with flight jackets, suits, and good ole' boots. The aircraft was an HU-16 "Albatross." The Plane Captain started reading the checklist and we soon were taxing. We flew for forty-five minutes. The lake outside of the aircraft looked beautiful with towering firs and spruce all around the outskirts of the lake. We landed in the water and soon a large boat pulled along side. We loaded all of our gear onto the large boat. The cabin was beautiful, carved from the fir tress behind and around. All of the latest facilities we brought up by airplane to make the cabin "top drawer."

By four o'clock in the afternoon, we started fishing. I had a ultra light Mitchell spinning rod and an assortment of fishing lures. I had great success with the Mepps lure. I landed a 14 inch salmon. We fished until seven-thirty. I started to clean the fifteen Brown or Rainbow trout that had been caught. After the XO and I finished with the trout, we put them in the cooler. The Commanding Officer was in the cabin making supper. We had drinks before dinner and soon the steaks were ready to eat.

After clearing the table from dinner and washing the dishes, a Newfoundlander came back and brought his guitar. He was nearly fifty-nine and boy could he sing and play with a drink of Canadian Club in him! I must confess that I was under the stress of being the lowly one in rank-I got plastered!

In the morning I had the proverbial hangover, as did the XO. We had coffee and rolls for breakfast as we took off to the area where the lake overflows to form a large pond. The base Commanding Officer parked the boat on shore and indicated that is was two thousand yards to great fishing. Off we go stepping behind the CO. I slipped and turned my right ankle. It hurt like hell. The XO saw how much pain I was in, but I assured him I was fine. As I stood up, the pond was insight. I wandered into the water till it covered my flight boot. Fishing was heaven. I have never caught so much trout! Thirty minutes later I told the XO that I was going back to the boat to rest my ankle. When we got back, I went to the dispensary to get my ankle x-rayed. It was not broken. I received crutches to help me walk. Tuesday I went back for a second time and they put a cast on for six weeks. I bet Jane and Beth did not approve of that.

From January 29, 1966 I gained a lot from this deployment by rehearsing in my mind the tactics that were given to catch submarines. The P-3A Deltic with the AQA-5, we had better luck in detecting and killing the nuclear submarine as it travelled home. The OPCON in Argentia is ranked below average by most Pilot/Tactical Coordinators in not only patrol but in surveillance concepts. The terms of surveillance verses patrol are definitely confusing. A patrol means going the rounds of an area for observation of the maintenance of security. Surveillance, is simply, a close watch. The Merriam Webster Dictionary leaves room for discussion concerning this matter. In order to fly a twelve hour patrol we must fly two and a half hours to onstation and spend six hours in this area. We rig and take pictures of every ship, trawler, merchant, tanker, fishing ship, and Elints, but what do we do with Russian submarines, conventional or nuclear? Based on this deployment in Kelfavik a diesel submarine once detected must need a fix as quickly as possible. This provides a quick attack, even simulated or if a real weapon is dropped on the target. The difference is the nuclear submarine has time to travel along the path that he intends to proceed. We as TACCO's need his course with a series of sonobuoy barriers five miles apart, called mini-barriers. To run a series of flights on this nuclear submarine is called surveillance.

The next morning I climbed in my aircraft with my crew helping me up the ladder. The plane made it to Brunswick, Maine is two point four hours. The XO put the plane the farthest away from the hanger. Jane was holding Beth as she was scared of the planes engines. All members of the airplane had loved ones join them. Beth thought I had missed the airplane but here I come on the back of a truck. Beth went tee-tee on Jane's pretty green dress. I kissed and hugged them both.

I had orders to VP-30 and I had a thirty day leave period upon leaving VP-10 for VP-30. The house that Jane was living in was base housing. She had somehow or another gotten out of the lease and moved into the base housing. The housing was nice, but it was time to move to Patuxent River, Maryland.

We said good-bye to the NAS Brunswick and headed South for Maryland in the last week of July 1966. We spent the night at some motel and arrived the next day at NAS Patuxent River, MD. We got a visitor's pass and went to public housing. We were greeted by a lady who had what we asked for—a small two bedroom apartment slated for Lieutenant Junior Grade. She promised that there would be housing across the street by next June. Jane wanted to see the house so I got directions to the apartment. It was upstairs and not air conditioned. I said I would buy an air conditioner and so we thought we would make due until June of 1967. That afternoon we signed the lease and planned to move in on Monday. We celebrated this momentous occasion by visiting my parents.

Bob Givler and Edna were Jane's folks and we went down to see them the next weekend. Bob works for Bell Telephone and smoked at least two packs of cigarettes a day. He talked all the time about his job. Beth usually liked him, but she could not stand Edna. The secret is, to get grandmother to wear her bedroom shoes that Beth would like to wear. One morning Beth arose early and Bob came in and took her in the kitchen. I had not made love to Jane in about four days and I snuggled up to Jane and said, "Let's make a baby." Jane agreed. I did not want it to stop, but Beth was at the door announcing breakfast! What's a fellow supposed to do?

The whole month of August I added to the apartment. The air conditioner, curtains in the living room, dining room, and of course the moving van arrived. We met our downstairs neighbors, and also LT Al Mouns and his wife Judy across the street. They were the first VP-30 couple that we had met. Al and Judy were from the West Coast and really liked Patuxent River. We cooked out with them and drank many Martini's. Little did we know, but Al had just won a twenty foot boat and motor. He won it in a drawing held the last weekend at the exchange.

The week before I was supposed to check in I went to the hospital to check on the cast around my ankle. The doctor looked at the leg and took off the cast. He gave me a positive report to give to the VP-30 officers. Friday was check in time. I went down to the Administration Department and met with a senior Chief. He looked over my orders and told me I did not have to check in until Tuesday after Labor Day. That being the case, I met a few officers and made my way back to the apartment.

CHAPTER 6

VP-30, NAS PATUXENT RIVER, MD

I checked in on Tuesday and reported to the Training Officer. He was excited to meet me and had a lot of good news to share about VP-30. In the Operations Department, I turned over my log book and was instructed to meet LT Ron Ellis. I gathered my flight gear, a May West, ear plugs, and newly refurbished hard hat to meet Ron Ellis in Building 420. Ron was teaching the same course that I sat through a year ago. He had drive and forcefulness that made him an excellent teacher. He called on me several times to explain who, why and what is just the way to do it. Ron had a great background of Naval experience, switching from officer to teacher and flying at VP-30.

VP-10 called me at VP-30 to let me know that my liquor would be at Air Operations on Friday at noon. Something else would be coming from the Pelican Pen of VP-44, CDR Ed Waller, the Commanding Officer formerly of the Air Test Center, was putting together a Tactical Note that was being published by COMFAIRWINGSLANT for review. CDR Waller had put together a study of all tactics, setting about to approve or deny them. The convergence zone was one of the creations that worked. The range of the convergence zones was reported to be always 25-27 miles in length. This range together with my thoughts Northeast of Andoya, Norway made me wonder. Also within the TACMEMO we were given several hints that could be used to promote the evolutions of CODAR. In short, here are the tactics that they discussed:

> a. Radar run in—After a CODAR fix is developed, the appropriate radar review is to fly into the wind and turn down

wind at ten nautical miles at 1000 feet and light off the APS-80 radar with high PRF to detect the snorkeling submarine.

b. CODAR Tracking Circle—This is used about a rough fix and it is usually ten nautical miles. Three CODAR plants are employed that can really fix the target.

c. Search patterns—In many of the search patterns that we rely on, all are not as accurate in position as they seem. Dropping at 1000 feet or 20,000 feet can make a drastic difference. For example, you drop your sonobuoys but you do not know the wind and it is completely different at sea level. This new TACNOTE is for you to drop all buoys and note the time of the drop. The next step is mark on top of the first sonobuoy drop. Mark the on top position and slew to on top position. The navigator takes the drop time and figures out the wind and applies it to all buoys based on the time of the drop.

d. VP-10 and VP-44 were involved in flying an exercise called Sunrise. This, by all means, was to prove that convergence zones do exist; what ranges should one expect a convergence zone to occur; and to correct the range previously quoted as "always 25-27 miles." VP-10 had studied the oceanographic text books and learned that the convergence zone range depended on the sea surface temperature. In warmer seas the convergence zones are at longer ranges than 25-27 miles. In colder seas such as off Andoya, Norway they can be much shorter than 25-27 miles. VP-44 had done all its operations in the temperate waters off Norfolk, where, indeed, the convergence zone range is typically 25-27 miles.

Lt Bill Tuallabee was the transit Navigation Training Officer whose shoes I would fill. Bill had been filling in giving lectures for the past three months. I sat in the back of the classroom as he started lectures that last for three and a half days. He had two classes; the first is made up of all first and second tour pilots. The second was made up of VP-30 Pilots and NFO'S. I had trouble with the lesson guides but I requested to take them over before the next class. The only things that upset me was getting off to a brand new start. The Navigation Dry

Swim was the last item of the class. This swim consisted of plotting ASW-1 sheets and these students need their computers, pencils, compasses, and dividers to finish the dry swim. Bill had to go somewhere and I briefed the class. I gave them thirty minutes to preflight before I started the UNH-6 tape. By and large it was an antiquated tape using tactics dated 1963. Brittingham, you have got to change this tape! The next day I got the keys to the office and the combination to the safe. I looked for a turnover book, no, you have got to be kidding me! Next I secured my lesson guided and half of the transparencies were out of date. Next I looked at my office supplies, which seemed alright. The Navigation logs were very old, in fact, the last time I used these logs were in VP-30 in late 1963! Good news, in my drawer were three new pointers ready and waiting for me. Clearly, I had my work set out for me!

The VP-44 TACNOTE was about to blow up because of the Sunrise exercise flown by VP-44 and VP-10. The results were discussed at a meeting in Patuxent River where the exercise would make or break the convergence zone tactics. The VP-10 had gotten new P-3B's recently back from deployment. These P3A Deltics were transferred to VP-44. The ASWILS was transferred to VP-44. This improved gear was learned mighty quickly by the 44 gang. With ASWILS VP-44 should have an advantage over VP-10 in Exercise Sunrise. Interestingly the flights were scheduled "high flight" of one squadron that monitored the low flight from the other squadron putting in buoys. VP-44 used the "always 25-27 mile" convergence zone range in their localization tactics, while VP-10 used 34-36 mile range predicted for the warm (80 degrees) seas off Charleston S.C.

A week later I was assigned to sit in a panel that was to look at and decide which tactics would be incorporated in the VP-30 syllabus. Lt Tom Ryan, the Tactical Officer, led the discussion and right away we got into a ruckus over the convergence zone. The NATOPS Tactical Coordinator was from VP-44 and excelled in it's call for the zones. Tom Ryan stood up and established time out; we took another tactic. We discussed tactical drift maneuver and we agreed we would try it on the ASW-1 plotting sheets. Eventually we assigned short term duties to have the work finished with our findings presented in two days. On Friday the group convened and everone agreed. The item was the ever popular convergence zone. Again the LT from VP-30 voiced his opinion and Tom Ryan read a part of the message that changed the range of the zone to 30-35 miles. The panel voted on the TACMEMO and voted 4-1 to include the tactics that we had worked on. The next task was waiting in the tactics on lesson guides, syllabus flights, a weapon systems' trainers, and included in the syllabus grading sheets that accompany the flights.

The flying started in my second month at VP-30. Just as I was promised, I did not have three months to "get my shit in order." This class of students really tore the NFO'S a new sphincter. Usually, the class represents eight crews, but ten crews were ready to fly. The first flight I had was a night nav flight to Lajes. The flight was prepared by the students and the Loran charts were different with each Loran station noted by the colors. The Howgozist chart was prepared and the Weight and Balance chart was prepared in case anyone needed it. The flight took off and the students did well. I did not track off these flights noting if the students were average, excellent, or border line with respect to passing. It was only two days when I had the next Navigation course. I got the slides from the NATOPS for the class. A Second Class Petty Officer showed me the Xerox machine to make the slides for the morning show. I started cleaning up the afternoon slide requirements. After sitting down, I went through my text and interchanged my slides to show the students. I came across some nude slides that would bomb your whole day. Oh well, what the hell, this was the perfect time to display them, just before lunch! I think I am ready to handle the class, but I will improve as I retain more information.

Jane was pregnant with our second child. We called Mom and Dad in Annandale and told them the news. Bob and Edna, Jane's parents, were excited and wanted to come to visit. Jane did not seem the same. Unbelievably, she did not want to be around me, and make love to me, are you joking? The medicine she was taking was not helping her and I knew it. We went to the doctor next week and the doctor discussed this with me. About a week and half later on Saturday, she become ill in the morning and evening. I kept Beth and put her to bed. Sunday it was worse. She vomited so bad that at 8:00 p.m. all she was bringing up was this yellow stuff from her stomach. I made arrangements with the downstairs neighbors to keep Beth while I took her to the hospital. She was about to vomit her life away. The doctor put her in the hospital on IVs and changed her medicine. I called my Mom, Inez, to come down for a week. Beth was glad to see her. We played together and went out to dinner several evenings. The doctor who had been treating Jane wanted to see me. I met at three o'clock for a sit down appointment. I was harassed by him about being a horrid father. He asked me questions if I wanted this baby and why did I marry Jane? I have never been as mad as I was that day. I told him that I loved Jane and cared for her through this exacerbating tragedy and dam him for the insult he had laid on me. He apologized and shook hands, but he had to perform an act to find out what in the world was going on with my wife and I before she became ill.

Jane came home Friday. Beth hugged her and we had supper together. Jane had soup and crackers that she was able to keep down. She did well, but just when my Mom starting packing to go home, she started vomiting again. She got sick on Sunday again. I returned to the doctor's first thing Monday morning. My Mom stayed until Wednesday when Jane returned home. She was home for good and I was glad she was in our apartment.

Many of the tactics flights are interesting. Tactics one is basic patrol with rigging, photography, and some time on the mining range. Tactics two through five deals with plot stabilization, both high and low altitude; basic Jezebel pattern laying; Logical Comparative LOFAR; and basic entries into the eight thousand and four thousand yard Julie pattern. The advanced crew can be utilized to incorporate Magnetic Anomaly Detection as well as SSQ-15 or pinger tactics. Tactics six was a night flight featuring searchlight runs off of Tangier Island, Virgina. We used to try photo flash cartridges until a local squadron VP-8 had an incident that nearly blew off the tail of the aircraft. This accident precluded the use of photoflash cartridges in the P-3. Flying at night was a pleasure because we flew a Julie pattern to show what an active pattern was like. Tactics seven and eight were basically the same with variations depending on what has happened thus far in their progress. Tactics nine and ten depended on whether sub time was available. The last flight of VP-30 was a catchall of information that was woven together so that the students got all they were required from the syllabus.

Logical Comparative LOFAR was a recommendation by the TAC-NOTE and was incorporated in the VP-30 syllabus. LCL dealt with the comparison of the strength of LOFAR on each sonobuoy. The strength of a signal, let's say a merchant signal, can range from a strength of one to ten. If a sonobuoy is dropped near the target the buoy can pick up cavitation from the screw noises and it will pick up the appearance of a closest point of approach (CPA). Another buoy may only show the minimum of characteristics of signature, or no aural screw noises, that will be further away from the merchant. So, for example, we drop a four buoy pattern, three buoys on the circle a 120 degree apart and twenty miles from the datum sonobuoy. Initially the Jezebel operator gave the following strengths: buoy 1, strength 7; buoy 4, strength 2 (cavitation); buoy 2, strength 7; buoy 3, strength 5. Next the navigation must know the ranges of the day for merchants. You can see that when we plot the strengths reported by Jezebel, we may have to put on our thinking caps. The Tactical Coordinator, the most high, almighty omnipotent Chief can grace the airplane his fix of LCL. In short, the target is left of datum and he is traveling Northwest. Wait a minute, I can not predict that as we adjust the range of LCL. Now we hurry and proceed into CODAR vis a vis the ten mile CODAR tracking circle if your are tracking a conventional submarine.

Jane was feeling rotten Halloween night and I came home with candy, bubble gum and Snickers bars. Beth was really excited in her costume. Beth and I were ready so we went out about six o'clock. We really had a good time trick or treating. She had a bag full of goodies and we came home after an hour and a half to show Mom. Beth was cute, but she did not know how to accept another child. She wanted one, but we will see. Tom Ryan called to invite us over for a glass of cheer. I told him of Jane's situation. Tom got his wife on the phone with Jane and she talked her into going over to their house. There were twenty or so people there, all VP-30 officers and their wives. They really took care of Jane. They were able to get her to eat a hot dog and some chips. The officers took care of me with drink, while Beth slept in one of the Ryan's bedrooms.

Dick Michaux was another friend of mine that was placed on one of the first VP-44 P-3A pilots that turned the Russian ships back creating a successful blockade in 1962. Dick went to the Naval Academy and went to preflight. He and I were both on shore duty. We took off on a night and day navigation flight. The pilots and navigators were all first tour. I had trouble with two of the pilots. Their charts were sloppy and they did not shoot the stars at all. I talked with Dick about this and boy was he mad with the same individuals! We decided that we would play the laziness by hand! The night before the day hop they were drinking when Dick and I left. At six a.m. we were up and had already eaten. At eight a.m. Dick, the NFO student, and myself were ready to get on the bus. We waited five minutes. Dick wanted to go to the plane right then. Dick had the phone number to get the sleeping pilots. The first tour and myself went to get the weather and filled out our preflight. About thirty minutes later, we showed the flight plan to Dick and filed it.

Forty-five minutes before take-off, the two pilots stumbled aboard the aircraft. They immediately got a cup of coffee and LT Michaux took direct care of them. We worked them every minute of the flight back to Patuxent River. I have never had such netherworld beings so inept with basic skills! I had to mark them down on the NAV 1 and 2 grade sheets.

Little by little I am changing the script of the Navigation Dry Swim. The players are ready, that is the three or four Second and First Class who are interested in this dry swim. The navigation logs had arrived and I have spent several days writing lesson plans and augmenting them with slides. The next step is to start building a turnover file. It would not be long before we had an Administrative Inspection of VP-30. Navigation officer or not, I had better get hot!

The VP-30 change of command would be occurring in November 1966. Commander Russ Roberts was to be my skipper again. We had a big change of Command and a reception at the Officers Club. There I met LCDR Ray Estes who works in the Training Department of Wingslant. I told him that I was a Navigation Training Officer and I was in dire need of navigation logs. The following week I was called from the Duty Office to pick up a box. It was navigation logs with instructions on how to fill them out.

In December Tom Ryan had a flight which was to be the last flight of the tactics' flights. Tactics 10 is a flight where anything can happen, and it usually does. I watched the nav preflight before we went out to preflight the aircraft. The aircraft was in pretty good shape, but the APS-80 radar was acting up and a new system was coming to replace the radar indicator. Finally the indicator was installed and the happy faces of the radar operator proved that we were ready for takeoff. Tom called the brief, the student instructors gave the brief including all of the ditching assignments. It was a nice day at 5000 feet when we marked on Salisbury TACAN outbound to the Atlantic Ocean. An hour and thirty minutes later we sent our onstation report. We began laying a seven buoy Jezebel pattern. The VP-30 Jezebel instructor called an hour later to tell me to look at two buoys. These had high hopes of encountering a Soviet submarine signature. I walked up to the cockpit to tell Tom Ryan what I saw. He got another pilot to relive him as went back to see the grams. Tom saw, he looked again, and said, "Mike you have got something here; I am going to set Condition Two and we will go from there." After the loudspeaker announcement we went into CODAR. Our target was fixed and we went into a CODAR tracking circle. We had the target proceeding west at about eight knots, then it changed it's heading to the East at eight to nine knots. We sent a real situation six report and we amplified it with course, speed, and time of each event. Finally, I said enter into SSQ-15 tactics. Tom said no; we lost contact with the submarine. We tried to regain contact but had been ordered to divert to Norfolk, Virginia for a visit to COMFAIR-WINGSLANT for debrief. The crew old and new were exhausted so we took all our logs and records to LCDR Sam Estes. He was quite happy that I was the TACCO. He took the tape and played it on the recorder. The look of the debrief caused concern but after thirty minutes they said no contact. I was sure there was contact, oh well, another day in the life of a likely sub hunter.

Lieutenant E.M. Brittingham was promoted during the week by CDR Roberts who called him into his office with Jane present. Jane pinned on the bars and that made me proud. The skipper, as I was leaving, told me that during the flight last week we did have contact. He congratulated me and that night all of VP-30 partied at a downtown Lexington Park Bar. We all got bombed celebrating making rank.

Bill and Mott Atherholt were in Springfield, Virginia. Bill and I had been keeping in touch. We had been invited to a New Year's Eve party. When we arrive at their house it was very cold and ready to snow. We had a great time reliving the old times in VP-10. Happy New Year and we welcomed in 1967.

The year of 1967 was one of worry and hoping. Jane was all right. The winter was cold and icy. Captain Roberts had me in his office expressing his concern about Mr. John Smith revolutionizing the way Jezebel was taught. COMFAIRWINGPAC, the West Coast side of anti-submarine warfare, had invited him to present his talk. Now he will present the talk to Naval Personnel Research Activity in San Diego in two months. CDR Roberts wanted me to attend, but first I was asked if I had the advanced course in Jezebel. Obviously I responded no and was scheduled for the course the third week of February.

The course was held down in Norfolk, Virginia at the Fleet Airborne Electronics Training Unit near the BOQ. There were about sixteen in the course. In one day we relearned everything that we had forgotten. We studied and looked at grams until 1630 (4:30 p.m.). The next day we worked on more information, the most interesting was the new submarines that have recently been deployed. The exam on Friday was one for the books. I did all right on the gram reading. What I did not expect was the twenty question quiz held immediately after the gram portion. I received my Advanced Airborne Jezebel Operator graduation certificate fifth out of seven completing the course.

The next month I went to see Dr. John Smith. A First Class Petty Officer, AX1 Brown, went with me to the speech. He had a completely new idea of teaching about Jezebel that was extremely complex in nature. He had many spinoffs of practice and this, shall we say, was boring to many. On our last day, we agreed to give our Commanding Officer a report about what we have learned. Apparently Dr. John Smith must have reached the magic light and now it is green; we will continue our pursuit of this objective.

It's now the end of June. Jane is suffering during our move to a new apartment. Several of my friends helped me move but I called movers to take the big furniture away. The actual moving took four hours, including placing the furniture. The new two bedroom apartment was a godsend. This was a much more spacious apartment in the bedrooms, kitchen, the living room was 20 X 14 feet, and the dining room was 12 X 12! I had Jane sit down with her ice tea while I sweated my you-know-whats'-off getting everything settled.

On July 18, Jane had funny sounds coming from her stomach. I took her to the dispensary where they decided to watch her for an hour. I started watching the news and about 8:00 p.m., we had a little girl. I stayed around to see that Jane was okay and see the baby. She was very cute when she slept.

Mother came down from Annandale to help keep Beth. Mother and I went to see Anne Driscoll the next day. Jane came home with Anne on the third day. Dick Michaex came downstairs to meet Mom and Anne. We also had friends come over including Al and Judy Mouns. Jane fed Anne and she seemed to like it for about two weeks, then it seems like she was always sick.

One thing I forgot to mention is that I was a proud boat owner. I paid $500, which was quite a deal for a 16 foot 35 horsepower Evinrude motor with a trailer. This is a nice boat that I would take down to the marina. Al Mouns and I used to make "touch and goes" on the harbor where we would pick up water skiers! Al, who had won his boat last year, was a wizard at boating. Dick Michaex really got interested in fishing. One day shortly after Anne arrived, we went down to the marina and went out into to the Patuxent River. We were trolling for rockfish. The gulls were orbiting the area a half a mile ahead where the Rockfish were breaking the water. I told Dick to reel in and, in a flash, I had the motor turning and a burning. It was hot in Patuxent River and you have guessed it, thunder was coming down the river. We had made many casts at the splashes and netted about five Rockfish. The storm was on top of us and it began to rain. I noticed I was just about offshore of the Patuxent Officers Club. I started the engine to head back to the landing site. The waves were furious. I told Dick that I was going ashore rather than lose my boat in this storm. It was really coming down when we hit shore. We both pulled the boat out of the water and we ran to a tree trunk for cover. Eventually, the rain stopped and we were soaked. We put the boat back in the water and went back to where we left the trailer. When we got back to the apartment, I said let's keep the boat, the fish, and everything to your imagination!

I have been busy at VP-30 during the summer. After this month at VP-30, I have logged 359.0 hours inflight. Variably, the tactical flights were doing great but the problem with CODAR kept me wondering about the CODAR plotter. The plotter is used to plot the bearings of the CODAR plants. If the "road" is zero-nine-zero true, the plotter is put on top of the plant 090 true. The bearings are plotted and the next CODAR plant is a right angle to the first CODAR plant dropped. For example, Plant Bravo is dropped on a road of 180 degrees true. Then obviously the CODAR plotter is facing 180 degrees. After about three ounces of Drambuie, I finally figured out a way to stop the infamous, erroneous bearing from sidestepping into the ASW problem. I took a 180 degree compass and laid it on the road of the fictitious course (say 090). The Jezebel operator then calls a broadside that correlates with a 090. I tried to work out a fix for this new design. I found the Xerox and copied the CODAR plotter. I wrote up a page on how to use the device. I contacted several of my friends who I thought would help me prove that this CODAR plotter really works.

In the fall, we went back to San Diego for another meeting. The Officers were put in the Admiral Kidd Bachelor Officer Quarters. LT Jim Beam of FAETU in Norfolk, Virginia stayed next door to me. He was in VP-23 and got assigned to FAETU for shore duty. The meeting required a lot of work and if the work was approved, there would be a Jezebel test that all NFO's and Jezebel operators would have to take. The next meeting will be in Norfolk, Virginia to make the whole thing interesting and a happy occasion for all of us.

The Administrative Inspection of VP-30 was announced a month prior to the date of inspection. Finally I had the players briefed and tomorrow morning we had a nice quiet setting to finish the recording of the navigational dry swim. Each person had been briefed on the player or playee that is to perform. After three hours, we sat back and listened to the tape. There is one Julie explosion that needs re-taping. On that particular phase of the recording, the tape was finished. I told all of the guys to join me in a beer. Dam, they all did for one or two hours. It was a happy occasion for all of us.

I had everything in order and ready for the inspection. LCDR Sam Estes inspected me and was impressed with the lesson guides, slides, and overjoyed with the dry swim. I had some students dry swims' graded and he looked over these with vigor. I went over the latest navigation logs and with that behind me, I rested my case. He opened up a few questions that were not relevant to me. He ask what did I include in the tactical navigation syllabus in the past year? I told him that I have included about all of the COMFAIRWINGS Notice of last year, including refinement of basic tactics to the convergence zones. I opened up the safe to show him the plotter device. He was so impressed with the plotter, he wanted to take one to Norfolk to have it made. He had several more officers to meet with, so I just shook my head and he went out the door.

In November 1967, VP-30 had a Change of Command. CDR Russ Roberts was being relived by CDR Josephson from an aides job in Washington. Russ was headed to Washington. I suspect he is going to NAVAIRSYSCOM. CDR Josephson was President's Johnson's aide, that was a position that must have kept him jumping! Jane and I both said our good-byes to Russ. He told me he wrote a top fitness report for me and to keep in touch in Washington. We later had an opportunity to visit him in Maryland, just outside of Washington, where he was living. We had a gala reception afterwards in the Officers' Club. I was reacquainted with many old friends as well as meeting people that I had a great deal of contact with in later years.

Christmas came and was good. By New Year's my daughter Anne was still sick. She had chronic colds and infections. The third week of

January 1968 Jane took her to the doctor. She called me at work to meet her at the hospital. Anne was a sight. She was in a plastic device breathing oxygen with an IV connected to one of her legs. I cried when I saw her although she was as happy as she could be. She was diagnosed with pneumonia that the doctor's felt they would soon overcome. All the grandparents came down to pull Anne through. She spent four days in the hospital before we could bring her home again.

I started my new job in VP-30 by jumping into the Tactics Department. I was assigned to the Search Officer who taught the basic Jezebel tactics that covers radar and electronic counter measures. Tom Ryan was still teaching the entire phase of flights and tactical procedures not discussed in present handbooks. I was introduced to new lesson guides that were really old with new information stuck inside the book. The old words "convergence zone" keep coming back to haunt the old decrepit TACCO. The genius of VP-30 decided to create a course of Sound in Water relying on the background noise and the many parameters that will affect sound in water.

Of all the forms of radiation known to man, sound will travel through the sea along the best and most efficient path. The uses of underwater sound constitute the science of sonar. An active use projector sound generated by targets is returned as echoes to a hydrophone. A passive or listening system uses sound radiated by the target.

The course was constructed by two VP-30 officers, one newly graduated from the Naval Post Graduate School. He capitalized on the sonar equation. The essentially simple sonar equation serves two practical functions. The first being the prediction of performance of the equipment currently being used. The second being the design of new improved equipment.

The basic considerations are the signal level at the receiver, background noise and the ability of the sonar operator to detect the signal in the noise background. The sonar equation is satisfied when the signal level equals the background masking level plus an additional minimum amount needed for an operator to just begin to detect the target. The passive sonar equation is:

$$SL - TL = NL - DI + DT$$

There are three types of parameters that are a part of the equation: Parameters Determined by the Target, Parameters Determined by the Medium, Parameters Determined by the Equipment. In the passive sonar equation the key parameters are: Targets Source Level (SL), Transmission Loss (TL), Receiver Directivity Index (DI), and Detection Threshold (DT).

The sea, together with its boundaries, forms a remarkably complex medium for the propagation of sound. As traveling through the sea, an underwater sound signal becomes delayed, distorted, and weakened. Transmission loss expresses the magnitude of one of the many phenomena associated with sound in the sea. The velocity of sound is an oceanographic variable that determines many of the peculiarities of the sound transmission. It increases with depth, salinity and temperature. Since salinity in the open ocean is relatively constant, and temperature is usually much warmer near the surface than it is at great depth, the sound velocity usually is higher near the surface and decreases with depth until the temperature becomes constant (usually about 32 degrees). At great depths it is possible for the sound velocity to equal or exceed the near surface sound velocity.

This is a fascinating course at VP-30 seemingly unlocking the boundaries of sound. The term "velocity profile" refers to the variation of sound velocity with depth or the velocity-depth function. In the deep sea, the velocity profile, obtained by hydrographic observations of temperature, salinity and depth, is displayed in the ajoining slide. In the surface layer of the sea, the velocity of sound is susceptible to the daily changes of heat, cooling, and wind action. Sound tends to be trapped or channeled in the mixed layer, just below the surface, called the seasonal thermocline. The term thermocline refers to the changing temperature in relation to the depth of the sea. This layer has a negative thermal or velocity gradient, simply put, the temperature and velocity are decreasing with the depth that varies dependent on the seasons. During summer and fall, the near surface is warm, the seasonal thermocline is strong and well defined. During the winter and spring in the Arctic, it tends to merge with the surface duct beneath the seasonal thermocline. This is the main thermocline where major increases in temperature over that of the deep cold depths of the sea occur. Located below the main thermocline is the isothermal layer that maintains a constant temperature of 32 degrees fahrenheit.

On every flight we order a Sound Velocity Profile. There are certain areas of the sea that each portion of the water column is used in analyzing its use of anti-submarine warfare. This is how we determine the paths of water that effect the sound propagation in this area. Another interesting area of the course concentrates on the deep sound channel.

The deep sound channel, also known as the SOFAR channel (sound fixing and ranging), was discovered in WWII. Downed aviators dropped an explosive charge that was fixed when the charge went off. More recently this technique accurately measures the fix for geodetic distance determinations and missile impact locations.

The course also covers Convergence Zones. These characteristics for convergence zones are in 30-35 mile ranges in temperate to tropical latitudes and 25-30 miles in cooler latitudes. The peak of a convergence zone is at 25 decibels above the level found in spherical spreading and absorption. This increase is called convergence gain. For deeper sources or receivers, the single convergence zone is found when the source and receiver are near the surface and split into two half zones.

Detection of signal is one of the more important topics covered in the course. This involves detection of signals in noise and reverberation. The input signal-to-noise ratio is required for making this decision at some pre-assigned level of correctness of the decision as "target present or target absent." At the pre-assigned level, the signal-to-noise ratio is called the detection threshold and refers to the input terminals of the receiver-display-observer combination. The words detection threshold imply two of the most important aspects involved in extracting a signal from the background in which it is embedded. First, the function of detection itself, and second, the existence of a threshold somewhere near the output of the receiving system.

The Figure of Merit (FOM) of a sonar system is the expected excess signal at the input to the receiver above that needed to just satisfy the sonar equation. This means that the signal-to-noise at the input exceeds the detection threshold and it can be expected that a signal present decision will be made with a level of correctness higher than the pre-assigned level. The higher the FOM the more likely the sonar system will make the correct detection decisions.

In summary, the figure of merit and the sonar equation are all one needs to know to employ the principles of underwater sound in designing or operating a sonar system.

Our third meeting of the Jezebel Training Conference was in Norfolk, Virginia in the Spring of 1968. We received grams with basic parameters of engines. We discussed various topics of antisubmarine warfare (AW) rating that was currently being considered by the Navy. Unfortunately, I was for it. I ended up being elected to present my personal beliefs about the rating. I was elected to present my opinion to the Commander from Washington, D.C. I had made some notes that morning citing information back to 1964. I recalled that a Jezebel operator that was an "AX," the radio operator was an "AT," and the Julie operator was an "ATN." Each of these individuals worked on the plane on the ground and in the air. I felt the Jezebel operator should be a part of a training division when on the ground to meet the demanding changes occurring with nuclear expansion, but should do nothing but fly. He was impressed with my comments and shook my hand. The AW rating was passed in a month.

In May 1968 a message of an overdue submarine in Norfolk, Virginia, caused every squadron to be launched. The USS Scorpion, an attack nuclear sub, was returning from deployment. The ship was overdue and had not been heard from. I was launched with a VP-30 student crew to assist the search along the route of the sub. This was almost 200 miles east of Norfolk. We were briefed on the sub's buoy markers and flares. We found a group of buoys and guessed they were a part of the same net. The second day we went further out, only to find more junk in the water. Two months later, it was learned that the sub was lost near Lajes, Azores. This was one mess and surely ninety-nine individuals did not want to perish. They found the hull. The rest was really left to the sub command forces to learn how the Scorpion perished. This was also the same situation when the Navy lost the

Thresher off the New England coast in April 13, 1963, CDR Earl Luka CO of VP-10 dropped a wreath at this position.

The heat of the VP patrol force abroad was about to ignite, Norway was to get the P-3B aircraft. The training officer unloaded this bit of information to the twelve officers that would be assigned to train them. We prepared lesson guides, weapon system trainers, and tactic flights that they would fly upon arrival at VP-30. We had a happy hour when they arrived to introduce the wives to one another. The officers were proficient in English and I could not foresee any problems with the syllabus.

I had the first class of officers, Jezebel, TACCO, Navigator, and Julie/ECM positions. I went through the navigation segment, then the tactics lectures. Tom Ryan picked up on the tactics criteria that lead into the Weapon System Trainers. I gave the brief and I knew the crew was the skipper's top-notch crew. The WST-1 started out as a series of mining runs. After six runs, I announced to proceed at 180 degrees for forty miles to lay a four buoy module. I did not say anything more. The Tactical Coordinator put in the four buoy module and did a Tactical Navigation Stabilization that was perfect. The Jezebel announced contract with blade rate, shaft rate, revolutions per minute, and classification of the contract. The TACCO and the navigators plotted all this information. Next the Jezebel reported closest point of approach on a buoy and he gave strength readings of two other buoys he had made contact. I was ecstatic about the professionalism of the crew. The entire scenario was over in three and a half hours. At debrief, I asked the Tactical Coordinator if they wanted a medal for completing VP-30. I could not find fault with what they were doing. In fact, I learned some techniques that would be good for other VP-30 candidates that received training from me.

The training went on for sometime. I really missed all of the antics of the Norwegian aircrew as I rotated back to the aircrew training in the United States. In December 1968 Tom Ryan and myself were selected to fly with VP-56. This crew had just transited to the P-3B. We went over to take a tactics flight with this crew. We sat through the brief and proceeded to preflight. We had been assigned to a ditching station in a training area normally used by VP-30. Things were not going well. The Tactical Coordinator was not directing this action aft. The PPC was taking the lead by overseeing the TACCO. I could not help myself, I was feeling a great deal of frustration at the end of this flight. Before we went to debrief, Tom pulls me aside to find out what my reaction to this crew had been. I started talking about the various things the crew had done and Tom stopped me. He had made up his mind. The PPC was embarrassed when Tom got finished with his debrief. Then it was my turn. The bottom line of this affair was they had to go on another flight before they were given a satisfactory grade.

Tom did the right thing. He went to Capt. Josephson, the skipper of VP-30, and told him what had happened on this flight highlighting the principal factors the crew had violated. The skipper assured him he would speak on his behalf. The next day the skipper of VP-56 called the skipper of VP-30 inquiring as to why the instructors were so vehemently critical in their actions toward the crew.

Tom and I were ordered back to the CO's office of VP-56 to tell why the crew did not perform and was given a refly for the flight. He went on to say that he received a verbal lashing from our Commanding Officer so get on with the program. After Tom and I finished, we accepted congratulations from the skipper. Two weeks later the VP-56 passed their flight with other VP-30 officers on board!

1969 brought a gala event when the New Year came, parties where everyone got drunk. The kids were growing up and having tubes placed in their ears. Beth and Anne used to have an ear aches every six months. The answer was to put tubes in their ears to establish a connection to the eardrum, in two or three months the tubes would fall out, and the problem solved.

I had began working in my lesson guides the next ADMAT was coming for VP-30. I typed all day until 4:00 p.m. on a Sunday. I later took Jane and the kids to dinner and had friends over when we got back. We got the kids to bed and opened a bottle of Champagne. At 11:00 p.m. our guests left and we still had half a bottle left. Jane was feeling drunk and attacked me. I finally got her undressed and she made love to me on top of the bed.

A month later, I came home from a successful grade on the ADMAT to find Jane crying. I gently held her and asked what was wrong. She thought she was pregnant. She went to the doctor and he confirmed the suspicion. The doctor was smart to put her on the exact medication she had been on before.

The need for orders kept popping in my head. Along with orders is the trip to Burbank, California for the Lockheed P-3C. We have already sent several maintenance men there for six months of training. The training officer approached me about a course that started in May

1969 that would last for five weeks. My orders were due to arrive in June. This meant no passover whatsoever to VP-30. I left all the decisions to the powers that be. Next week I was called into the Executive Office of CDR Gene Tansey. CDR Tansey had called the placement office and I was to be extended for one year. This seemed acceptable to me and to Jane after speaking to her at home. She has been doing well with her medicine. Early in May we said our good-byes as the C-54, a reserve airplane, took us on a ten hour flight to Burbank.

This four engine aircraft, that must have been twenty years old, finally landed in Burbank after an eleven hour flight. We unloaded the plane and spent an evening in a hotel in Los Angeles. The next day was Sunday when I contacted the Lockheed representative to pick us up at the hotel. The motel was something out of the past, it was cheap, relative to the prices in downtown Los Angeles, and the only drawback was the smell of marijuana present on the second floor! The motel staff had a happy hour for us that included wine, snacks, and draft beer. We met people who lived there, stayed there might be a better word, and discovered the twenty by thirty foot pool. Last but not least, there was a go-go strip joint a hundred feet away that featured all nude dancers. Yes, what a way to see Burbank under the disguise of being a beatnik.

At 9:00 a.m. Monday morning, I represented VP-30 by giving orders to the appropriate staff. I was told that our class was meeting at 10:00 a.m. with twenty other agencies of the Navy, including test and contractor facilities. The remainder of the day was spent showing how great the P-3 was, but look out because we have a better system with the P-3C. This plane can run circles around it's adversaries. In my view, we spent a week wasting our time. We had a two hour lecture followed by a question and answer period. By 1:00 p.m. Friday afternoon we were excused and I received a phone call from VP-30. The skipper, Captain Coughlin, wanted to know how the course was going. I was ready to come home as were a few of the groups on this week's course. I told him if the instruction was not up to par, I would bring the entire group back with me.

The class began at 0730. We were given two NATOPS manuals. One covered the basics of the CP-901 computer system through the Logic units and loading the computer with tape drives. The second manual went into some detail of the parameters of each tactical display operators; Tactical Coordinator, Multipurpose Display (MPD), and the Navigator/Communicators Display.

The week went by fast. After learning how it speaks in a factor of eight (computer language), we had learned all about the computer. On the second week, we went to the P-3C aircraft and took turns loading the computer. I just about loaded my computer, but I dumped (the computer went down) the system. Once the computer was loaded, we did several things to the program so our instructor would know what we were doing.

The main thing about running your computer is by checking the TACCO's power control panel in the MPD. At the top of the control panel, there is a run switch light, a stop switch, and OV TEMP switch light coming from the computer. When the stop light comes on you can Bootstrap the program. The start switch below the run light is activated and will cause the computer to enter recovery bootstrap routine. The tape that has all the documentation on it goes back to the beginning to start putting the program in and going to the point when the program failed. In the light "stop" position, the manual position creates a single bootstrap mode for a single start sequence.

There are three logic units that control the computer and link all sensor and navigation functions. The logic units control all symbols, markers, range circles, movement of the aircraft, keysets, all auxiliary readout displays, sensor displays, and the pilot's display.

The Navigator display of the inertial navigation system is to determine the geographic position of the aircraft inflight and to provide accurate information to guide the aircraft to it's intended geographic point. The INS-84 (inertial naviation system) provides altitude (pitch and roll) and true heading measurements. The INS has two inertial sets, INS-1 and INS-2, that provide dual source accuracy to increase the mission success. A two axis accelerometer is the primary source of information for the inertial. The gyroscope exists to establish and maintain a level of reference for the accelerator that provides altitude and heading information. The latitude and longitude positions can be inserted during the ground alignment.

The Tactical Coordinator's display consisted of the unit called the ASA-70. This is a multiple display made up of the sensor (data), readout, and four power panel displays. The Multipurpose Data Display (MDD) displays digital data consisting of alphanumeric symbols or conics. The details of cues, alerts, and other display symbology are available through the matrix select and readout labels on the keyboard panel. The TACCO tray contains thirty-six matrix select switches, sixty-nine monofunction switches, forty-four keyboard switches, and a trackball. The tray switches enable the TACCO to select MDD displays, insert tactical data to the display and into the computer program. It also may select navigation modes of operation, select TAC-NAV, launch search and kill stores, control the magnetic tape transport, and control the data link system.

The basic reference system for the ASA-70 is the flat-earth X-Y coordinate system. The center of the display represents the point of tangency for the X-Y plane with all data positions being expressed in nautical miles ranging from two to 1024 miles.

Two other things that deserve mentioning are the Ambient Noise Meter and the Data Link System. The Ambient Noise Meter is set aside to handle SSQ-36 bathythermograph sonobuoy. I know this sounds familiar, when the buoy is dropped it is assigned to a certain channel. To read the noise that the sound monitors is in the change of temperature versus depth and the buoy prints out a velocity profile. The other interesting system is the Data Link System that is a communication link providing an exchange between computers of tactical data with other aircraft and participating units. Tactical data is accumulated by the operational program and selected date is encoded by the link 11 format. The TACCO then selects local contacts for transmission to other units of the data link net. The AQA-7 acoustic processor/display system were the highlight of knowledge about the P-3C. Unfortunately, both lines of sensor one and two were vacant in the airplane. The instructor said we would get them in a month! The DIFAR system that receives signals from the sonobuoys, can be analyzed and classified for the purpose of locating submarines. Data is recorded on chart recording (grams), cathode ray tube displays and noise on the headset. The DIFAR processes signals from either active or passive sonobuoys.

In the cockpit of the P-3C the ASA-66 takes over as the main system in the antisubmarine warfare. The ASA-66 is a 7.6 inch cathode ray tube projector and visual screen readout that assists a pilot in pursuing a sub. The display is positioned on the main instrument panel and by the capability of getting all the inserts that may be received or processed.

The pilots tactical display presents symbology of an acoustic tactical display. It shows range scale, alerts, and other important cues. The computer program does not allow symbology to overflow into the outer peripheral segments. The ASA-66 display is broken down into two mile segments like the ASA-70, ranging from two to 1024 nautical miles. The scale readout is dependent on the pilot's initiation of increase of scale.

The remaining two weeks were spent training in the air and covering left overs relating to ordnance. The first flight was exciting. We entered the airplane to first tackle the navigation station with the latitude and longitude positions in the ASN-84. We started the inertial program by filling in the fly-to-points. There is space for six positions, probably from the Patuxent River, Maryland to Lajes, Azores Air Force Base. We did many things that were unusual to us. We got onstation, in the desert somewhere, to try the TACNAV and saw how the drift would be applied to the tactical or appropriate aircraft dead reckoning position.

Finally we received a test that was a brain teaser. I think I got about at 3.2 grade out of a 4.0. The test showed how hard and stressful the past five weeks have been. Lockheed did know what its doing—providing a centralized computer aircraft that would replace all other models that they have built for antisubmarine warfare. The study of the two manuals that we completed covered strategic and never-ending views of the P-3C aircraft that would continuously be corrected and modified until the next answer to patrol aviation was realized.

In summary, this had been a tough course, regardless of brass, silver, or gold we were whipped through computer technology, maintenance of gear, and preflighting the airplane from bottom to top including the satisfaction of the NATOP's manuals. This was not a course for Tactical Coordinators. For an initial course, Lockheed did a credible job, however, VP-30 needed the logistics of how the system worked. There were many systems that were unavailable to be included in this five week period. DIFAR training including the recorders and associated equipment would be included in VP-30 when they were delivered to Patuxent River. VP-30 sent us to do a good job but the inclusion of other commands hampered the effectiveness and manageability of the course. Lockheed has the expertise, knowledge, and experience to teach the first computer driven airplane. I think the answer was hidden behind a computer chip that maybe revealed in coming years.

The C-54 aircraft finally got us back to Patuxent River. Jane, Beth, and Anne picked me up. Jane was happy to see me and had really gotten pregnant. She was sick but not to the extent of throwing up. Beth was five years old and about to start kindergarten in September. Anne would be two years old next month and she was practicing reading elementary books.

I took a few days off from VP-30 to take the kids out to the Crab Place on one of the islands. Summer has been beautiful this time of the year. The squadron was getting ready for the P-3C Tactical Navigator course coming up in three weeks. I was entertained by two surprises. I received my orders to take my NATOP's exam in the P-3B aircraft. The change of orders were to Deputy Commander Fleet Air Wing Five. Why, I wondered? That was not the surprise that bothered me. LT Cox, the NATOPS instructor, said if I should not take the test, then he will report this to the Commanding Officer . This really burnt my ass. After five weeks of studying the P-3C, I must go back and restudy the former non-computerized P-3B aircraft.

It took two weeks of relearning the old system. I took an open book exam that I filled out in the first week. The closed book exam got right down to the nitty gritty. I passed it but could not understand why answer C said it all. The day of the NATOPS flight I briefed the crew and ended with safety drills and assignments. I went out to the aircraft to begin preflight. The ASA-16 was sick and their maintenance team was trying to fix the gear. I continued on the inertial system with the alignment. Fifteen minutes the ASA-16 was declared up. I began my preflight and finished it prior to the brief on board the aircraft.

The flight was tiring and the instructor, Lt Cox, was having drills that required action on all hands. The tactics portion of the flight went well. The Jezebel operator announces a Yankee nuclear sub on a sonobuoy. This lead to a three buoy contact. Just as I was about to reach to a new tactic, the Jezebel operator had screw noises on a sonobuoy. I elected to mark on that buoy with MAD standing by. We got a MAD man, an active buoy was dropped, and we rapidly bombed the sub. At debrief Lt Cox said I did a good job. He was meticulous in noting any violation when the crew conducted the multitude of drills on the aircraft. Forty-five minutes later, we were through with the flight. Two days later I checked my log book to find that Lt Cox had filled out my Qualifications and Achievements as follows: P3A/B NATOPS Evaluation, TACCO Qualified. Since the date was June 25, 1969, I wrote in the next column, P-3C TACCO/NAVCOM Instructor. One reason that there is not a NATOPS officer for the P-3C is that we are gearing up for the first three squadrons that will transition to the P-3C aircraft.

The first surprise was my orders and I finally went over to see my new hangar. The Administration Officer did not know about these orders. I met some old friends but I wondered about this trailer in the hangar that was connected by long wires and cables to the hangar for power. I did find out that these were sea duty orders for me to assist in carrying out the duties as assigned.

July was a busy month with Beth's birthday last month, Anne's birthday on July 18, and my birthday is on July 30. They invited us up to Annandale, Virginia for the weekend. I wanted to go fishing on Saturday. We arrived Friday afternoon and went out to dinner. Dad was working very hard at the Coca-Cola Bottling Company. We had drinks and ordered the girls' their meals. We got home before dark and decided to sit out on the patio. Dad and I went downstairs to check out the fishing gear. Dad had started me fishing when I was nine years old. I remember the time when I caught my first fish at the falls in Goose Creek, near Leesburg, Virginia. He surprised me when he gave me a brand new Mitchell 300 spinning reel. I then started to put some line on the new reel. Dad got some Drambuie and the line got on the reel one way or another. We gathered up the two buckets that we used for bait. We had a net that was 6 X 4 feet. One of us would position the net over and around the stones so we could catch hellgrammites. The aquatic insect larva is caught by lifting the stones and brushing them with your hand in front of the net. After two or more stones are picked up, I will help Dad pick up the net and find hellgrammites, crayfish, and mad toms that look like Catfish.

Four thirty in the morning was mighty early but I got up and boy was my head crying for Excedrin. We had a cup of java and headed for Front Royal, Virginia. The Shenandoah River is a pretty site and continues its flow through West Virginia where it meets the Potomac River at Harper's Ferry. We had ham biscuits, scrambled eggs, and bacon at the restaurant in Front Royal. I almost forgot the coffee, but we headed South on the other side of the Blue Ridge Mountains with the river flowing on the right. We stopped at a boat rental facility overlooking the river. We hauled down all our gear and the motor. Dad hooked up the motor and I shoved off, heading for the ripples a mile up river. As soon as we got there I jumped out into three feet of water to hold the boat while Dad got out. The right side of the ripples was where I pulled the boat over the crashing, bubbling water to move it to shore. We caught bait and then fished. I have never felt more at peace. This satisfied my view of life looking down on the glorious view of the mountains and the Shenandoah River.

August was a busy month with Tactics Lectures and training flights with the P-3B trainers. The P-3C guys were to the wall with training. I was working on the lectures. The problem finally came through, the orders were causing controversy between VP-30 and the Officer Detailer. The problem was solved when I agreed to continue to help VP-30 train P-3C and other P3 types regarding tactics lectures and encompassing issues. It sounded good to VP-30, but have they touched base with Deputy Commander Fleet Air Wing Five? VP-30 had just woke up in early August and found out that half of their P-3C trained Naval Flight Officers (including me) have good orders and were moving on to Post Graduate School or elsewhere. The object is, they are a hurting motor scooter until they can get some NFO's trained as Tactical Coordinators and Navigation/Communication Instructors in the P-3C. The earliest they can reach that goal is November 1969.

After Labor Day, Beth started kindergarten and I started P-3C training. I spent a good time in the airplane training and correcting the ground training in Building 420. The orders I have say that my last day was September 30. I went to the Wing to show them my orders and report. The Administration personnel said that Captain Barnette would not be in until he returns from traveling. I had them arrange for him to see me as soon as they could. Two days later they called me and would like for me to see him the following Wednesday at 2:00 p.m. On Wednesday I met Captain Barnette. He is a mild mannered man that wanted to know about me. I started back in 1964 with VP-10 and then transitioned to the P-3A. I discussed the many jobs I had held in VP-30. I ended my monologue with my selection into the ground school in Burbank, California for the P-3C. I shared with him my surprise to return to Patuxent River to find orders. The Captain interjected that be was happy to have me aboard. The squadrons that were transcendent were good and he needed me to debrief their work. He spoke of another project that I will be in charge of, the Mobile Operational Control Van. The gang down in Norfolk passed that van for me to train and utilize when the opportunity arose. He ask me if there are any questions. "Well Captain," I said, "this sounds like a dream come true." I asked if he had gotten briefed on my orders to his command? As he lit his cigarette, he said, "No." I just about shit my pants! I told Captain Barnette the "Tale of Two Cities." It started when I got home from Burbank and progressed through VP-30's "mister fixit" evolution whereas, I would stay in the replacement squadron and go to DEP-COMFAIRWING Five at the beginning of 1970. Captain Barnette's face was getting redder by the minute. I finally explained that I had to see you first because you had not been approached about my situation since I had received my orders in June. It was quiet in his office. He smiled and looked me in the eye and finally said, "Mike, we have a problem and I am going to fix this situation." He told me that he would arrange a meeting with the Commanding Officer of VP-30. He had to meet with him anyway about training deficiencies and this would be a perfect time to ask about me. He wanted me to understand that he appreciated my honesty and he trusted that I would say nothing of this conversation. He ended our "conversation" with an invitation to come over to the Wing and get settled. I stood up and thanked the Captain, relieved that I did not get my ass chewed.

The next day I went to the Wing and introduced myself to the Operational Commander. He and I sat down to discuss the staff. He took me around the offices and finally the Wing Operational Control Center (OPCON). There were three or four Chiefs there that were AW's, the kind that I like. The gear was brand new. I did not want to tie up the Commander. That afternoon we had to go down to the hangar and get in this van that I had remembered. His name escapes me but he was the technical contractors' representative to train new members in use of the van.

A week went by and the Captain wanted to see me. I went to his office and told the Yeoman that he wanted to see me. The Captain stood and welcomed me with a cup of coffee. The Captain said he had a drawn out conversation with the Commanding Officer of VP-30 about me. Evidently he had not advised the Captain on changes, modifying orders, or "behind the back orders." First of all, I have granted that you make a list of what you can do at VP-30 and give the list to me so I will show it to VP-30. I promised that I would present the list to the Captain in five working days. One week from today I gave the Captain a list day by day of activities that I would help VP-30 through 31 October 1969.

With the days growing shorter and the leaves beginning to turn, there was a nip in the air as October came around. Jane was due anytime and I had already alerted Mom. We had invited guests over to spend the night, which meant the cots were set up in the living room. This was a helicopter pilot who was leaving the Navy for a pilot who ferries the oilmen back and forth to the rigs in Louisiana. We had drinks along with his wife as I cooked barbecue for dinner. At six o'clock the next morning, I dressed in my military uniform. I went into the kitchen and started coffee. By the time I started the bacon, I had awaken the guests. Jane came into the kitchen and looked like she was going to have the baby. I asked her what was wrong, but she dismissed the whole thing as the baby moving. Beth and Anne joined the group just as the bacon, eggs, and toast were served.

After saying goodbye to our friends, Jane started to get dressed. It was 9:00 a.m. and she was concerned about the labor pain. I was getting excited and wanted Jane to go to the hospital. "No worry" she said as she stepped into the shower. I called the office and told them I thought Jane might be ready to deliver; I would keep them posted. Jane was dressed at 9:30 a.m. I asked if there was anything I can do, but no that is not the way to act! Finally at five till ten, we pull up in front of the base hospital. I helped Jane inside and her doctor came around the corner. He saw Jane and he asked a nurse to have me sit down. The nurse sat me down in a hallway where women gave birth. It was 10:30 a.m. when I saw the nurse again. She asked if I was Mike Brittingham. I replied, "yes." She told me I had a son. I jumped and shouted out "a son!" Immediately four women who were nursing their babies poked their heads out of the doorway!

Edward Michael Brittingham Jr. was his name as agreed upon by Jane. The doctor stopped in and told us of a hernia operation that must be done. We both agreed and the next day he was operated on. Mike was a good baby and he sure snuggled up to his mother's breasts.

I took a box of cigars to VP-30 to celebrate the occasion. I was nearing the last days of work. In order to leave VP-30, I must turn in a lot of secret documents. I was working on this when a call came in from Keflavik, Iceland relaying that I had made Lieutenant Commander early. I was very pleased. I told Jane, but this started a new brain wave which should get me a three bedroom apartment in Patuxent River, Maryland.

CHAPTER 7

DEPUTY COMMANDER
FLEET AIR WING FIVE

Mobile Operation Control Van was now mine to learn for training and getting the van operational. The van was in charge of a Technical Representative who taught the rudiments of all the gear stowed on the van. This van was a "tractor trailer" about thirty feet long. The back of the trailer was eight feet wide yet the communications equipment expanded to about eleven feet wide. This was where the radio communicator sat with two UHF's, VHF's, and high frequency radios each. These were secure or unclassified radios which dealt with a mobile fixed antenna that was set up outside the van.

When you walk into the van you were presented by a brief/debriefing room the mobile van had to meet the crew to be briefed. The briefing room consisted of a display of what the mission would be. The presenter of the brief was capable of getting the communications down pat as well as the route to and from onstation. All logs and charts would be passed to the crew with all danger areas noted. The particular submarine the crew may encounter would be discussed by the AW on duty. He would show the grams of the contact of interest to the Jezebel operator, his primary mode of operations, and his speed of advance throughout the area where we may have detected him. The radio communicator would go over with the watch analyst the frequencies that would be used for High Frequency communications both covered and in voice connection. As a backup he would be issued all useable frequencies. The rest of the van was tied in with an intercommunication net that allows contact with any areas of the workspace. One final item, the tape analysis consists of UNH-6, UNH-1 and UNH-4 tape playing and recording. The van had been tested a year ago in Lajes, Azores, and received excellent reports.

In addition to the van, the brief/debrief function of the Wing carried a tremendous load on "all hands." Many of the qualifications were commenced by forming of crews in a new aircraft. Such was the case with VP-56, 24 and 49. Many of the basic quals were modified or done away with. The old Sniffer, searchlight and several other quals have been scrubbed. The P-3C crews are plagued with the new Low Lite Level Television Qual and the basic quals have been improved. One of the more memorable times that I had in ASCAC was debriefing a crew that had dropped a live MK-44 torpedo. The run was set up by a small boat that recovered the torpedo after it was launched. Everything went according to Hoyle, but the torpedo did nothing but run, then after four minutes it dove and imploded at depth or it exploded when the pressure was more than the torpedo could handle. After the tape of the event was heard, the Wing Five Duty Officer called on the secure phone COMFAIRWINGSLANT and told them the results of the four live torpedo drops. Ten minutes later, the Wingslant duty officer wanted the tapes ASAP. This required getting them down to Norfolk on the first flight launched tomorrow.

Another harrowing event was a OCEANSYSLANT qualification that the crew had communications with the facility and thought they had the qual. We had a ticker tape set up with them. I hammered out their call sign and shazam; they answered me. I asked them about the qual and what parameters they held on the contact. They answered and it was just one tenth of a number off on the Jezebel gram measurement. It was classified right and I give the crew credit because it was the only merchant within fifty nautical miles.

In January 1970 I was informed that I would get an award and to have my uniform restriped. My promotion to Lieutenant Commander at least a year and a half early so I had better be prepared for the inspection. Captain Burnett was the inspecting officer and he gave each one of his Wing Five staff a thorough visual "going over." He spoke briefly about the present condition of the staff and the coming events of the next six months. Incidentally, he also commented on the excellent appearance of his men both officer and enlisted during his inspection. He then called two Chief Petty Officers and gave them medals. He called me to step forward. Jane was in the audience when he recognized me as LCDR and shook my hand. The next award was a pleasure for me as he read the Navy Achievement Medal. The Navy Achievement covered the period of June 15, 1967 to September 30, 1969. This was the improved manual plotter that I had manufactured from the CODAR plotter. ASW was improved by the plotting speed and accuracy. It has received an excellent evaluation by the VP-30 squadron instructors. After the Captain pinned the medal to my coat, he shook my hand again and that made my day.

As the van compliment continued to increase, I was called in to see the Commander about something important. He wanted me to go to Springboard for a month and grade qualifications. I would fly down by squadron plane and return by the same fashion. The needs of the squadron were well in hand. There were plenty of ASW-1, navigator charts and other logs are there in place at Roosevelt Roads. In other words, I packed a separate list of each item and forwarded it to go with me on my fun filled trip to Roosevelt Roads.

We arrived in Puerto Rico on Monday with three flights needing to be debriefed. I jumped right in and finally caught up by 2300 hours late Monday night. I went over to the squadron spaces and met the Officer in Charge and told him I was available from 0800 through seven or eight that evening. All of my extra logs, charts, was set up on the debriefing table so the squadron will take them as required.

The space provided for the ASCAC was pitiful. Since there was only myself, I was busy as a "one armed paint hanger." There was no stipulation as to when the packets should be turned in and essentially the qual was a qual when turned in for me to grade it. Secondly, there were no antisubmarine warfare analysis to check if the contact was gained, if CODAR was employed, and if "syn and cal" were used every 15 minutes during the qual. Julie and MAD tapes were under my review. In summary, the list of things that infuriated me made the big hit parade when I got back. Captain Barnett said he appreciated the work that I had done, but he was pissed off with the shortcomings of the ASCAC that I had left in Springboard.

In two weeks time I was working with my van personnel and I met my Executive Officer, a Lieutenant Junior Grade who came up from the Oceanographic station at Eleuthera. I introduced him to all and told him to get next to the Technical Representative and learn all he can about the van. As you might guess, I was destined to leave for Roosevelt Roads again with a LT and four men were going to help train the ASCAC in Roosevelt Roads. This would greatly increase their proficiency, expertise, and give them more quality time as an ASW quality control analyst.

What a difference three weeks make! It must be my perspective, but the ASCAC was completely functional with all equipment operating and a new Watch Team to train in Roosevelt Roads. This ground-swell of enthusiasm caused me to generate a watch bill which put me on days and the other officers on nights. The Chief Petty Officer divided his watch team in half and we started training and grading the quals that came in. The third day I was satisfied with the progress we had made as we are tracking and the new men are performing. We had a couple of problems that we over came. The first was on landing the aircraft after a ASW qual. The crew had to report to ASCAC within thirty minutes. The second rule pertained to logs, records, and the tape of the flight. If you do not have a tape, forget the qual. The third and final rule is do not try to "smoke one through." This happened to me and I caught hell for it. The Commander raised hell and said he would take the exercise back to Jacksonville and get it graded. I told him to go ahead and get it done, but the qual will not count because it was not in the area where Jacksonville has priority. He walked off and tomorrow he did the same qual and made numerous attacks. When I finished the paperwork, he shook my hand and said he was sorry he got so pissed off.

Back in Patuxent River the van had grown to its last number of people. The total number was twelve, but I suspect that nine or possibly ten will have to do. By being at Springboard for the second period, Norfolk had been trying to activate the mobile van. My Executive Officer had been doing some work researching the measurements of the trailer to see if a C-130 plane could take the van to a new area of operation. He briefed me in detail and finally the work came in that the trailer will be disconnected and moved outside the hanger. Incidentally, a new device or a new sound device placed aboard a frigate was being tested next week. On Monday we received a top secret message. The facts were simple, put the van in a C-130 and remove the van from the C-130 and set it up to be operational as quickly as possible, and test the high common net and receive the necessary signals that are being broadcasted. We have a week to prepare for this test. I had a meeting of all hands and I advised them of the highlights of the message we had received.

I left the mechanics of loading and off-loading to the XO. I told him I would be watching and passing information if necessary. I would provide a tight-knit arrangement and have the sentries monitor the area and have badges produced for the crew that should permit them inside the van. The next three days were tedious as we had constructed a "pull the van out of the airplane—to operational." We went over the final checklist at eleven o'clock. We did not find any mistakes. The yeoman typed the checklist and gave the copies to the XO.

On Monday we received a message and we can expect the exercise to begin the next day at 0700 hours. We went over the details again and made slight changes to setting up the van, but everything looks good. The next morning a C-130 pulled up to the hanger and shut down it's engines. It took all morning for the van to be "squeezed" into the C-130. Frankly I thought it was too big but the van made it with scant clearance. We grabbed a sandwich and started to get the van ready for the signal. "Mark," I cried, and we began to unload the van. We moved the van with a tractor truck and stopped it about 300 yards behind the P-3 airplanes. Just as quick, the guards marked off the area of the van and placed a rope fifty feet about the van. The military police were mean bastards and to get inside the barrier you had to show identification. The next step was to secure the wheels and open the back door. The first person in was the Communication man and his assistant. Immediately they began to push out the radio section of the van. Next and most terrifying step was get out the portable antenna. This was massive and three to four men put this together in thirty minutes. Yes, it was cold but I have never had a team that worked so well with one another. The last manuever of all was brief turning on the high frequency radio. To be sure we were on line we had a communicator check with Norfolk. The communicator okayed our connection and switched to the assigned frequency. The frequency was clear and the voice at the end of the line was not cooperating. We checked the out and input boxes but to no avail. After an hour of listening and recording of this sound I contacted Wingslant and reported our progress. They said to monitor and record for one hour and then to secure the van. I walked out to the van and kept the radios working for another hour. I congratulated the men and told them they performed precisely. I did not know at the time, but they wanted me tomorrow morning with the tape recording in Norfolk. COMFAIRWINGSLANT was situated on the water in Norfolk. The planes would taxi to the building and behind the building the taxi director would inform you, turn the plane 180 degrees and secure the two engines on the port side. I came down the ladder with the tape that we made yesterday. I was greeted by the Tactical Development Group which took my tape. LCDR Danny Wolkensdorfer introduced himself and he had several questions about the loading and unloading of the van. We talked about the tedious loading, which included many options for aircraft loading. The LCDR was elated when I told him how much it took to become operational. Another gentleman entered the room and spoke with Dan, and, in turn, told me of the successful operation of the tape. The data was picture perfect and he requested no information was to be released to me.

In May 1970 the Operational ASW Exercise was scheduled for VP 49. Commander Bob Wisdom and CDR Gene Tansey were the Captain and Executive Officer respectively. CDR Wisdom was a former member of the ANEW team where he was responsible for many exchanges/updates to the P-3C aircraft. The team from Deputy Wing Five were selected and then went over to first Tactical Support Center. The center was built with the P-3C in mind. The officer in charge was head of the center and had seven other officers, AW's, and all of the maintenance help that worked out to about forty or so personnel. The team received a thorough going over of the system and its parameters. Each briefing room was explained and there the Antisubmarine Warfare operators went to the displays that quickened the results contained on these tapes. This was really the dream of the future and all deployment sites will have this system on the East coast.

The operational exercise started by numerous attacks and then came the dry period. The TSC showed many flights have had contact with the conventional United States submarine. The DIFAR was not working that well. As soon as a DIFAR was dropped, the bearing sometimes lagged behind the true bearing and then about ten or twelve minutes in the water, the bearing will tend to be right on. In my perspective, VP-49 needed some work before deployment, in essence, the operational ASW mission was given a thumbs up with VP-49 deploying in July.

One morning I was called by CDR Gene Tansey. He wanted me to come over and talk to him. Gene was a great guy. He had been a tremendous athlete and he liked to party. He wanted to talk to me man to man. Gene shook my hand and asked me to sit down. The XO wanted me to come to VP-49. Before he got to me, LCDR Pete Smith was grounded for an undetermined amount of time. He was the skippers tactical coordinator and that left the squadron one tactical coordinator short. Pete

Smith was the tactics officer and with the gap coming they would certainly fill that replacement. CDR Tansey stopped and wanted my comments. To begin with, I was astonished. I wanted to go back to flying, but what will that do to my career. Essentially, I had been in sea duty for one year. If I went to VP-49 would it be for two years or one year? All the parameters began infiltrating my brain along with a gigantic headache. I told CDR Tansey I would like to talk to Jane about this and tomorrow I will give him my decision. I asked him one more question, where would I find myself in the order of ranking the Lieutenant Commander? I would be at the bottom of the pile; fourteenth of fourteen.

I went home and I had a drink with my children. Beth was bubbling about her year in the first grade; Anne was telling us about her pacifier; and I was feeding Mike a bottle. I told Jane after the two kids were asleep about my visit with CDR Tansey. I related the ins and outs of such a move. We discussed the ramifications this would have on our lives and my career. First of all, we would need to have a three bedroom apartment. I went to Public Housing and gave my upcoming status. The lady said that there would be two openings in July. I accepted that and signed the list. I called CDR Tansey and he went ahead and called the officer in charge of assigning LCDR's to sea duty orders.

The problem was solved just before the squadron deployed. I was to report to the VP-49 in August and sure enough we moved in about ten days before I went to Iceland. We had a moving van from Lexington Park move us. The kids were happy as they liked the abode and we moved in by adding drapes, rugs and necessary needs in the kitchen. Boy was it hot! The last of July and the first of August I put the small air conditioner in our bedroom so that the air got back to the bedrooms.

The day before I left to join VP-49 I was packed for the trip. Everything that I could do to the house was done. The grass and bushes were cut; new plants were put out and the apartment looked nice. Everyone had a bed. Mike was still using the crib and the girls had bunk beds.

I told the kids good-bye that I would be back in November. I gave each child a kiss, with Jane being the last. I told her I would write with the address to reach me. As we roared down the runway, I said a prayer that I will do the best to cover for the lack of P-3C experience over last year.

CHAPTER 8

VP-49

VP-49 Deployment N.S. Keflavik, Iceland

Keflavik, Iceland was located on the Northwest shore of the Reykjanes Peninsula on Faxa Bay. This fishing port was booming as all of the Iceland's trawlers were tied up there. Iceland's international airport was booming and the Air Force F-102 were on hand as well as the new P-3C Orions.

The oceans of the world cover 71% of the surface of the globe. The planet or "blue planet" is the most dominant fixture as depicted by pictures taken from space. The ocean is regarded as the last major frontier on earth for the exploration and development of resources necessary to sustain mankind in the future. The ocean is a hazardous environment for man due to ice, storms, great depths, and the submarine.

The first geography of the oceans and seas was to map the physical geography of the sea bottom done by a US Naval Officer Matthew Foutaine Maury in 1850. Maury showed a rudimentary generalized knowlege of the North Atlantic Ocean. Increased cable laying (called submarine) revealed even more knowledge of the topography. This work gave little help for those who sought the details of undersea mountains, ridges, hills, slopes, and trenches. Knowledge of these became strategically important in matters as diverse as the employment of nuclear submarines. All of the oceans may be used for strategic purposes. Their great depth, vast expanse and freedom of navigation on the high seas leaves one to wonder their strategic vulnerability.

A vital element in Naval Strategy is judging the actions of potential threats and countering them by deployment of additional forces.

Major powers use intelligence gathering ships (Soviet AGI's); gate-keepers at entrances to critical areas; vessels cruising with electronic earshot of bases; ships charting other ships (tattletales); subs tracking other submarines; aircraft and helicopters using sonar or magnetic anomaly detectors; sound surveillance systems, including sonar arrays on the sea bed or within the water to detect a submarine; fixed hydrophones to the sea bed; and satellite monitoring. The United States had the greatest coverage of the systems while the Soviets had acoustic surveillance devices that were not as well developed.

It took seven hours before we touched down in Iceland. I spent most of the flight getting to know the names of the crew and the various aircraft systems that I trained on in Burbank last year. The Bachelor Officers Quarters consisted of two buildings. The Air Force liked the first floor for some reason; this was set aside for F-102's that flew there permanently. The second BOQ was an overflow that housed traveling dignitaries or other Air Force officers. They put me on the second floor of building two where the Lieutenants and below were housed.

I guess since I was the lowest on the LCDR seniority list this was the best place for me. It was a nice room with a bathroom, but something I noticed, it was still daylight. I unpacked most of my suitcases and proceeded to the officers' club.

The officers club was jumping! A band played on Wednesday, Friday and Saturday night. I went in where the band was and I saw the skipper and the XO. They stood and greeted me. There were several guys that I have met before. One gentleman was Bob Prehn, a damn good pilot. We met in VP-30 and his wife recently had twin girls. We drank until 12:30 a.m. and I was wondering if I should get to bed. Bob said don't sweat it, the Commanding Officer said we don't have to go to work until 1300 today; that being the case, I had one more for the road.

That afternoon, I went through the check in process. I went to the dentist, doctor, and lastly to the squadron. Finally, I saw the XO who welcomed me again and said I was the assistant Tactics Officer. Also I was on the Commanding Officers crew and he explained the crew ready duty cycles. That was enough for me, so I thanked him and went down to the Tactics Office.

The Tactics Office was vacant. There were books on table, but no one was in. The VP-49 board had all the officers written in chalk. I picked up the "white stick" to write my name under the Asst. Tactic Officer slot. Fred Wright was the Tactics Officer and I did not know a single person on the list. With that I left and locked the office and turned in the key to the Duty Officer.

In the NATOPS world I had to become familiar with the Tactical Coordinator position system, but there were no textbooks I could find. I had the two volumes of information that I had last year. There had been several changes in the software but this information was unavailable. The APN 70, the Multipurpose Data Display really helped me. The clouds of smoke blew out the rest of the majority of the systems.

In my room I studied the Sensor One and Two stations. There are two stations for the Jezebel operators. Both are duplicates of each other. Sensor Station One is designed with a recorder and several switches which will allow grams to be printed on the Lofargram display. In other words, the operator can monitor eight sonobuoys at a time, four on the grams and four on the Bearing Frequency Indicator (BFI). The operation I selected was single frequency or a specific band for searching a frequency that the target might emit. The sonobuoy controls above the Bearing Frequency Indicator display are the channels that you are holding in the water. The BFI also displays the active ranging sonobuoys when used for localization. Most important is the DIFAR passive analysis acoustic signal processing and display. I must remember to monitor the DIFAR sonobuoy for at least ten minutes after the sonobuoy has been deployed. This is printed on the grams or likewise on the BFI.

Larry Vice was my Navigator-Communicator. He was doing a nice job. He used the system well and taught me several things. We went out on my first flight as the initial flight on the Echo II submarine. The Echo II SSGN was a fine nuclear submarine; it rotates the sail structure to expose the Front Door radar. This radar can guide the SSN-3 missile that covers up to 300 miles. There are eight cutouts of the hull where the missiles are fired from. The Operational brief gave us the point or position where we will start laying a barrier of eight sonobuoys and move toward the intended submarine by another barrier of eight buoys. We should monitor the barrier for two and a half hours, then without contact we lay one more barrier.

After the brief was finished, we gathered up our gear and went to preflight the airplane. My gear preflighted well; then the ordnance man gave me my sonobuoy load. I have to type in all those buoys. I finally got finished just before engine number two was started. We took off and then we were clear to set Condition Three. Half way to onstation the computer bombed. I looked at Larry and he said we would try it with the skipper driving the plane. I got a additional chart that duplicated the Navs chart. I set up the chart with some circles representing sonobuoy drops and proceeded to lay the second string of sonobuoys. With the sixteen sonobuoys I briefed the Jezebel operators to monitor the buoys. At first, I was not sure they were listening to every sonobuoy or not. In essence we left station with no contact and the weather there was overcast, rain, and wind gusting to thirty knots. The next crew did not relieve us as we had the first flight on the submarine. The next flight which was eight hours later had contact and the Echo II was tracked by the next eight flights.

LCDR Fred Wright was a kick in the ass. He was sharp, but he told me that he didn't want tactics, but go for it and he will support me to the fullest. I told him that I was discouraged after volunteering to help VP-49 and now I can't catch a submarine (the Echo II). I asked him some pointed questions; such as, who he had relieved tactics from, and had there been any training with respect to Comparative LOFAR, DIFAR sonobuoy problems, and AQA-7 listening procedures? Fred's face was red and he told me that Pete Smith left the squadron grounded and he took over in June. Yes, I knew I had found a problem. So I told Fred that I would set up a training session for all NFOs starting next week.

The following week we had a NFO meeting and I explained some of the things that we should know. I started talking about Comparative LOFAR and I was interrupted by a Lieutenant wanting to know why all this stuff, can't the Jezebel operator do it? I drew three buoys on the chalk board. Each buoy had the following strength. "Where is the target?" I asked him. He looked befuddled! He did not respond, even though I have not given him the maximum range of target. So then I proceeded and gave the range of 15 miles and showed him the probable area where the target was. Next we talked about monitoring a sixteen sonobuoy pattern. We talked about monitoring sonobuoys. With the AQA-7 you can put four buoys on your recorder and four sonobuoys on the Bearing Frequency Indicator (BFI). Once on the BFI you can scan for the frequency that is most prominent. This idea gave more flexibility in the way Jezebel operators achieve contact. After thirty minutes I said that's it and the bashful chap made an apology to me. He said he had never heard of CLF but he learned something from me.

The deployment had been slow for the first half of our deployment. Our airplanes were having a rough time staying up. Word came out that a Yankee SSBN was coming around the Norwegian coast and headed out for a patrol in the North Atlantic. The Yankee was the first modern class which was completed in 1967. This submarine will carry 16 SS-N-6 missiles and also carries eighteen torpedoes. This submarine uses a propulsion plant similar to that of the Victor SSN.

The ready duty was launched and they had contact but not enough time to fix it. The ready duty passed by secured voice this data and an hour later they were tracking the target. This went on for three flights and the skipper launched with me as his TACCO. We got onstation and the airplane has already left station. According to the tactics at offstation we were to drop one or two Alfa and Bravo sonobuoys. The A buoy is the position of the target and the B buoy is the bearing which the target is traveling and this position of the B buoy represents the course and speed for one hour. I marked on the Alpha buoy and went 190 degrees true for ten miles, in other words, the course and speed of the sub, but where is the submarine printing on the sonobuoys? I called the skipper and told him that we had no contact, but we have course and speed. I suggested that we go thirty miles down and start a barrier again. I got a roger for that and we went down thirty miles and started the barrier. The barrier was in and we kept monitoring the buoys. After about two hours the Jezebel thought we had contact. We flew to the sonobuoy and dropped a DIFAR sonobuoy. We waited for ten minutes and then we had a bearing. This was no indicator of a submarine so I told the pilot to mark on top of the DIFAR and head out one five zero. After the mark on top the pilot said that he had a Soviet trawler about five mile ahead. We were not doing what we were supposed to do. Anyway we went down and took pictures of the trawler which had all the characteristics of many antennas on board. After three more passes, we climbed back to patrol altitude and our relief was talking to us on covered uniform high frequency number one. Finally we left station and I was really pissed off. The operators showed me the grams, but they did not show me the BFI's which I knew therein was the possible submarine.

Every month each squadron sent out a monthly message which relates maintenance figures, administrative deficiency, and operation effectiveness. The Operations Officer LCDR Lee Barrier would send a "take-it-for-action" on the message and this would have a due date of the first day of the month. I was working on something when LCDR Chris Mills, the Assistant Operations Officer asked for the operations input. The input was due tomorrow by the Commanding Officer but he wanted it by 1600 today. Well, I open the safe and there has been nothing done to this report. I looked at my watch and it is 8:30 a.m. I went to the squadron communicator and got all of the purples for September. By 1100 I had all of the purples and was madly writing the Soviet Yankee operations. By 1200 the draft was finished. Commander Wisdom came in the Tactics Office and gave me the particulars of the rest of the messages. He told me to go ahead and type up the message and he will be back to sign the message out. I took the message to the typist and told him I needed it in a hour and a half.

I was finishing lunch when the communication yeoman presented the message all typed up. I checked over the message. I found a couple of mistakes that I sent back to the yeomen. The Commanding Officer was right behind him. I told him I have proofed the message but no one including the Operations Officer and the XO have not seen it. The Skipper said that was all right and walked out with the message. He was pleased enough with it and signed the release. That afternoon during Happy Hour, Lee Barrier approached me to find out if I had worked on the Operations Summary. I told him that I had started work on it this morning at 0830. I finished the rough draft by 1130 and the Commanding Officer gave me all the information so I typed it for him. I corrected it and he signed it. Lee smiled and he regretted not being here. As a matter of fact, he and Chris Mills were in town.

In the middle of October, our crew left for Lajes, Azores to do some loading qualifications. The facility was booming along with many transports lined up on the line. The first load was a torpedo that required three or four Air Force Military Police tying down area fifty feet around the plane. I was watching the whole evolution. That afternoon the special weapon drill was finished without fail. Later that afternoon we went downtown and bought several things; shoes, table clothes, etc. We are supposed to leave for Keflavik tomorrow so we planned one more trips to get wine and other things before we left. I think we took eighty cases of wine loaded between the various segments of the P-3C. Finally the lights of Keflavik shown through the night as we descended to land, and made a series of splash landings with all that bubbly on board.

The news of the squadron was another flight against a nuclear submarine. The ready duty was launched and gained contact right away. The eighth flight was out and it looked good for VP-49. We were in a standown until the end of the week. Anyway the planes were holding up and this looks like a twelve or fourteen event launch. The next day back I drew a summary of the latest submarine launch. The skipper liked the sitrep (situation report) and so he released it.

The last thing the Crew 1 did was to work out some tactics for our submarines. The United States Navy was worried about new escape routes to the North Atlantic. There have been Soviet nuclear subs coming down on the right of Iceland, and sometimes they go through the Iceland-Greenland Gap. The message sent to Iceland was primarily discussing the area West of Greenland. The place of concern was Baffin Bay or in particular the Davis Strait. This time of year there is still some ice falling in the water. The water appears to be isothermal for a great distance in this bay. We were given a track of water and were told to detect and track during our onstation times. I ordered the sound velocity packet and set up tactics so that we could do our best.

We left Keflavik and heading West. About two and a half hours we let down west of Greenland. We marked on top the area and I proceeded laying a micro barrier. The sound of the buoys made me hold my headset as the crashing resembled ice. Soon one was detected; we went to DIFAR to track him. Fifteen minutes later the second submarine appears. This was an excellent tracking exercise. After three hours we said we were through and the Skipper climbed up and finally we were heading east back to home plate.

Commander Bob Hall was our new Executive Officer and he would be number two when the present XO achieved command in late November. CDR Hall was presently getting the lay of the land and learning the names of the officers. With two more weeks remaining in Iceland Fred Wright and I start wondering about this brief that accompanies the return from deployment. I gathered all of the flight data and began building this brief. Word came that we should talk about the sub tracks, how long and what was the significant breakdown of the aircraft, or is it just the associated gear that made the difference. At the end of a two week period, we closed the Tactics Office and I packed up our gear.

The P-3C deployment had just about terminated and its time to look back on the first deployment of this new airplane. VP-49 was produced to take the P-3C to Iceland, but the supplies were slow in getting to the deployment site. The Woodpeckers, the fine feathered bird mounted on the plane's vertical stabilizer, flies among the elite and attacks to be the avengers of the Russian submarine force. This three and a half months of being in this squadron makes me sad, but clearly I am now at my peak of tactical ability. The problematic climb from being P3C Tactical Coordinator was gained through many trying episodes. The crew—certain crew members, were not performing—kept me apprised of this situation and the unwanted members will be leaving the squadron when we return home. The OPCON's idea of sending out planes to gain contact is an excellent idea. If contact is gained, then launch all planes if possible and schedule long extended flights as nessary. VP-49 did extremely well by training through sucessive periods of contact times. Next year the Tactical Support Center will be operational and a substantial gain will be realized and the squadron will peak regardless of its willingness to succeed.

VP-49 NAS Patuxent River, MD

The weather was identified at Patuxent River, Maryland. We landed and there was Jane and the kids. I hugged Beth, Anne, and finally I held Mike. He was just a year old and talking a little. Jane kissed me and so did the girls. I could not even try to get the luggage loaded. I finally got the baggage loaded into the car and away we went to our house. Beth and Anne really helped me get into the house. The kids showed me what they were doing in school and Anne was showing me the different things she had painted. Mike was by my side and I had given him a piece of candy. Jane was laughing, they were happy and by now they knew I belonged to them.

We had dinner and all of us took our baths. Mike was really cute. We watched television with the kids until 9 p.m. After all the prayers were finished, we kissed them goodnight. Jane and I opened a bottle of champagne and watched the tube. We were starting our second bottle of bubbly in a half an hour. I laid down on the couch so Jane could lie down with me. She snuggled and kissed me. I was getting aroused and she began to take my pants down. We placed the blanket on the floor and we fell onto the blanket to a complete climax. I said I loved her with all my heart. She held me close and after fifteen minutes she wanted more. I gave her more and she was satisfied when I fell asleep holding her next to me.

The gang was back to work on the deployment brief. We had a meeting with the Commanding Officer and the XO to present a rough draft of the brief. Commander Wisdom made very little comment and asked who was going to give the brief. The XO said he was not sure, then he said that Fred and I would give the brief. That required extra hours to decide what verbal garbage would we say. By 10 p.m. we were ready to speak, but now the typist would figure the keys!

The first step was Deputy Fleet Air Five and his staff. We went through the brief and the wing was really impressed with our handling of essential information. We answered questions and wrote comments that we had to modify. The big show was just before CDR Wisdom was relieved by the Admiral down in Norfolk. The plane landed in Norfolk and we climbed down the ladder into the briefing room. The Admiral and his staff came in and were seated. The Skipper started by stating the deployment, how he assesses it, and here was the brief. Fred Wright and I unveiled the brief and after thirty minutes we had an audience. We thanked each one, and then we were open for questions. The back and forth question and answer was proving what we had said. A Captain just made that statement which rang through the entire briefing room. The Admiral stood up and congratulated the Skipper and his band of happy campers.

Bob Wisdom was relieved by Gene Tansey as Commanding Officer of VP-49. CDR Wisdom was a happy speaker as he wished the best for the "Woodpeckers." CDR Gene Tansey was a native of Boston, Massachusetts and his idol was the Boston Celtics. CDR Tansey was a fine pilot, a super athlete, and a fine party drinker. Both my wife and I told them how much we have appreciated their support during my short start with the squadron.

Commander Bob Hall was my new Patrol Plane Commander on crew seven. Bob just assumed the second of command (XO) and he was eager to fly. We had a crew meeting and I got to meet my sensor Station One, Two and Three. Sensor Station One was nicknamed Pappy Moore and Sensor Two, was George Meeker, but he was young. He could hear a sound of mud squeaking at 10,000 fathoms! Sensor Three was young and slightly inexperienced. He just made AW3 and was willing to learn the ropes.

The first thing that happened was Springboard. The idea intrigued me because we were low on advanced qualifications. We arrived at Roosevelt Roads and found that we had room in this hangar for office spaces. We went, saw, built the office, and erected a sign identifying our squadron. We participated in making quals and we attacked all the subs that we ran into. We took plenty of tapes so that we could record the computer as well as the UNH-4 tape recorder which processes all

LOFAR, DIFAR, and active pinging sonobuoys which had pertinent data towards the achievement of the qualification. The final day at Roosey, we had a crew party, and the men got bombed.

One of the associated tasks of the Tactics Office was to brief crews concerning the movements of the United States nuclear submarines. This was top priority and it went beyond "never, never land!" About a year and a half ago, the US submarines were being detected just as they were going in to port. This was unheard of, so the submarine force clamped down, the intelligence tripled there watch, and I'll be dam if that didn't happen again. COMFAIRWINGSLANT called a meeting and decided to develop a new procedure to catch an intruder. The Tactical Development Office designed a plan and issued it to certain individuals in the squadron. I picked out four crews who were to handle this sensitive information. The first crew I briefed I wanted the PPC, TACCO, Sensor One and Two. To back this up I got a tape of one of the submarines, fast attack or a missile boat. I went through the brief and answered all the questions. Lastly the UNH-6 tape recorder was played giving the sound of the target. About 4 a.m., they were back. They had good news, and I reported it by secure phone. This was not always the case. The skipper called for me two days later and wanted to see me. The Tactical Development & Evaluation people wanted to see me and the other squadron that handled these missions.

Monday morning I was at the WINGSLANT Tactical Development only to be meet by LCDR Dan Wolkensdorfer. We talked and finally we were joined by two other members coming up from Jacksonville. We went through the whole routine and I quickly disagreed with part of the plan. After about five hours, we got our shit together. The next day we waited for the typist to correct the rough draft. Finally it looks good!

Lockheed had finally delivered a NATOPS manual which in turn, we received a copy from VP-30. It was sketchy but required a lot of work. The exam was coming around and the NATOPS TACCO was flying his pants off. I was scheduled for a check and gave quite a checklist of things that the instructor did not know. I am sure he made life interesting for the other TACCO at VP-49.

During the winter months, the Tactics Division held a big part of the tactical development in the squadron. We were asked to provide an airplane to help the new replacement helicopter pass its necessary tests. My crew went out and believe me we went off the North Carolina coast line. The Helo was assigned to a ship where we checked in and reported onstation. The nuclear submarine was currently underwater and we were told to go North and drop a string of buoys ranging fifteen miles. We rogered that and went fifteen miles north and laid a five buoy pattern. The spacing was three miles and we covered about eighteen nautical miles. As soon as the sonobuoys were laid we made contact on the nuclear sub. I reported the contact to the ship. The Helo was taking off and the ship turned him over to me. The sub was approaching one buoy and the Helo was headed right for the sonobuoy. The Helo dropped a pinger on the LOFAR buoy and he gained contact. We were at Angles ten and the Helo at Angles two (we were at 1000 feet and the Helo was at 200 feet). Sensor One and Two were reporting passing the buoy and I vectored the aircraft to fly north to lay another buoy. The next buoy went in and suddenly the Helo gave an emergency call on guard and he was returning to the ship. I gave word to the pilot that I was going to track the sub. The buoy made contact so I dropped at DIFAR buoy. This was a most pleasant exercise and we attacked the sub four times.

CDR Bob Hall was a strange man but he thought out every obstacle. He was concerned about our move to Jacksonville, Florida. At the same time he was talking to the Detailer about different things and they mentioned my name was coming up for orders. Bob Hall was in panic condition one! So now, what gives? The significance of this matter was these orders were only for a year. So I wrote a letter requesting another year at VP-49 and the XO knew what to put in his endorsement of my letter.

The move to Jacksonville was on everybody's mind. LCDR Pete Cressy has been designated "Mr. Jacksonville" and he went down with some senior petty officers who agreed to help with the move. Pete briefed the wives and had the names and addresses of Realtors, rents, and anyone in Jacksonville/Orange Park area. Jane was upset when I told her of my orders plus the move to Florida. I told her my orders were a down right mistake and the command had sent a letter changing the orders for another year. We talked about renting a house for a year, which was the best plan. How could Jane get down to Florida and back without the children? Clearly we will have to sort this one out when the time comes.

The FAETULANT facility was offering a course which utilized all carriers, battle groups, and destroyers tied in with the antisubmarine squadrons coupled with attack submarines. The course consists of lectures and then the group is divided up into several sections. The first week in Norfolk, we spend in classrooms and the later half, we worked with convoys and then we simulated an assault on Norway. This led many to discussions and may have led us to reconsider tactics prior to the second week. The second week put us as a modified trainer which had to be learned prior to taking off (simulated of course). All of the information must be ordered by the standard ASW movement and planning doctrine. The plane reporting onstation had to have a ship guarding his safety flight. This was matriculate at best, but after one knows what to do, its a piece of cake!

Just to the left of the living room is a door that leads to a porch. I had a good idea when I went to base and they gave me enough plywood to close in on the long wall and there I put a replacement window on the front of the house. It looked pretty decent as I had gotten a fake fire place for petty cash. I moved in a rocking chair, a single bed, with wrapped up pillows, a rug to cover the concrete, and finally I got Chris Mills to help me move my television set to the den. We had a party to celebrate the den!

The final day of being home was beginning to run down. Jane and the kids are getting nervous and wanted me to hold them. Mike was really learning how to walk. He walked with me and he even went with me to the package store. Jane helped me pack and then wrote down things that she should look into the event we rented a house in Jacksonville. The continuation of my orders still had not come through. Why in the hell can't something evolve as it should for me? What is not a parable, a metaphor, or hyperbole is what Big Ben has drummed up for me.

VP-49 Deployment Keflavik, Iceland

We took off from Patuxent with a full load. The airplane was packed stem to stern and who would believe that we had twenty people on board. CDR Hall talked with me briefly and I decided that I would inform the crew to walk only as a necessity to and from the head. Iceland had not changed much. We landed and parked on the line. We carried our operational bags and Larry Vice carried all his communications gear into the duty office. Here they had lockers to store this gear and we had locks to place them on the outside of the lockers. The room assignments were the same as I wanted the same room that I had last deployment. The room was the same, but dirtier than hell itself. I borrowed a mop and scoured the daylights out of the room. I ran over to the exchange and brought some wax. I waxed my room and so did my compadres on the second floor.

The Tactical Support Center had arrived at Keflavik. The second day I was there, we went through the TSC and what should my wondering eyes see but LCDR Hagy. Jim was a buddy of mine in VP-10 and was happy to see me. We talked and his wife Judy and their children were in base housing here. We parted and promised we would see each other at happy hour. The briefing was clear and was more like last deployment. The search for a nuclear sub favored this "walking barrier concept." This put in barriers ahead of the sub so that this crew could walk towards the target and eventually gain contact. The layout of the Tactical Support Center was all over the place. The Jezebel facility was miraculous in that the sonobuoys were played back in record time. If contact was gained, they could go back and play real time to see if it was a contact or not.

The Tactics department has a good program going. The weapons program led by LT John McCallister has been getting everybody qualified in the loading exercises. I have set up a tactics review board where we bullshitted each other about this and that, but we created TACFACTS (tactical facts) that we published and authorized each crew to try these in real life.

The first evolution was a Soviet Yankee (nuclear sub) was coming down into the North Atlantic Ocean. The ready duty launched early this morning and the launch sequence was established. The Yankee class sub usually deploys every sixty days. This sub is probably going around Norway and cutting through Greenland, Iceland, United Kingdom Gap (GIUK) to go onstation East of Bermuda. The Yankee has been known to travel at ten to twelve knots and go on patrol at four to six knots. We launched in the afternoon. We got on station and we had buoy contact. Sensor One had briefed me that there was only the A buoy in the water. We marked on top this buoy and barely was their contact on it. I called the XO and I was going where the TSC said to start my barrier. Down thirty miles we went and started our barrier. We gained contact on the forth and fifth buoys. Sensor Two reported they both had up doppler. Sensor Two was a lad who had set both sonobuoys of the subs signal on the Bearing Frequency Indicator. He looked at the presentation and saw that the sound from the sub was higher than normal. In other words, I had the sub coming into my barrier and now was time to place DIFAR to track the bandit. DIFAR reported up and the initial bearing was good. Descending until 2,000 feet, the aircraft marks' on top of DIFAR 7 and goes into DIFAR sonobuoy drops which form a v-shaped pattern.

In review, the DIFAR buoys were seven, eight, and nine; five miles between the three buoys. All buoys were up and pointing. In fifteen minutes I got a aural contact on the center buoy and five minutes later a close point of approach (CPA) on buoy eight. Then all hell broke loose, Sensor Two, who was monitoring aural, came up and announced he was turning. I listened and he was doing something beside turning. Sensor One said not to worry, he was checking to see if some one was following him. Yes, he was right. In five minutes time, he was back on course and it was time to plant more sonobuoys. I planted four move DIFAR barrier and got CPA information from them all. The relief aircraft passed over position A buoy and we were relieved onstation. After landing we walked to the TSC and we were met by Jim Hagy the debriefing officer.

The third of July I went with the Hagys on a fishing trip. We went about an hour and a half drive to Chain of Lakes beyond the Whale factory. I brought my ultra light gear and Jim said Judy would include me in lunch. The weather was breezy and I started fishing in the water. The first fish I caught was an Artic Char. We cut up the Char and used the bait to catch Trout. I hung into a Trout that I couldn't believe I landed it. It was three and a half pounds of beautiful fish. We caught several fine fish. Judy invited me over on the 4th of July with a guest as we caught three large fish and several others that we kept. I called Judy the next day and told her I was coming with Larry Vice and will bring the wine. Larry and I arrive about 1700 at their apartment. It was spacious and Larry had to meet the three children. We sat down and talked about the good 'ole days. It had and was still raining outside, but I will take another glass of wine. Dinner was served, and Judy really did a good job. This meal was out-of -sight and reminded me of my wife and children.

One of the many tasks that I had in the States was the security of our sub forces. This came into being when the TSC wanted to see me. I told them I was the team leader and I was responsible for briefing my crews. With that verified, my crew took the first flight. It was a daylight flight which I was an Elint/surface ship finder. We took off, rigged what shipping we found in the area east of Iceland and I went down through the Gap off of Farol Island. The Rockall Rise was a permanent small part of the ocean before the bottom falls out as it enters the North Atlantic. The next point on the chart is a little island. We found the island so we worked on top and headed east. We arrived to our drop point about ten minutes early. I suggested we might look around because we had the radar on standby for the last thirty minutes. The pilot reported no contacts so we laid the pattern. The aircraft commander climbed back up to 20,000 feet and there we waited. I listened to the buoys and I hear him coming out of the background noise. I was going to alert the Sensor One & Two but they out guessed me and said they had aural and gram contact. The sub drove through the buoys and I tried to find a renegade skunk. No luck so we went back by the island and climbed altitude and headed back to the TSC. The briefing team was ready and so were we. The briefing officer checked our logs and records. He said we did an excellent job. I related to the crew that being a good crew means everything to a TACCO. Keep the good coming and will find submarines.

One night I was home doing something when a knock came at my door. There was a call from my wife and I can call her at four o'clock in the morning. I set my clock and I was at the TSC at 0400 in the morning. I reached her and she apologized but she found a house for rent in Orange Park, FL for $275.00. Jane told me about the house, four bedrooms, a den, and she said she could adjust to it. "Take it," I said. I will be home in October on leave, and we will move to Orange Park then.

The next evolution was the Echo II SSGN. Indicators of the sub movement suggested that it would go to the Mediterranean Sea for deployment. The ready duty launched and did not gain contact. The flight behind the number one flight gained convergence zone contact of the sub. The third flight gained contact and fixed the submarine. We had flight number six and we had contact relived to us. I became scared when after three penetrations the Echo II reduced its speed. The range of the Echo II was 12-15 miles, but after the submarine pulled back his speed to 4 knots, the submarine got very quiet! After an hour of this slow speed the target started back up to eight knots. When listening to the sub the Echo II had a squeaky shaft that seemed to permeate itself through out the water. The TSC was jumping as the ready duty was launched on a Charlie Class sub. An Extendex on Echo II and another on Charlie, Brittingham get your troops to bed for they will be flying in 14 hours!

After a restless sleep we had a brief to go against the Charlie Class sub. This second Extendex was eating us up with airplanes going down and aircrews just plain worn out. This was the last flight on the Charlie. During preflight I got everything in place. We briefed on board and I asked how everyone felt. Let's go get the bastard! We reported on station and found the turnover buoys with contact. Incidently, we are working in water due East of Iceland.

The waters are filled with merchants and fishing boats. The Charlie went through two DIFAR fixes point of approach, then he checked his aft by making a three hundred and sixty degree turn. He then reduced his speed and I never saw him again. Back at the TSC we went over the tapes and we held the Charlie an additional thirty minutes.

CDR Hall knocked on my door and said we have a brief in two hours. I checked the clock and I had been asleep for ten hours. Thanks for waking me. I got up and took a shower. The TSC was still going as I was the twentieth flight on the Echo II. The flight was almost two and a half hours away from Keflavik. The turnover buoys were hot and I listened and I heard the scraping sound, I'm home! The sound kept me entertained for three hours and as we were getting ready to turnover, another sub started under the sonobuoy which marked or fixed on the Echo II! That sub was the Charlie that eluded me on the sixth flight of the other Extendex! The flight, which the TACCO is Lee Barrier, marked on top indicating he has the problem. What is he going to do? Is he going after the Charlie or what in the hell is he going to do?

We got in contact with the TSC about 150 miles and told them on UHF covered that we redetected the Charlie. I gave the position and the time. The P3C landed and secured the engines and I ran with Pappy (Sensor One) to the Tactical Support Center. They confirmed the Charlie and put a message for them to concentrate on the Echo II.

It was the first time that submarines have interacted with each other that men were on duty at the debriefing facility.

This evolution was one of the greatest accomplishments I have even been a part of. Two nuclear subs in one week! The supply of operational sonobuoys is at a low level. I had ready duty about five days later and we were issued a standard load but not to drop until authorized. We left the squadron after one o'clock and the result was to take a nap. We ate dinner together at the Officer's Club. We sat in the back of the club so no one can see you. After an exciting hour, we were jumping into our vehicle to go to the movies. Nine o'clock we were back in our rooms; at 9:30 p.m. we were instructed to launch ready duty. I threw on my coat and sprang to the door, just as Larry Vice was coming to get me. We ran to the ready duty truck. Larry told me the duty office called for us to report to the TSC immediately!

The TSC was running about telling us what he wants of us. A Golf class conventional submarine was located east of Iceland. Building of the Golf class conventional submarine was begun in 1958 and finally twenty two were constructed. Three diesels, 3 shafts, and electric motors were the propulsion drivers equipped with eighty four or eighty-six men. This type of submarine has an extremely large con-ning tower which has three vertically mounted tubes and hatches which are used for launching ballistics missiles. The position which he gave me was only 250 miles east of Iceland. The debriefing officers said we were authorized SSQ-38A LOFAR sonobuoys. These sonobuoys could be set for twenty-four or seventy-two hours set at three hundred feet. The buoy spacing turned out to be thirty-nautical miles. After we have received information we bolted down the pas-sageway and ran to our airplane which had engines three and four run-ning. Up the ladder and number two was started, I got up to the TACCO's station and I heard "Set Condition Five." Larry said he would take a quick condition five and I put on my Mae West. The pilots were anxious so I told them we were after a Golf class sub. At forty-two minutes after notification, we took off. I briefed the crew and wanted lookouts when we arrive onstation. The cloud cover was against us, so I decided to stay at eight thousand feet. The first buoy went away and in about four minutes there was no contact. The moon was out and we wondered what the cloud cover could do to the moon. The second sonobuoy fell and still no contact. I swapped seats with Larry in order to let him get some training. The third buoy went away and I was standing beside Larry. A moment of excitement come from Sensor One and Two. Sensor One announced to the TACCO that they had got him. I asked Larry what should we do. Larry said to go to DIFAR. I gave him a thumbs up and we planned two DIFAR about the LOFAR sonobuoy in contact. DIFAR first came up with a good bearing and Larry was going to drop the other sonobuoy so we can get a reliable fix. The second DIFAR went out and the plane was flying through the air, because if the Golf sub realizes that a aircraft fixes him, he will pull the plug or dive. Larry got the point which crosses the other DIFAR bearing and its time to descend and mark the DIFAR and proceed down the bearing line. As we descend we broke out of the clouds at nine hundred feet. The pilot announced, "mark on top." Dead ahead lies the Soviet Golf on the surface at nine nautical miles. The Sensor Three operator cried, "MADMAN!" The Golf class finally realized what was happening and decided to pull the plug. We were on top of him and dropped another SSQ-38A. The sub was going 090 at three or four knots. The LOFAR sonobuoys kept track of him while Sensor Three was having a ball. Needless, to say we had no SSQ-47 on board! After thirty minutes we climbed back up to eight thousand feet and had a cup of coffee. I told Larry that he did an excellent job of finishing off the Soviet Golf.

Sixty minutes later the Sensor One reported a submarine and asked if I would come help identify it. Both Sensor operators were monitoring it. The sub was a diesel electric and the signature was part engine and blade. I assumed, that it was a NATO submarine. But, what is the Golf sub out in this area? What if he decides to snorkel or come up on the surface? We dropped our final three buoys to encircle the submarine but to no avail. The Golf is a strange bird, but I had decided to query the debrief about this strange occurrence. The long and short of it was a French diesel was snorkeling and the Golf was not surfaced or snorkeling after we had marked on top of him.

About ten days later we were getting anxious about getting home on leave. The crew got a ten day period and we went down to the terminal to see if any flights are going to the east coast of the United States. There was one flight that left at 0600 in the morning. We signed up for the flight which went to New Jersey. From there we could rent a car to Patuxent River, Maryland. I guess its better than nothing at all!

We had one more flight before we left for home. The flight consisted of SSQ-36 sonobuoys that were dropped in one part of the sea.

The rows were made up of buoys, for example, when you dropped a buoy the "BT" recorder will come one and record the buoy down to one thousand feet. Air speed, time, and the ground speed must be in sync to let each buoy drop and be recorded. Jim Hagy, our briefing officer, went over the drop sequence. I asked if there was anything else we should do. Jim though a moment and them he asked me to remain. The other gents excused themselves and walked out to the plane to begin preflighting. Jim parted the curtains and he showed me where he briefed Crew six that intercepted a Yankee class going back home from a deployment. He did some calculating and gave two positions the sub will be at. I copied these positions down and told him I would bring grams of the Yankee.

The P3C Orion roared into the night as our "BT" plane, loaded with thirty six sonobuoys, took off and rolled out two zero zero true. After condition three was resolved, I came on the speaker and told the crew let's get ready because after the BT buoys are dropped, we will see if we can catch a Yankee going home. We are going out of the way, but we will make our six o'clock takeoff for home! Finally the last BT buoy went out and the aircraft picked up a Fly to Point which I have put on my ASA-70, my TACCO's display. The next point was an hour later and that was the second drop. Larry Vice and I had prior knowledge of this and we should be there right on time. Sonobuoy away and the next Fly to Point was dead ahead at zero three zero at twelve nautical miles. The SS-41A came on line and both Sensor 1 & 2 cheered as I had the sonobuoy on aural with contact booming in. I called the PPC and told him to drop the next and head home. With that, I went back to see the grams. I mean to tell you, they were marvelous. Then they punched out the second buoy and believe it or not Ripley, the sonobuoy already drawing on the second buoy. Shaking hands, and being with the crew is doing what you are suppose to do. The grams of the Yankee were made ready for the Tactical Support Center. The tapes off the second buoys were thrown in just for laughs.

It was midnight when we walked into the TSC. The logs and the tape recording were being fed into the computer. The TSC AW analysis knew what was happening and Jim Hagy walks in. "How did it go, Mike?" he said. I replied it was okay. God damn, he said he discovered the grams of the Yankee. He was happy as an Icelandic salmon. We went over the flight I told him we had been back to pack our bags as we go on leave at 6 a.m.

One minute after four bells, the four engine jet took off for McGuire Air Force Base, New Jersey. I got three and a half hours of sleep and I had my bags packed. There were five guys together and believe you me, I slept most of the way home. We landed at an Air Force Base in New Jersey. We collected our bags and started shopping for a rental car. In ten minutes, we had a rental car and we had two six packs and assorted snacks. The trip went without any problem and after two hours we stopped and filled up the mens' room. The drive took us about four hours to Patuxent River, Md. I asked everyone if they were all set and had notified their wives and loved ones. They were all set and they dropped me off at my quarters.

Jane and my children met me. I could not believe that I was here. We went inside and I asked Jane what she wanted me to do. Five minutes later I was taking down the drapes in the living and dining rooms, and cleaning the bedrooms. The moving van comes tomorrow which is Friday and we will go to Edna and Bob's house in Richmond after the moving van leaves. Early in the morning the van arrived. The man was nice and weighed about 230 pounds. He has two assistants and they begin the arduous task of packing up the Brittingham family. I went out for doughnuts and Cokes. The man from the housing facility came by and gave us an up, which means we passed the test. Finally we were ready as I rented a U-haul. I carried Beth's bedroom furniture down to Edna's for safekeeping. Beth wanted to ride with me so in she goes. She's wearing a baseball cap that she slept in on the way to Richmond.

The next day was spent carrying up Beth's furniture and shopping. Mike was really growing and so was Annie. One thing that I forgot was dropping the car off for a lube and an oil change. The bill was surprising as he put a new muffler on the station wagon. One more surprise and you can forget Orange Park, Florida! The next day was goodbye to the grandparents as we struck out for Florida. I stopped in South Carolina to get a motel room and watch the Washington Redskins game.

Monday we stopped in Jacksonville and called housing. The housing people said the moving van was there and they wanted to move us in. I talked to the moving man and he would meet us at Orange Park. An hour later, we toured him to our new rented home. This was a beautiful house with a lawn in need of cutting. The house was open and the rental representative gave us the key. Off I went with Mike to get some ice, Cokes, beer and some snacks!

The house basically was a living room, den with a fireplace, a huge kitchen and breakfast room, four bedrooms, two bathrooms, and a double garage. The movers really packed the house, not to mention the patio outside the den. By the time rolled around it was 5:30 p.m. and we wound down. The movers joined us in a beer and wished them luck as they rode off.

The next four days were very hectic. We took Beth and got her into school. Anne was put into day school. Mike was being such a good baby. We went to the commissary, the Navy Exchange, and finally we went to the liquor store. We also went to the post office, telephone company, and made deposits on everything! Next I began to think how I was getting back. Finally I took a flight from Jacksonville to New York. There I was scheduled to fly Icelandic Airlines to Keflavik. Friday I was amazed that I have unpacked everything, stored most of the winter things and did not see much of Jane the last eight days. Fair wind and seas, my family, I must get back to Iceland and finish my deployment.

I got to New York without any sweat, but I had a brisk walk to make my flight to Keflavik. I stepped aboard the plane and it was packed. I found my seat as the engines were started. I did not know much Icelandic, but boy did they speak it. I arrived at about four in the morning. I caught a taxi which ran me by the duty office where I turned my leave papers in. I got a flight schedule and the taxi driver ran me to the BOQ. The flight schedule indicated that nothing was going this week end and I had the ready duty on Monday. Now I was going to sleep.

Monday morning it was dark and I was out preflighting the airplane. Everyone leave a great time on leave and let's kill submarines!

I did not know it but the crew was ready to go for a ready duty brief. We all walked down the ladder when CDR Bob hall said "Mike I want you to look at the nose of the aircraft." From the pilots windows downward to the deck are symbols and pictures of submarines equating to fifteen that I have been blessed to find. I almost broke up but I thanked the aircrew for their support and promised them that there is more coming!

The end of the week marked another flight checking our nuclear subs. Sunday was blustery and the winds were howling something fierce! The Commander of the brief/debrief team gave the brief and had us write down the position of the drop point and the bearing of the sonobuoys in thousands of yards. It seemed to me that this was going too far but, let's play the game. After the brief and what few questions we asked, we proceeded to do the preflight. At precisely the right time we took off and did our normal ship surveillance. After three hours of looking, we shut down the radar and headed South. The Rock Hall Rise where we saw the volcano, marked on top, and began our run to the designated drop point. Everything proceeded according to hoyle, but there was no contact. We listened, and we paused over the grams but no contact. We altered heading a different way because we had no contact which was a signal too.

Meanwhile at the TSC we brought all of our records including the magnetic tape of the flight. We looked at the display and nothing was seen of the U.S. nuclear sub. I wrote up a narrative describing the flight and indicating no contact. I felt dismayed about not having contact, but I left the TSC and had a beer before taking a shower. In the middle of the shower someone was knocking at my door. The OPCON officer wanted to see me ASAP. I called the Duty Driver and he took me to the TSC. The Commander was there who briefed us, and he had a problem that won't go away. In other words, how does one articulate that I fucked up! That was the case for the jury to decide. The defendant, namely me, asked to start with the brief, which went over and then shifted to the TSC monitor which showed the aircraft position where I dropped the sonobuoys. I then asked the prosecutor (the Commander) for the brief book which has the correct latitude/longitude for the drop. The brief book showed the drop point as being nine miles off what was given me. The CDR checked the green which tasked the flight that I carried out and it was nine miles off too! The Commander's face was red and he conceded that I was right. Even more intriguing as this case unfolds is; how does the CDR admit he is responsible for the blame of this whole greened event?

I rode back to the BOQ and I thought I had better see CDR Tansey. Commander Tansey was briefed thoroughly and he commented to me on the handling of the situation. He said he would do two things, first, he would check on the message tomorrow and, second he would talk to the Operations Officer about this individual's conduct during and after the brief on Sunday. With that taken care of, we had several beers together.

NATO has an exercise every year in October. The planning begins in the summer and includes the British, and numerous players including Norway. The concept of this exercise is to protect Norway and let the Norwegians keep the red submarines from taking over the Northern advantage of the fjords which protect this country. The participants of the exercise included the P3C aircraft, British aircraft, a US convoy, numerous submarines, and a massive communication net.

We flew many missions and the second event there were more subs involved. We were protecting the Norwegian coastline with a barrier of sonobuoys. The sonobuoys were eight hour setting and were set thirty miles apart. We got onstation just about darkness. The sonobuoys went out as we were at twenty-thousand feet. We monitored each buoy and suddenly we detected a US FM 10. This was a diesel submarine which started snorkeling and was planning to attack Norway. The mileage was at least one hundred and fifty miles and we had at least a half an hour left onstation. The XO was driving so we cruised our way north and I talked to the Ordnance man about two DIFAR sonobuoys. We began to slow down as we approached thirty nautical miles. DIFAR went away and Sensor One reported it up. A good bearing put the submarine to the left of the LOFAR buoy. I put in another DIFAR sonobuoy and this sonobuoy gave us a fix and then the aircraft went down to 1000 feet headed to the fix with which was eight miles ahead. Commander Hall was going to cut his approach lights on at three miles. Hang on sports fans, at three miles out we had a surfaced submarine and we simulated killing him dead in the water. Yes it was an FM10, US submarine which they gave us credit for the kill.

The festive occasion is multiplied by the party of VP-49. This party is a celebration of deployment, going home, or whatever its a real blast. The party starts with lunch and it goes for hours. The VP-49 band is playing and our crew is certainly keeping time with the music. Another time the enlisted club invited Larry and I to hear a group that was on their way to Europe. This band sounded like Chicago or The Four Freshmen.

The last thing that had I had to do was truck down to Lajes and get one special weapon qualification. We flew a ship patrol down and we rigged ten ships with pictures. We stayed at the BOQ at Lajes and got showered and went to the Officer's Club. The bar was packed and we roll the dice for drinks. We spent about forty minutes in the bar and ambled on down to the dining room. Matues' is the wine that your always get in Portugal and since Lajes is Portuguese, well you get the point. This exceptional wine which comes in two varieties plain or bubbly. Steak and wine is our favorite.

The weapon loading in the morning went well, so we went to play golf. The course was large and very soggy. We finally quit after nine holes. We went back to the exchange and bought linens for dining rooms and bedrooms.

The next morning we stopped by the class six store and got cases of wine. The next stop was the Lajes OPCON. Yesterday we saw the Petty Officer in charge and told him we wanted a surface flight back. The only thing he had was an Elint with a possible Zulu class conventional sub near the ship. We took that flight and I know what I had to do. The airplane was loaded with wine so we had to walk around the cases. After about an hour I briefed the crew before we went onstation to take a sweep of the area and to shut the radar down. About three quarters of an hour had passed when the radar suddenly came on. The Sensor Station #3 reported two contacts that were both on the OPCON briefing board. We were on our way to intercept the first radar target. It was a Group 4 tanker; we needed to turn North to intercept the elint. The Fly to Point was still there and at ten miles the PPC called contact dead on. The look out stations were manned and I looked out to see if I could see him too. I caught a glance of the Elint and then I saw a snorkel in the water. I yelled to drop a buoy and said to do a three hundred and sixty degree turn. Condition One was set. The Ordnance man said he threw out a DIFAR sonobuoy and Sensor One said they had contact. I alerted the Sensor 3 for MAD contact. As we were approaching the marker, Sensor 3 reported a MAD signal. The sad story is we did not have anymore sonobuoys! I drafted a contact report and we got another MAD contact. We have established a course and speed but the Russian trawler has started making revolutions and it headed for the DIFAR sonobuoy. After twenty minutes we have lost contact with the Zulu sub. The Zulu attack sub is a conventional class which has diesel-electric, direct drive, and battery mode coupled with 3 shafts. The submarine can reach eighteen knots on the surface and sixteen knots submerged. The sub is not the answer now, but we have got to find the crewmembers on the trawler looking for the sonobuoy. We made several passes at the ship and finally the DIFAR sonobuoy sank. I was a happy sailor and we climbed altitude to head toward Iceland.

I spent an hour going over the grams that highlighted the battery mode of operation. The Zulu went about two or three miles and she faded out. Larry told me that he has finally got through sending a contact report. I drafted the final report emphasizing the blade rate that was characteristic of the Zulu.

Clearly, the deployment was almost over. Fred the Tactics Officer, had been keeping track of the extendexes and has made a chart of each evolution. The TSC officers have been doing additional analysis on particular flights which pointed out to the crew what went wrong. We had not decided how to present the mission debrief but we are full of ideas. Evalulations of work done in Iceland was one of shear unmitigated luck.

The Tactical Support Center gets its' contact by several means. He can relay on NATO, i.e., the Norweign Patrol aircraft (P-3B) contact, or other different ways of passing this information to the P-3C aircraft deployed to Iceland. These submarines were flown on, gained contact, and then it was in the operational boundary of Iceland.

VP-49 launched the ready duty aircraft and deployed a walking barrier. At debrief a convergence zone contact was detected on a Yankee class submarine an hour before the crew left station. The contact was never printed again. The flights were called off and there was a strange feeling that something went sour. Several days, namely three days, went by and suddenly the TSC was alive and they had the ready duty launched on the Western side of Iceland. I don't remember describing Iceland, but it is a island ringed with volcanoes but there is room for a Soviet transitor to reach the North Atlantic. The only land mass to the West is Greenland! The ready duty planted a walking barrier and gained contact as it was relieved by another P3C. We flew five or six flights on the Yankee. We had no other medium holding contact, but we held on through thick and thin. Further South we held contact on decreasing ranges, five miles to three miles at slow speeds. It is, without a doubt, VP-49's greatest success on deployment! The TSC was greatly overjoyed when we brought back on grams to prove we had spring tail feathers and a chisellike bill like the "Woodpecker" who it uses to drill out those Russian submarines to protect our countrys' freedom.

Many parties precluded the final days of deployment. Our skipper will have a Change of Command in Patuxent River as soon as we get back. The advance plane had all ready left and the wives were worried how we would get to Jacksonville. The party the night before going home was a stomach-grabber. I have finished packing when four guys came into my room and dragged me to the party. I am afraid I drank too much, but I nearly slept all the way home!

We got to Patuxent River and we could not believe this place. All of the squadrons are moving and we hear that VP-30 is moving too. We got off that aircraft and, for the last time there is an airplane ready to take us to NAS Jacksonville, Flordia. An hour later we were off to our new base. Jane and the kids were waiting for me. I got all my bags, Beth and Anne helped me, and Mike, Jr. was so cute but careful not to leave his Mom. The deployment brought some goodies for the Brittingham fledgings. Top priority was to make a fire in the fireplace. I called a firewood man that night and I had a half a cord of wood delivered the next day. I never thought of this, but I paid for freshly cut pine logs. What a disaster, but burn, crack, pop, and let the screen to the fireplace do the rest.

The Change of Command was held in Patuxent River and Jane plus others did not attend. I and fellow officers flew up a day early and stayed at the BOQ. We partyed most of the night and formed ranks at the ceremony. At the Officers Club we had plenty of guests. Of course the Commanding Officer was Bob Hall. He deserved to be a Skipper, I wonder how he must feel! Gene Tansey was a fine C.O. He sought me out and by the grace of God, brought me to VP-49. I knew him back in Fleet Air Wing Three and as Executive Officer of VP-30. I am glad I accepted the challenge and performed my maximum where he stood guard over this squadron.

When the dignitaries, the Admirals, and other coequal partners left, the "after the Change of Command Party" started. The party got wild at times; Tansey got thrown in the pool and such antics as that. The Commanding Officer came over and laid a few things on me. I was the new Assistant Operations Officer for the next ten days. I was to schedule at least fifteen hours on the flight schedule. Secondly, he wanted the new crew list to start getting there aircrew qualifications. These are simple and I know what they are.

VP-49 NAS Jacksonville, FL

Well on Saturday, I bought a second car, a Volkswagen. It was a 1968 coupe with standard stick shift. It was white, but after I cleaned it up, it sparkled. At the new hanger the Operations office was big. The flight schedule was left wide open and so I accepted the task. In two days I had rocket firings, mining drills, and in one week, I had six crews ready for Charlie status. The C.O. came in from leave and the X.O. reported that I was tearing down the walls getting quals for everyone. The C.O. stopped in and said that we should get ready for the Wing Eleven brief. The brief went went smooth, but Fred has to work out some verbage with me. We took the brief to WINGSLANT and they were very pleased with the presentation. On the way back to Jacksonville, the skipper thanked me for my unannounced Asst. Operations officers job. He wanted me to take over Freds job as Tactics Officer.

On December 31, 1971 we went to Capt. Bob Hall's house. His rented house is right down the street. About five o'clock, a Canadian

Officer (VP-49) stopped by and had a few drinks. Jane and I got dressed up and went to the party. I don't know how, where, or what but boy, was my head hurting on New Years Day. We had a party whereby we had invited twentyfive or thirty squadron officers. I cooked the spareribs outside with my sunglasses on and a Bloody Mary nearby. Our party was a tremendous success, but I overheard that someone had let the air out of one of CAPT Hall's tires! That didn't sit right with me, and as a matter of forgetting, I could not remember last night!

Monday at work I called a meeting of the Tactics Office. I laid down the plans as to how we would operate. I laid out a new plan that would make each officer a briefing officer. This task was a "tough road-to hoe"! I was included on the list and I told them about the submarine brief which I notified the Tactical Coordinators of these crews. There were some interesting sidelights both to and from concerning the various topics that I broached. I was happy and told the officers if there was a question, comment, or otherwise I can be reached by phone. Suddenly, the Operations Officer Chris Mills wanted to see me. Chris had a message that the C.O. wanted to take. I read the message and now I guess I will go. The message ordered us to pick up a NAVAIRLANT Vice Admiral and a staff of 10 and go on a European, Mediterrean, and Iceland trip to be back to Norfolk in ten days. This trip was supposed to leave on the day after were are welcomed to Naval Air Station Jacksonville. I was to select nine of my crew including the C.O. Also, the plane had just put the Low Light Level Television (LLLTV) on the airplane. The system was not working too well, but we will have it fixed post haste.

The squadron inspection was crowded as the Mayor of Jacksonville was there and so were the Admirals who were stacked in a succinct file. The Commodore of Wing Eleven welcomed the participants and especially the wives, enlisted and the officers of Patrol Squadron Forty Nine to Jacksonville. After one hour and a half we adjourned to the Officers Club for lunch. We had our lunch and then the guest speakers had their turn. The C.O. then stood up and I knew it was time to head up to Norfolk. Jane went with me to take me to the hanger with my suitcase packed. On the final day of January, we took off for Norfolk. We got there in one and a half hours. We tied up the aircraft and we planned everything to a nats' eyelash. Four o'clock in the morning is not pleasant, but we were getting everything onboard. One thing was missing, where is my camera? We took polaroid pictures of our crew and had them mounted as the dignitaries came onboard. The Skipper briefed them by loudspeaker and thus we were ready to taxi. Everybody was sleepy and so it was a quiet flight over to Rota, Spain. The two star had a brief tomorrow and so the preflight time was in two days. The Skipper decided that we should go visit the Bodegas and sample some of there sherry. The next day we did that but the February wind was out of the North. We settled in at night and had dinner at a Spanish restaurant.

The preflight was early the next morning and the LLLTV on, we were watching the rabbits outside in a field about a thousand yards away. I placed a First Class Petty Officer who showed the scenario on the Sensor Station Three display. The flight to Sigonella went smooth. The visit was only eight hours and they had a short hop to Naples, Italy for the next two days. This picked me up but backed up my routine, causing a lot of stopped up noses and colds. John McCallister had a serious cold and went to bed. The Skipper, Jim Allphin (our new navigator), and I went out to eat.

The Naples weather was bitter and the wine was great. The exchange was a highlight for the next day. The pizza topped with anchovies was just exquisite! When we arrived at Athens, Greece we had a long awaited stay. The visitors had to meet the carrier group, so they departed within twenty minutes after we had secured the engines. Everybody was sick on the airplane. We took John to the Air Force doctor, and he received medicine that could control his breathing and two other containers of pills that were decongestants. We crashed that night and the next morning we began to feel somewhat better. We walked around Athens and walking through the ruins of Parthenon on the Acropolis. As if this was fun, we had a call to go see the Air Force Communications at the base. The Skipper and I went down to find that the VIP party will be ready for pick up tomorrow at Naples, Italy! You could have pissed off the Pope, but Bob Hall was inflamed. I quieted him down and when we got to the hotel, we notified the crew. Furthermore, I invited the crew to eat with us and both the Skipper and I got slouched.

The stop after Naples was London and we arrived on a Friday night. We stayed at a hotel and John was feeling better, so we saw the sights. The main attraction was an old English meal. The girls wore bawdy attire such as big bosoms, and long skirts. Every once and a while, the Knights fought with their swords like a Northern Norseman. It was fun and the food was so, so. We met several stewardesses who were having fun. Afterwards, they joined us and had drinks at a pub. Quite a time we had, but protect one's vigilant!

The flight to Keflavik took off and I recognized the officers were slightly hung over. The operational part of the brief was going to be conducted during the flight. Once onstation, I showed them (the ones who really cared) the shipping on my ASA-70 display. Then I dropped two Difar buoys and demonstrated tracking and establishing a course for the merchant. Finally, I concluded my demonstration by marking on top the merchant. Several questions came up which I answered but the bulk of the material was from days gone by. The weather at Iceland was shitty, but we got in with no sweat at all. Keflavik was busy as hell, but the VP-56 Duty Officer was ready with wheels for us. We went over to the Club and saw some of the friends we had left behind. The preflight the next day was well worth it because we were headed home. We arrived at Norfolk, Virginia and we had to offload all of the baggage of the entire plane. The bombay was unbelivable! NAVAIRLANT representatives were inside acting as if their duties were spectators, lovers, or which ever you would like to call them. I was infuriated that we had to load all the bags of these individuals to claim them. And then, the audacity of them refusing to accept other baggage for men who were going to claim them. I told the customs agent that we are going home and when they decide the items were not claimed, they should lock up the gear. All of our baggage went back on the plane and as the sun set, we were in the sky headed for Jacksonville.

Jacksonville, the Tactical Support Center was brand new. The men assigned were not checked out, but we were new and among the experienced back from Keflavik TSC. The C.O.'s crew, Crew 1, took off and did some quals. One of these qualifications dealt with turning off the radar at 10,000 feet. I ordered it and we laid a four buoy module. We got contact on a merchant ship and I laid a Difar sonobuoy. We got a decent point and so I offset the bearing and dropped another sonobuoy. The second sonobuoy gave me a fix and I marked one mile South of the contact. The crew picked up five quals on this flight. The TSC looked at our evolution and our grams were matched with their AWC Chief who was coordinating the analysis. After twenty minutes a Lieutenant came out of the replay room and said the qual was no good because the radar was left on! I hit the ceiling! Where was the tape of the aircraft? He said follow me and the tape was already loaded. I asked him to call up the radar parmeters. He did but it was secured at 10,000 feet, approximately 75 miles before onstation. The Lieutenant was red-faced, so we got the qual.

The most interesting flight of the month turned out to be a destroyer twosome against a U.S. Nuclear submarine. We got this green (a message that orders the flight) and we read into the green the services or exercises the destroyers wanted. We reported onstation and we were told that the exercise was about to began. The Airplan, called for the airplane to go South for twenty miles and search towards the destroyers. At twenty miles South of datum we heard voices saying we are underway. Sonobuoys are at a premiem, being the home squadron, you only had twenty lofar and no Difar sonobuoys to use. The range of the day is poor, but we laid a barrier of buoys. Pappy announced we had contact on one of the buoys in the barrier. Two acoustic sensor operators were working their behinds off trying Comparative lofar, Iceland techniques, and noise/closest point of approach. Sensor One and Two both said the sub was heading North, so I put three buoys ahead of the sub about five miles to the North. After 16 minutes I told the destroyers he was headed 010 degrees at 12 knots. The destroyers, however, were busting there ass trying to gain contact on the submarine. After marking fixes of the submarine, I generated a track of the submarine and created an intercept point which I was going into a four minute circle. I caught the intercept point and we entered the MAD or 4000 yard circle. The C.O. was updating what we were doing and here comes the destroyers stumbling into the middle of a 4000 yard circle!! We stayed in the pattern for 2 sweeps and we got a MADMAN on the Northern boundary. Commander Hall got on the UHF and reqested permission to attack. No word was spoken from the surface ship, but as we passed the orginal mad mark, fifteen seconds later we got another MAD indication. From that point we entered another 4000 yard circle further North. Again we gained contact on the Mad signal. It's amazing what is going on in the Command and Control (ASW Coordination or whatever) aboard one of these ships. Bob Hall was about to come down from the sky but I mollifed him and when we get a MAD contact, kill (simulated) the bastard. "MADMAN," shouted Sensor Station Three and we did a three sixty degree turn so that we can fly over the point to another mad contact. We get it and now I compute a weapons fly-to-point, open the bombay, and the C.O. is communicating with the ship. Ten seconds to drop, and there must not be a bonafide officer handling the problem. "Hold the drop, hold the drop," said the C.O. followed by a Mad Man. He was so pissed that I told him that we had better climb up to one thousand feet. The only comment I can make is, boy you wait until you have seen the narrative of the flight, or purple.

Data Link was big on the assignment for VP-49. We sat down as our electronic equpiment increased, so we taught ourselves how to use data link. The four crews that were selected were to report to me. As the lead "linker" I gave them the grid lock position that we used onstation. The surface ships are testing their equipment so we should include all appropriate anti-submarine data. We launched early one morning and when I got there the cloud coverage was beyond belief. I then broke the 360 degrees into four ninty degree segments. Once we had Grid Lock inserted in the data link matrix readout, we simulated sonobuoys and managed to send and receive from the ships. An excellent system, but I would like to see more use of this important antisubmarine system.

Technically, the Tactics Officers are busting at the seams with respect to paperwork. I have never seen a more organized Tactical Fact distribution within the crews. A particular crew creates an idea and puts the plan on paper. The tactics officer prepares a TACFAC and all crews may use or not use this way of doing business. After a month a tactics board will decide if the squadron should prepare a paper and send it to the Wing.

Another part of the tactical process is getting into the ASW Weapon System Trainer. The 2F87 trainer was a fantastic, almost realistic, machine that we had to prepare a tactical syllabus to get maximum advantage of the weapon system. As a matter of pride, this trainer molded many candidates rapidly to become early Tactical Cooridators.

Early in April, I got a call from the duty office that I was wanted by the Commanding Officer. I went to his office and I was joined by six other officers. CDR Hall had just returned from Wing Eleven and it seems that the squadron in Bermuda was, shall we say,"having trouble." The squadron, a P-3B, was working a Yankee nuclear submarine. The Yankee has a set of patterns which it will follow until its' time to head home. At four or five knots the undersea Soviet vessel can transverse this distance yet will not put out the noise or signature. With that said, the C.O. said we were destined to go and help them gain contact. We sent four crews and their airplanes. My crew was going, but not the C.O. Crew one flew only once but it was on a pre-dict of over twenty four hours old. We used sixteen sonobuoy barriers set for three hours. After two and a half hours we were to move thirty miles up the course line and drop a new barrier. Not even a sniff! At any rate, our crews did not have contact, however, the squadron at Bermuda regained contact and we were headed home.

In April I got a letter from Lieutenant Commander Ron Martin and his wife Jordan. Ron and Jordan spend three years at VP-3O and then became Commanding Officer of Naval Facility Barbados. The letter triggered my mind and suddenly Jane was interested. I did some checking and I looked into a Air Force C-141 which was flying to Antigua, which carrys supplies to the Communication Center. I then booked a flight from Antigua to Barbados. Next I called Mom and asked if she would come down for a week. She said she would like to have someone to come with her. The next day she and Elizabeth (Buggie) would enjoy coming. On Friday, two weeks later, I met them at the Jacksonville Airport. We had a great time that weekend and Monday afternoon Jane and I headed South. We stopped at Patterson Air Force Base and checked in. We were all set but Jane had not got-ten her shots yet. She got all but one shot and Jane was as sick as a lit-tle puppy dog! Oblivious to pain, Jane and I climbed aboard the C-141 and eventually we got to Barbados. After engine shutdown a tall six foot five inch black policeman with a pith helmet, shiny white belt, and short white pants, came aboard the aircraft and said," I say, is Commander Brittingham onboard?" I stood up by my seat and repeat-ed, "Yes sir, here I am"! The policeman saluted and advised me and my bride to follow him. I was dressed in whites and Jane was sportily attired. I would have guessed, but we walked inside the airport and there was Ron drinking a gin and tonic having the time of his life!

Ron and Jordan wined and dined us, even when sailing in his thir-ty foot sailboat. His rented house was super and Jordan really had it laid out nice. A special event happened three days later. A British destroyer, H.M.S. Phoebe sailed in town and the U.S. officers plus wives were invited to a formal affair. The mess dress blue was author-ized and I was wearing tropical white long. Ron said no sweat, that his officers are working on my uniform. The only thing I own was my underwear! The night of the event, they arrived with my uniform. The only thing different was a humongous set of miniture medals. Finally we arrived at the ship. I pushed Jane up the ladder because she didn't want to bend over as she had a topless dress on. We no sooner got on the main deck, we were beseeched by the lads carrying drinks. We met the more important people of Barbados and skipper and his exective officer of the ship. I thanked each officer for the formal dress I was wearing. I thought the uniform was outstanding until I was accosted by this lady Geraldine Smith, who wanted to know what the medals stood for. This was so, and suddenly all the officers of the Naval Facility laughed, cheered, and clapped when I had given those wrong answers for all the wrong medals! Geraldine was John Smith's wife, which of course, he is Deputy of the British Commonwealth of Barbados! This is a time in my life that I will never forget Also it is a milestone when I can look out on the water offshore, and realize that there is so much more in my life to possess.

By and large, the visit was worth all the tea in China, so the saying goes. We left Bridgetown aboard a DC-8 destined for Miami, Florida. Interestingly, I arrived in the United States with four dollars and a Visa card. We checked out a rental car got lunch from McDonalds and we were on the road to Orlando. We turned in the car and we are glad to see the VW! Shortly after nine o'clock we entered the driveway in Orange Park. What a reunion! All of us were talking, so I went and had a beer. The greatest story I overheard was Mike, my youngest son, telling Grandmother, "Don't go near the water." The reason for this is apparently Mike is obsessed with the idea of the St.John's River which flows by Jacksonville is a danger to him. Believe me, this was perhaps the greatest getaway that Jane and I will ever have.

Three nights after we got back, a LCDR Joe Kuckelkorn called from Washington and wanted to know where I wanted orders to. I told Joe that I had not made up my mind but I was open for Navy War College. The main reason he called was COMFAIRWINGSLANT was interested in me. Wow, this was really impressive to me. Joe said there was no decision at this time, but he wanted to know what was my preference. Amazingly enough, I got a call from CDR McKissock, the training officer of COMFAIRWINGSLANT. He introduced himself and said he was calling to congratulate me for coming to the staff. I pleaded guilty to the charge, but yet I had no orders. He told me of a Tactics Manual meeting in June and he thought I might come and additionally the staff wanted me to attend a meeting concerning Personal Qualification Standards that the team was developing for each station that mans the antisubmarine airplane in WINGSPAC. I think the concept started about two years ago, when VP-30 distributed its grading sheets (UBAA's) to all of its sister East coast squadrons. VP-31 wanted the lesson guides as well for review.

The Tactics job was about to boil over with many projects coming due. The squadron Tactical Notes were a big hit with the Tactical Coordinators. Also, the Mining Officer was to kick off a mining exercise, and the ECM Officer had just spent five to six hours with all the NFO's in class and in the airplane to acquire the ESM capability that was just installed in the P3C.

The WINGSPAC Personnel Qualification Standards (PQS) was held in Naval Training Center at San Diego. The WINGSPAC Training Officer went over the brass tacks of the PQS system for a day and a half. We were divided into three groups, the Pilot, Tactical Coordinator, and the Navigator. After three hours, we had not accomplished anything. The next two days we structured the pilot training syllabus with the satisfaction of our group in San Diego. The biggest avenue of concern is to take it slow and discuss all the issues before making the actual steps of a PQS grading sheet.

I returned to 2784 River Oak Drive in Orange Park exhausted. I received a card from Joe Kuckelkorn saying that my orders are being readied. Beth had finished the second grade and was showing off her grades. Anne had completed kindergarten, while Mike was just turning three. Beth was really excited to go back to Maine. Jane and I talked about building a house. We thought that would be the best thing to do. I told Jane that she might be called up to Brunswick, Maine if I needed her to buy a house.

I left Monday morning for NAS Brunswick, Maine. I met with LCDR Paul Griffin. He told me that I was to see CDR McKissock about a report on PQS this morning. Paul told me he had heard the news of my orders. He began to feel me out on whether to buy or rent. Paul told me that he just moved in about six months ago. He spoke highly of a builder named Ray Reindeau. He offered to call and make an appointment with the contractor if I was interested. Ray was above board in his dealings with Navy Officers. He was developing the area where Paul lived and there was an empty lot four houses up from Paul.

The Tactics Manual meeting got off to a busy start Monday afternoon. There were many chapters of the manual that needed changes. Immediately I started many of these changes. At 1630, we all got together for happy hour. The next day we covered much ground and I left at 1500 to meet with Ray. I toured the land and decided to build on the vacant lot near Paul. That night I called Jane and she was to come up to sign a paper to build the house. We met again on Thursday and signed a deal with Ray. The house had four bedrooms, living room, dining room, kitchen, den, basement, and a two car garage for $44,000! We only needed $1,000 up front to seal the deal. Jane and I attended a function at the Officers Club for the FAIRWINGS staff. We met many people including Rear Admiral Hadden and his wife. The next afternoon we met with Ray and Jane had all the colors, kitchen cabinets, and light fixtures picked out. We would leave Maine without knowing what we had done, but we were going to have a real house!

In July the squadron was involved in many facets of a patrol squadron. First things first, the Minex was performed by the Woodpecker aircraft. I flew in this exercise, but I practiced because I thought I was flying in the real Minex. Our practices showed that there was a discrepancy in the software program. A serious correction was wired out to Burbank, California which was routed to Warminster, Pennsylvania for correction. Finally we flew without the change and got a conditional up regarding the minex. Another hazardous trick ruining our whole day, is the Navy Technical Proficiency Inspection (NTPI). NTPI means the loading crew, that consists of at least seven people, and you are to load a live Mark 44 or 46 torpedo and then load a special weapon. This represents a "mind bending evolution" which is subject to flunking the exercise on the least insignificant misuse of the critical procedures. We practiced the loads many times and with my doing, we had observers, mainly other squadrons, critique our loads. I think this was a job done professionally and I was pleased that we had such a high score on the NTPI.

In mid-July I started packing and it was a mess. The things that we have been hauling around for ten years just cannot cut the mustard. I advertised the VW car and had a middle aged couple come by with their daughter looking for a jalopy. The car was cleaned up and I had the brakes repaired, oil changed and lubed. They took a spin and fifteen minutes later I sold the car. Beth and Anne were running back and forth. They were playing with a ball. The next door neighbor offered me a beer that I accepted. Beth was chasing the ball and anyway she started running toward the fence and vaulted over the broken fragments of wire on the fence. The poor girl did not make it as the strands of wire broke up the back of her leg below the knee. She was hurting as I ran to get her. Jane heard her crying so I told her that I was getting a towel to stop the bleeding. After wiping the underside of the leg I took her to the base hospital. I carried her in the emergency ward and thus waited for a doctor to see her. Clearly, eight stitches were required to sew up the wound. Beth was sorry as all souls should be, but she recovered before we hit the road to Maine! There is more to follow!

As we traveled through Richmond, Annandale, and Brunswick, Maine, I felt a soft spot in my heart for CDR Bob Hall. I first met Bob on deployment, not knowing just what makes a man like him tick. I had a rough time relearning the P-3C aircraft, but it took momentum to excel. The first crew I flew with in VP-49 was a selfish bunch, less one or two individuals, who though they were really 'hot shit.' I recognized the deficiency of the two Sensor operators and I tried to correct it and I did it by sharing my responsibilities as Tactical Coordinator. On the other hand, flying with CDR Bob Hall was a godsend. This is my turn to say that I am at my peak as being a Mission Commander and a Tactical Coordinator. In 1971 on deployment I gained contact, convergence zone or whatever, and was on top of every submarine except one, the US nuclear sub that the Operations Control Officer made a mistake or his intended position. That is a part of knowing your men, testing them on their decisions, and the joy in noting that they are the best crew in VP-49! I honor this and maybe I will cross paths later on in life with Bob Hall. The period of 1970 to '72 includes many of the techniques used to solve the ever present ASW problem. P3C tactically is worth its salt once the aggressor is found. The Woodpeckers promoted by me and my NFO's have made it a place where we demand respect, and we get results.

At last, we start up the road to visit Bob and Edna and Jane's parents. We arrived and visited everywhere in Richmond. We even went to the Richmond baseball game which Mike junior liked. Then from Richmond we went west to the Blue Ridge Mountains and drove up the Skyline Drive where we found deer to feed. We followed the Skyline Drive north to Front Royal then onto Route 66 headed east to Washington, D.C. We stopped at Manassas Battlefield and the kids seemed to be interested. We saw a ten minute movie which told about the battles that were waged there. Mom was waiting as the children ran to give her a kiss. Dad got home right on time to hug and kiss the grandchildren. Mom and Dad wanted to hear about the house we were builidng. The house was, for lack of a better word, a manison. It had all the modern conveniences. We expected to see them Christmas time.

The Ford station wagon was cleaned, polished, lubed, and packed for New England. We left at 5:00 a.m. and stopped for donuts and coffee. I don't know what happened, but we were way ahead of schedule. The car was not doing well. I had the radio blaring when Jane called my attention to the thumping noise coming from the motor. I pulled off the highway and got a mechanic to look at the car. Forty five minutes later, we were back on the road, feeling finer than" frog hair," really not knowing what is wrong, what had happened or who gives a darn!

We arrived in Brunswick and stayed at the Holiday Inn. The kids thought this was a great idea and went swimming even though it was 73 degrees that Labor Day weekend. I called Paul Griffin. He was glad to hear our voice. He and his wife Kitty were going camping in Northern Maine and we were going to use their house for the weekend. He gave me some orders for the cat, the birds, et cetera. We moved in to the Griffins' House on Saturday just as it began to rain. We realized our house was not ready as we looked at it today. Only the basement was dug and the concrete blocks were laid outlining the walls of the basement. Ray mentioned that a house was available until ours was ready to be moved into. I took the family by and what a hell hole to live in. I guess there was not much choice in this matter. The bedrooms were small and everything was small. The kids did not look very happy but I kept reminding them that just wait until we move!!

On Sunday about 1:00 p.m. Paul and Kitty drove into the parking lot. Paul and Kitty met the gang and they said it did nothing but rain an so they came back to party. We had a great discussion time from who's who to another! Thirsty as always, we laughed as we ran out of beer and I went out to get more.

KILO CLASS SS

FOXTROT CLASS SS

CHARLIE 1 CLASS   Nuclear Guided Missile

ECHO II   SSGN

YANKEE CLASS BALLISTIC MISSILE SUBMARINE SSBN

CHAPTER 9

COMMANDER FLEET
AIR WINGS ATLANTIC

On Tuesday, Jane put the kids in school. I checked into WINGSLANT and met with Don McKissock. The first officer I met was Captain John Moberly of Canadian Maritime Forces. John was a navigator which was sort of like me. He had many hours of flight and he was familiar with the P3C program as well as the Argus Bird. John had taken most of my job since LCDR Thompson had left in August. I took over the antisubmarine training and my superior was CDR McKissock. I looked for a turnover but to know avail. I was shown a lower left desk drawer and there laid the problems, heartaches and long overdue deadlines that dragged my job to an endless solution. The first object which needed attention was the Tactical Reference Manual and Tacaid that was still festering after the due date of July. The notes of the meeting which I attended we lost, or so it appeared, and there was nothing to support the changes, which for a fact was thoroughly discussed and approved before we broke up in June three months ago. There were several point papers that seemed interesting but the dye was cast, but what fact or factors did the decision overturn? Another factor is that at COMFAIRWINGSLANT there was also FAIRWINGFIVE. As it stands, I am both of these individual czars. This is an interdirected task which thrives on attainment to do the job of ASW, and has the Admiral to do the praising of a job well done. And finally I see that the Patrol Wing Eleven is made up of ex P3C men and those in the Wing are going to the P3C squadron. On the other hand COMFAIR-WINGLANT has one P3C officer—me! This headquarters must draw more P3C officers so they can make things better for all concerned.

The next day at work I calmed myself and in walked Don. He gave me two messages which needed answers right away. I started work on them and made two phone calls. The man on the opposite end was of P3C background. I put the message together and started working on the other one. This message wanted to know when the tactical manual will be out and several other menial subjects. I set out a plan that would cover all subjects by the end of the year. The Tactical Reference Manual was high on my list to finish but I felt this would be on the way to Navy Tactical Doctrine Activity in Washington, D.C. by the end of November 1972.

October 1972 was certainly a cold time of the year. We went to all the local stores and bought winter snow suits, winter or more dressy coats and we went to L.L. Bean in Freeport to get the type boots they wanted.

On Monday, a message arrived that concerned the meeting to be held in Canada at the end of this month. The list of goodies that our friends wanted to hear about were the P3C and numerous items that John Moberly had listed. The P3C was a general conversation item, but the main item of concern was the Tactical Support Center.

On the third week in October, we met with the builder and we walked through the house. The rooms were there but there is a hell of a lot of work to be done. We set the date and we hoped that this would be acceptable. The housing office notified and we began to get ready. The move date was to be at the end of the month. I took off and the furniture was moved in. After eight hours the moving van left. We had finally moved to Topsham, Maine. The kids got home from school and helped us with arranging bedrooms. At eight p.m. Jane and I were exhausted. And furthermore, I had planned to go to Canada tomorrow.

The trip to Canada was three days of fun parties and I fathered a terrific cold. The 'Canucks' were really super people and they plotted alibis among themselves to get you completely inebriated. Strike three, they got me completely, knee walking drunk. The next day, we spent giving presentations. I gave the P3C brief and followed with the Tactical Support Center brief. This led to a barrage of questions. Finally I stopped fielding questions, because we were running out of time. That night I went to a fellow officers house with John. We met his wife but that did not go over well, so we left and went to a bar. The third day we all gave our comments and then we left to meet the plane. I do not know about you, but I thought I had seen enough of Canada for a while.

Back in Brunswick, I started working on the changes to the Tactics Manual. I got started and was called to a meeting which needed a message which condones the outcome. I look as far as chapter eight, Jezebel, which threw me for a loop. All the notes, requirements, and the typed changes to this chapter were vacant or lost. With this in mind, I spent many nights going over making corrections. The aircraft that all three Patrol Wings had were P3C, P3A, P3 Deltic, and P3B. This was not all, some aircraft have AQA-5 installed ready to transition to the AQA-7 Difar installation. So in other script, the authenticity of the Tactics manual must relate to the type of system, model aircraft, ect. if it is going to be productive. Finally in the middle of November, the manual was sent to Washington, D.C. for illustrations and printing.

Christmas was a big day including Frank Spruill, who was divorced and with his girl friend; his two children; and his girl friend's son. They arrived during Christmas and they had a marvelous time. They arrived at our home just after dinner in the snow. The kids played in the snow along with the Brittingham youngsters.

Winter of 1973 was a rough one, with the Northeaster the prominent threat bringing snowstorm of amazing depth. The word from Washington, D.C. was that the Tactical Reference Manual was besieged by many queries, which meant I had better go to Washington. I called my parents and told them when I would be coming down. The facility was busy as draftsmen were drawing patterns, without meaning, or leaving out major parts of why this procedure was necessary. After spending two and half hours reviewing the material, I asked the supervisor if I could make changes to the manual. I began to make changes at 0700 the next morning. By lunch time I had marked corrections on the rough drafts of changes from the first seven chapters. The chapter on Jezebel was a horror show and after lunch I spent the entire afternoon on numerous things like convergence zones!

That night I rode out and visited Mom & Dad. The food was familiar and the liquor was superb. Dad was getting old in life and its a wonder he continually gets up so early in the morning. Mother still works in the family circle of the church. The next day was another day of checking the last chapters of the reference publication. After lunch the pages under rough markings were reviewed and were acceptable. Some needed revamping and back to the drawing board. Next the diagram which pertained to the sonobuoy patterns were sighted. Only a few needed touching up. Friday was the final day and I was going back to Brunswick. I had five more hours in which to bless or have the Tactical Doctrine Agency send the data before they publish the book.

Finally, the last day in Washington arrived, I looked over the charts, figures, and view graphs of what they had designed for the tactics publication, although it allowed, I wanted to see five items, ASAP, before the publication went to press. I thanked all convened and left Washington to meet the plane at Navy Air Facility at Andrews Air Force Base in Maryland. NAF sure looked familiar after I raised my hand there some eleven years ago!

Beth was having trouble with the back of her leg. The tear was promoted by Beth jumping over a wire fence and tearing the upper part of the leg just below the knee cap. Beth had torn open the wound and the dispensary said that a surgeon in Portland, Maine is the man to see. One afternoon Jane, Beth and I went down to Portland to see the doctor and he said that the surgery has to be done over. He said that Beth could have the procedure done in his office and then we could take her home. A week later I brought her down and she handled the operation very well. I almost bought the farm when I looked at the operation, I almost passed out. Beth was woozy when she came out of it and slept the whole way home. She had little problems, but the doctor said the US Naval Hospital in Jacksonville certainly did not do her leg any justice.

When I got back to Brunswick I was astounded by the happenings' of the week. The Admiral of COMFAIRWINGSPAC was asking the Admiral to visit WINGSPAC and met with his constituents about various problems they had encountered. Very quickly the messages arriving stating the meeting, times, reservations, and a list of agenda. Commander McKissock was very adamant about most of the issues and wanted a position paper by Wednesday describing the problem, action pertaining to, and giving a position to be later decided on later on by the Admiral of COMFAIRWINGSLANT. There were many problems of the Atlantic verses the Pacific squadrons. The first was the readiness posture of the squadron. The West coast squadron had a new readiness grading system which could, with out a doubt, set new records of achievement throughout the halls of antisubmarine warfare. The Atlantic force was not quite right because the advent of the P3C had already replaced half of the East coast squadrons. In other words, the readiness publication was out of date and a conference was scheduled in two months. The list goes on and we are dismissed to motivate, regurgitate the answer and put in proper format before Wednesday afternoon.

The WINGSLANT/WINGSPAC conference met at Moffet Field, California which started with twelve people including the Admiral. We met for a half a day to give there positions on each topic they had chosen to talk abut. After lunch we broke into separate groups which talked about three or four items of discussion. My group bickered back and forth on the qualification manual, Personal Qualification Standardization, nuclear & sub weapon loading standards and a new way of developing tactics. The end result of this meeting was that little was shared by the opposing counterparts. A raisin when used in desserts as something excellent, or something attractive must be given in return for a favor. Thereby, the matters that were brought up before the Wings were to be studied and were to be discussed before the next meeting to be at the East coast at headquarters in Topsham, Maine.

This was no surprise as this was the first time the WINGSLANT and PAC meet together for sometime. This was well-worth the effort to meet, and prepare for the challenges that we must meet. This was about time that the Tactical Reference Manual reared it's ugly head and wanted to know what the hell it was going on right now and what new techniques we would have in the future.

As part of my duties as Tactics Training Officer, I led the transition of AQA-5 aircraft to AQA-7 Difar aircraft. Being a part of Fleet Air Wing Five, I also ran ASW Exercise , and any target of opportunity exercises. My first experience with subs was when I went to Groton, Connecticut to brief a U.S. FM-10. The sub was tied up to the dock and we went aboard to talk to the skipper. I introduced my self and began the brief. The Captain was very precise and asked many questions. I answered each question and included the exact nomenclature that the skipper and his Operations Officer wanted to hear. We exchanged snorkel times so that the aircrews could get contact and we allowed only forty minutes snorkel time.

In the late Spring of 1973 there was a staff meeting which ordered myself and five other members to a study panel. This panel was to perform the following functions:

a. Develop a new organization of the Commander Patrol

Atlantic Fleet and his subordinate wings, Fleet Air Wing Five in NAS Brunswick, Maine and Fleet Air Wing Eleven in NAS Jacksonville, Florida. This edict came down from Naval Air Atlantic and centered on the manpower need to fill these billets.

b. Additionally, another operation that should be created by this command to fit in with other operational tasks.

c. Create the officer/enlisted manpower for both the two Wings and the supporting admirals command staff.

This six member board was pulled from the staff and spent a day on who would do what. The main project that they have for me was to get the manpower required for the Tactical Support Center. Fleet Air Wing Eleven had one, but we have to plan a new Wing Five which gets' a TSC in a year. After receiving Wing Eleven's manpower, the shit hit the fan. Taking the manpower that was planned by NAVAIR-LANT, the Wings would be deficient if we had a full compliment of men in the TSC. We bitched back and forth within our group. We finally called for help to try to alleviate this situation. In other words, can six officers man with below manning in all critical areas? After two and a half weeks the Wing Five and Eleven billets were filled by minimum numbers. The administrative and maintenance groups of the three areas were still not finished by the rest of the committee. They fought on as I was leaving for Jacksonville for a meeting concerning the Qualification Exercises for the P-3 aircraft.

The meeting was held with the Wing Eleven representatives. The main problems were with a conventional submarine; several grammatical bumps in the exercises; throw out Julie entirely, and numerous changes to the advanced exercises. Prior to these meetings, I sent a message requesting inputs and told them of a meeting that I would hear their case. I argued with everything that they had to say. I quickly took the floor and verbally thanked the squadron and Wing members who had put a lot of thought and desire in making the recommended changes. So back to Brunswick with another project and I will have it done as soon as I can.

CDR McKissock was smiling when I walked into the office. I briefed him on trials and tribulations of the Jacksonville trip. He asked me if I had read the boards, the answer was no. Don told me that they were going to hold a conference on the ATP-1 and associated manuals which concerned the surface ship Navy. He said they were considering a common manual for surface ship ASW. I went to the meeting and worked cleaning up the earlier plans and incorporating them in the TACAID [tactical aid] manual. I brought the revised trial with me for a chop before they went ahead and published.

My house was in a state of emergency with respect to the grass. All along the road was a ditch filled with rain water. In the middle of the week I contracted a dump truck and two loads full of dirt and top soil. I was ready at 0730 Saturday when the first truck arrived. He dumped the dirt and twenty minutes later he brought the top soil. I spent the rest of the day with Mike's wagon dumping the dirt across the width of my lot. Then came the top soil and then mixed in the grass seed. The whole front lawn got some dirt in spots and boy was my body sore. Sunday we went to church and when I got home the kids went inside to change their clothes. I walked to the end of the drive way and looked at my wonderful job. Overnight numerous small twigs fell from the trees so I bent over an picked them up. After three or four minutes I had more than a handful so I started to stand up and my body would not straighten! I cried for Jane to come help me. The front door opened, and Jane came running out. She helped me into the house and fixed me a place to lie down in the den. A visit to the medical facility prescribed me some pills which promptly knocked me out. The next day my back was no better. Jane took me back in my pajamas and I was waiting to be x-rayed when the head of the dispensary noticed me. After determining the problem, he told me to follow him. His office was big and spread out. He told me to lie down on the cot. The cot was hard and my back was killing me. The doctor told me to relax my legs. He picked up my left ankle and began shaking slightly, and then he pulled my leg which gave a resounding crack. Next he told me to relax and he did the same thing to the right ankle. The doctor told me to standup. I was standing straight and tall with a little pain and tears were rolling down my face. He told me to go home, get in bed, and he showed me how to sleep without knotting up my back. I went to work Thursday and at 1300 hours Friday I saw the lead doctor and he did the same treatment I had earlier. I do not know whether he is a chiropractor or not, but he certainly calms my back.

Paul and Kitty Griffin were in the thick of things. We went to cookouts and parties with them and had a swinging good time. We celebrated New Year Eve with them. Another party up the street was attended by the four of us. What a time was had by all; it was hangover time the next morning. Kitty and Jane had certain differences which relate to having to put up with children, or just plain tension which leaves one in a state of unrest. Kitty used to pick on Jane and then she came home crying. Both Jane and I tried to correct the problem but at the next Wing function, the girls were at it again! Paul did not like the job or the Wing. He surprises us all with orders to the Navy War College in July. Jane talked it over with me, so we had a party for them. We invited sixteen people (including ourselves), all were the favorite friends of the Griffins. We rounded up four bridge tables and set them up in the living room. I had bought eight bottles of light wine and several other brands. We had shrimp, peanuts, crackers and dip, and something exotic for dinner. The wine served before dinner was gone and the second bottle was empty before dinner was finished. The standby wine, the infamous basement dribble, was served (Matues') until the supply was depleted. Coffee and liqueurs led the way with dessert. Then the bitching began and soon Kitty was voicing her complaints. They left in July and I think Jane was never happier.

Living in Maine was an environment for lots of things to happen. Mike Jr, case in point, developed an interest in hockey. He was four on October 24 of 1973 and athletic enough to skate. In November I noticed a sign for the youngest bracket of skaters. The call said four or five year olds so I looked with Jane for advertisements for used skates. I found several ads to call. I centered on two candidates and on Saturday, Mike and I went checking. The first stop was very expensive, but the second stop was a winner. Bauer skates were number one as far as Mike Jr. was concerned. We bought these skates for a song. Then we went to the sports shop in downtown Brunswick. I bought him a hockey helmet, stick, shoulder pads, and gloves. What if he did not like the sport? Oh dear, we will cross the bridge when we come to it! Mom and the girls could not believe all the money I had spent. Mike put all his gear on and right away I saw he needed socks and raw hide shoe strings.

We arrived at the hockey rink at 0700 on Saturday morning. Mike's team of misfits as they were called, got dressed and I helped him string his boots. I opened the gate and Mike skated and fell; got up and skated to the gang of twenty soon to be hockey players. After forty-five minutes of practice, Mike skated over to me and was ecstatic! He was almost a skater, having only fallen five or six times. After talking with his coach, I enrolled him in a skating school during the Christmas holidays at Yarmouth. I went on leave about ten days during the holidays and took Mike and several others to these skating lessons. The distance was not far, but the snow was worse than ever. Since the practice started around one o'clock, the end of the session was kind of touch and go to drive home. Mike would go on and make hockey his sport of choice!

Apparently, the Navy was closing the navigation training at Corpus Christi, Texas, and permitting the U.S. Air Force to do the training for the NFO's in California. The meeting presented all of the parameters and explained the course curriculum. After the meeting, CDR Oak Osborn ripped us apart; he wanted to know this information by tomorrow morning. CDR Osborn was from WINGSPAC and I believe he was in the training area of expertise. There were these officers and we talked over the problems; however, I can't remember what the pressing urgency of the topic was. The next morning the senior officer reported the finding to him, which alleviated the whole matter.

One of the saddest moments of my life was witnessing CDR McKissock leaving WINGSLANT. He was headed for NAS Brunswick as an Administrative Officer. I don't know what happened. There was a failure during his career that causes a release or dismissal from selection for Command which killed his chances in the Navy. He worked me, pressured me, and I have the highest respect for him. Wherever he goes, he will never lose his devotion to the ASW cause.

The overall threat of imprecision lies in the minds of true Naval Officers. The WINGSPAC organization was pushing for something and that no one has yet not defined. Clearly, the Tactical Reference Manual was never divided into certain proportions so that this document could be included in the ASW category as a basis for all airplanes including the P3, S-3 and the SH-3 variables. This is the problem, where COMNAVAIRPAC really does not know where to go. The visit to San Diego was a thing of beauty. The S-3 Replacement Air Group was there and the S-3 was striving to be one of the leaders in ASW. The onset of the meeting stunned my colleagues and myself with many old hands fondling ASW. The admiral's aide was there and he talked for about twenty minutes. He gave what he considered the high spots of their plan. I stood up and stomped down vis a vis the plan and advocated the unified WINGSLANT/WINGSPAC stand that we need a united front with the intent and purpose of ASW alone, with battle groups, and with other aircraft. We need the Tactical Reference Manual and the TACAID which will give us this step to vitalize and improve our effectiveness. A great mass of emptiness blunts the WESTPAC crowd. Finally, the aide stood up and canvassed the room to ask questions. There were very few questions. We won the battle!

The last WINGSLANT meeting was the second Tactical Reference manual. We had good coverage from battle fleet air wings. The Training Officer led off the meeting and passed it on to me. I spoke briefly commenting that the manual was getting into shape and I wanted to leave it in a respectable condition. We worked for three days and took time out for a lobster and clams. The final day of the conferences, people were impressed with how we changed the tactical concept of the manual.

September, I got a call from LCDR Bob Howard, a detailer, as a matter of fact, he was destined to be the Commanding Officer of Patrol Squadron Forty-Nine. He wanted to know what I wanted for my next assignment. I was apprehensive that I had another year in this assignment. Well, he said he had me slated for Navigator on the USS Independence. He spent several minutes describing his annals, which gives him a coveted Commanding Officer of a squadron. Finally, I spoke and said that I did not really yearn for shipboard duty, but let me talk with my wife and I will call back tomorrow. By now I was fit to be tied. It was time to go home and have a hefty shot of bourbon! Jane was upset, and so were the kids. I slept little that night, and when Captain Zeisel came to work I went to see him. I related what I had heard from the phone call, thus what should I do. The Captain acknowledged the fact I did not unequivocally want carriers but I would take something as long as it had to do with a VP squadron. I confessed that I went back to squadrons much too early. I wanted to do the right thing, could he help me? That morning Captain Zeisel called the detailers and put a stop to their navigator assignment. They offered the COMFAIRMED job, which did not ring a bell with me. I saw the Captain late in the day. He told me that he was sending a message to the Admiral for further information about the billet. As I understand, the job is manned by an O-5, who is leaving in November. I think I will wait and see what the Admiral thinks of me first. In a matter of days the message was answered by COMFAIRMED/CTF

Sixty-Seven who listed the prerequisites for the job. I qualified for all (including basic mining) but I feel I needed quick refresher in electronic warfare. I contacted Norfolk and found a course which filled the bill. With that taken care of I felt that I was "locked in" to the job at Naples, Italy.

It came time to sit down and have an "all-Brittingham" conference. Beth was excited, but did not want to leave Topsham; Anne, wanted to go to Naples; and Mike was upset because they would not take him into the first grade and there was no hockey. Jane was leaning toward Naples, but CDR Sheets called from Naples and related that he was my point of contact. He had already sent many pamphlets, housing needs, and many other things that would be coming our way. He said that the Sixth Fleet will be having an exercise during the middle of November and I could come over with VP-11 who is tasked to do this commitment. You could not have guessed, but I got sweet talked into delivering two dogs to a Marine Lieutenant Colonel!

A year ago we at COMFAIRWINGSLANT formed a body to analyze our staff and the various commanders to assess our needs and agreed to present this to the Admiral on our staff. Effective organization means a lot, but it requires a dedicated and unrelenting devotion to the job set before the officer assigned. The Admiral agreed with the findings and we went to Norfolk, VA, the next week to present this study. NAVAIRLANT was ready for us and we had several questions. The brief had a few shortfalls; namely men! In essence, the three star admiral bought the whole ball of wax. Soon the changes were made to the manpower, logistics, maintenance, and operational control, whereby the new name of Commander Patrol Wings Atlantic was adopted the next year.

My final talk to the detailer, Bob Howard was a one-way conversation with my remarks about not taking the navigators job, but my orders are on the way. VP-11 took me and the dogs to Rota, Spain. I talked to a Petty Officer who had the watch while I waited to check in to BOQ, rest and take the dogs for a walk nine hours later! Finally, we took off for Naples and landed there three hours later. The dogs had a new home and I finally meet Bob Sheets and his wife.

The staff was very cordial and I was introduced to the man I am relieving. I spent one day reviewing the tasks that I would be responsible for. The two VP squadrons, one in Sigonella and one in Rota are my bailwicks including the Tactical Support Center and its operation.

The squadron assigned in Rota has four planes in Lajes Air Force Base to effect the squadron split deployment. This gets hairy, but wait until January 1975 when I take over!

Bob and Joanie showed me the town of Naples. We ate out every night, and I visited my long lost friend the Lieutenant Colonel and his wife for supper. Bob introduced me to a gentleman who would find me a house to rent. We looked at several houses which overlooked the town. I took notes and promised that Jane and I would contact him when we arrive in late January.

The Chief of Staff was Captain Bradley. I met with him for about an hour. He told me of his exploits as a Naval Officer in command of a ship and other important positions. He asked many questions, my position on many things, and lastly he asked about sensitive issues about ASW. He was concerned about many things and finally he wanted a worker and resolved officer. I told him not to worry, I am willing to serve, and serve I will. I have three safes; one of those deals with mine warfare, top secret minefields, and other interesting goodies.

When I got back from Naples it was cold as hell. My relief had checked in and was learning all the tricks of the trade. We had many items for sale and the new Operations Officer rented my house. The Christmas of 1974 caused us to recount the memories and think about the trials and tribulations of Naples. I sent our new Datsun down to New Jersey and away it went. The only car that I had left was a Ford station wagon which was a 1967 model. I sold it for $450. The last week we were moving and suddenly I realized I did not have my travel orders or my family's passports. I called Washington for help. The next day a Chief flew up to Brunswick with tickets, passports, and everything needed. I think Don McKissock took us to the Portland Airport and we took off to Boston.

Logan Airport was busy. The kids including Mom and I packed five large suitcases. We have everything from soup to nuts. The TWA Airlines had its big 747 ready and we went aboard. The flight was crowded, but what the hell our family is going to Naples for three years. The flight went quick, so fast that we stopped in Paris. We were permitted to go off the plane but stay within the confines of the rest area. We arrived at Rome at twelve o'clock. We got our baggage and we were directed to the Naples departing area. We checked in and found that there was a flight leaving at four o'clock. They took our baggage and we sat down to wait the agonizing three hours. The controversy was that Alitalia Airlines was on strike. We waited and asked what time the flight leaves but, the passengers were notified that boarding had commenced. We got onboard and shazam, we took off for Naples.

By the time we arrived at Naples the sky was light but darkness had bedecked the land. Bob Sheets was waiting for us as I suspected. We were exhausted and we check into the American Hotel just outside the gate of the Naval Facility. The Sheets, bless there hearts, gave us dinner which we could not finish. Night ended abruptly back at the hotel.

CHAPTER 10

COMMANDER MARITIME SURVEILLANCE AND RECONNAISSANCE FORCES U.S. SIXTH FLEET

The next morning I was groggy with sleep as I heard someone knocking on the door. It was Bob so I told him to wait in the lobby and I will be right down. I got dressed and told Jane we will meet for lunch. The trip was to check in at the facility, and finally housing. This being finished, we ate lunch at the main cafeteria on the basement floor where the CTF-67/COMFAIRMED lives or resides on the ninth floor. That afternoon was consumed putting the children in school. Beth we got in and Anne will go to school eventually at Pini Maria Elementary, North of Naples. Mike was busy working on something. He got tired of that so he found a book more to his liking. The school administrator asked, "How old is this child?" I told the administrator that he was in kindergarten in Maine and then found out he was to young to start school. The lady stood up and went over to introduce herself to Mike and ask him if he knew his ABC's. Mike automatically recited the alphabet. Then she asked two other questions and I knew he was in the first grade.

My first day at work was a ballbuster. I sent out ten confidential messages which were related to sonobuoy allocation, loading drills, numerous Fleet proposals, and NATO trivia which could be solved at a later date. Captain Bradley wanted me to go to Gibraltar with him to meet some of his contacts. We left the next morning in a seven or eight seat jet destined for Sigonella. This was my first deployment, as you may recall. We jumped off the plane and right away we meet LCDR Pete Baxter who was the Tactical Support Officer of Sigonella. Pete and I had been trying to meet each other since 1966 when we met at Norfolk during the Tactical Reference Manual reviews. Pete had a heavy hand in things over in the Mediterranean. He acted as our man in the know regarding the deployed squadrons and what they could do in a pinch. The Royal Navy was at hand since they had offered us a ride to Gibraltar. The Brits' had a new airplane, the Nimrod, which was a superb aircraft. The Nimrod had four jets which kept it out of water and had an impressive view of things inside. The console was centered around the head, shall we say, the Tactical Coordinator, and branched out through the sensor system which displayed an impressive acoustic ensemble. We climbed aboard and we took off. We proceeded to get a brief of the airplane and shortly thereafter, we observed them taking pictures of a Soviet Elint.

We landed at Gibraltar and we were meet by several dignitaries. They escorted us to the BOQ and we were on tap at happy hour. We made many friends and then it became time for dinner. I was with the British flyers and they suggested that we try something different. I went with them and we enjoyed the sights. The Spanish had a guard posted preventing any of us going into their homesite. The Brits' were briefed on this and we were aware that Gibraltar was elated as being a sole survivor.

The next morning we went to the airport where there was a brief set up. This was a NATO brief and I was prepared for the rapidity of this ordeal. The British were very highly proficient in making radar contacts and relating them to know Russian subs. Case in point, a Nimrod was staying out of Cyprus and South of Souda Bay, Crete, there was F-35, Foxtrot sub reported to be in the area. Do you catch what I am saying?

That afternoon we went to see another old friend of Captain Bradley's. The car was stopped, and son of a bitch, we were at the Mediterranean Sea. The sea was beautiful and suddenly it dawned on me. As I listened to the brief I suddenly remember a Foxtrot going home or leaving the Mediterranean. This purchase is a blessing in disguise!

Jane had met the real estate man and went on a trip with him. He showed her a house in downtown Naples, one in Pozzuoli, just outside of Naples on the shoreline which separates Naples from the island of Ischia. The last house that she saw was beyond where she wanted to live. She was dissatisfied, disgusted and ready for some wine. We talked it over and over. We wanted to check out the area, so I bought a Fiat for $800 and we went hunting for a house. We settled on Parco Cuma which looks nice since one of my LCDR's lived there. He had a nice place, a reasonable price, and not too far from work. We looked closer to town, but these prices were way too high. Incidentally, let's talk about lira. The rate for lira was 660 lira per dollar. This equated to paying one thousand dollars for 660,000 lira!

The next step was to go to Rota, Spain and meet the squadron and the soon to be TSC. The file that I had on Rota was packed with details. The ASCAC was composed of very few officers and enlisted. Many ASW enlisted were ordered to handle the TSC. The computer software and hardware is all trickling in and the site has been bull-dozed, so lets bring the TSC on! The ordnance officer of NS Rota is a tough nut to find, much less talk face to face with. When we arrived, we could not find him, so I told the Petty Officer that I was going to send a message that will require loading of mines. I made sure that the Petty Officer knew exactly what I meant.

The squadron was tied to Naples for operational tasking. This tasking comes about three o'clock in the afternoon. It is difficult to task/mount up a flight, including twelve bodies to fly for ten hours. Sigonella squadron may launch the ready duty for a night, whereas the Rota ready duty has a two hour launch time. To accompany this, there are numerous Pilot flights, tactics warmups, and their Naples tasking also makes the Sigonella squadron wait for orders. This is the problem with the Sigonella squadron who has to wait for the same Naples task-ing. The Rota squadron has a ready duty which has to get off the ground in two hours. To accompany this, there are numerous pilot flights, tactics warmups, and there are weapons loading drills which I intend to determine if they can do it. I went to the phone and called Naples. I identified myself and I said, "Send, the message." The time was five minutes after nine. After I hung up the phone, I spoke to the TSC officer and told him to expect an Operational message immedi-ately. My next meeting is with VQ-2 and I headed in their direction. The meeting was informal; I wanted to be known to a few officers since I was on the staff. There is another job for CTF-67 which pro-vides for the operational responsibilities, maintenance, and the intelli-gence gathering of VQ-2.

Naval Station Rota had an excellent Officers Club. I went there and ate with the squadron officers. They had been in Rota for several months and the last leg is coming before their deployment terminates. Immediately, the Squadron Duty Officer came in and recognized me. We stepped outside and he showed me my message on the loading drill. Then, he wanted to know what to do about the message, even though the communication station sat on it, the squadron got the message an hour and a half later. Nothing has been done. I told the duty officer that he had better get the ready duty out and load what ever the message called for. Pissed off as ever, I finished my lunch. By 4:00 p.m. the weapons load was complete. I had made up my mind that next week there will be another revenge loading drill.

It has been fifty days living in the American Hotel and believe me it is becoming a drag. My car suddenly showed up and I went down to get it. The orange Datsun looked good and I would drive it back to the compound where I would get the tags. The most exciting news with regards to the house was a Major in the US Air Force was ordered back to the states. The Major was on leave, so we met the next door neighbors and then had an Italian to speak with him. The father delegated his son to handle his home in Parco Cuma. His son related that he wanted 280 thousand lira for rent a month. That made it $420 American dollars per month. Yes, it was steep, but I had to say yes. We were far overdue as far as housing was concerned. The house was beautiful. The home was surrounded by gates and a chain fence. Inside the home the left side was a dining and living room with blinds covering the windows. On the right side of the entrance was a moderate bathroom. The final room on this floor was the kitchen that lead to the backyard. The second floor had three bedrooms and a giant bathroom. The bedroom that I and Jane have looks over the houses with the water and its' volcanic island as the backdrop. The basement, was a unique experience. There was every available amenity you could imagine A kitchen, bathroom, and fireplace. The movers arrived and began to unload the furniture. We purchased an old piano. When the men started to move it, the piano fell into seven or eight pieces. The movers left and we started marking things or we moved them downstairs until we had time to shuffle them to their rightful positions.

Standing the watch was quite a task. We had about eight or nine Duty Officers which handled the watch section. The Duty Officers shared a Saturday and Sunday watch which was sort of a Command Duty Officer position. The watch turned out the greens for both Rota and Sigonella which was mentioned briefly when I visited Rota. The routing of greens, tasking and special remarks were bugaboos that were resolved by the secure phone in the Operation Control briefing room. The calm, collected, and consistent behavior of the Duty Officer is paramount. Be aware and for Christ sake do not let Captain Bradley nail you! He will call you at least one time at night for you to make arrangements for some meeting or by ploy as the main action proceeds. At midnight and all the work is done, I went and lay my head down for four hours. The Petty Officer would awake me, either male or female, it did not bother me. After throwing some water in my face, I washed and shaved and put on my tie. The next thing was to get a cup of coffee. Next was to get a brief of what has happened, and then to sort out Captain Bradley's messages. At 0700 the gang, which normally ran the Operations room report for duty. They began to build the Admirals brief which takes place at 8:30 p.m. That in a nutshell, is what I do during the COMFAIRMED/CTF67 day.

A message from COMSIXFLEET came down and before I got to my messages for the day, he wanted me right away. Captain Bradley wanted me to set down and he read parts of the message concerning the use of rockets, MK54, dummy mines, and numerous other shapes that were stricken from P-3 use at least four years ago. I reacted and said that the messages were full of fluff. Captain Bradley was leaving and was all set to call them (COMSIXFLEET). I calmed him, and he let me draft the outgoing. I contacted the squadron at Sigonella and talked with their weapons officer. Much to my surprise he is coming up to Naples tomorrow. I gave him much of the data, but I wanted to see the NATOPS manual which gives precise parameters for carrying of all weapons. The next day I was right and the yeoman made copies for me to show the Captain. The next day I had a draft ready for release with numerous appendages for Captain Bradley. The Captain was so pleased that he went in and showed the admiral how COMSIXFLEET did not know what they were talking about. It does not take much to piss off the admiral, but he called me in to help him write a personal message, lambasting the use of P-3 and the weapon system. The messages were rolling out of CTF Sixty Seven towards Northern Italy the home port of Vice Admiral Turner. The messages were viewed and an officer came down from the flag ship and was corrected by me.

The tactical situation in the Mediterranean is a wide awakening to the young first tour tactical coordinator. I have studied the water conditions and I am still grasping for why we cannot get contact. Let's try

Rota. The incomer's are the Charlie, November, Echo II and the Victor Soviet Nuclear Submarine force. Outside the straits of Gibraltar there are rows of sonobuoy barriers put in by the patrol aircraft with no more than a mile and half spacing. The barrier or cobweb of sonobuoys is in effect for as much as twenty four hours. In order to do this, the Rota OPCON must contact NAF Lajes to get permission to set up a new command structure that satisfies CINCLANTFLEET. Back to the coordination, the CTU 84.2.3 launches out of Rota to drop buoys inter alia, to gain contact and track the submarine. Aboveboard, the United States submarines are waiting for VP contact so that they can follow the Russian submarines. That gets sticky, further in the Mediterranean. Now let us talk about the Sigonella squadron. Why does the P-3C flying out of Sigonella become more proficient in finding conventional subs while struggling with the Russian Nuclear submarine? There are several known "resting stops" for the conventional subs (Foxtrot and Juliette Class) along the way. The P-3C normally patrols these anchorages at least once a night and invariably gets a Soviet sub tied up to a Russian Merchant or a trawler that has certain electronics on its mast. The nuclear submarine problem equates to that of the Rota squadron. During certain times of the year the convergence zone area of the Ionian Sea becomes active. This characteristic becomes prevalent now when all of the sudden, the P-3C that was monitoring the barrier gained contact. He went to the sonobuoy that was in contact with the nuclear sub. He placed four buoys at cardinal headings about the sonobuoy. The four contact buoys were five miles from datum. Only half of the buoys had contacts when the Tactical Coordinator recognized the phenomena of convergence zone detection. The area to the West of Sicily is Tunisia and Tunis to the North and Malta lies to the South. This stretch of the Mediterranean Sea is not as deep as in the Ionian Sea, for example, this length of water is filled with channels and faults along the ocean bottom. The ranges can go from three to four miles, but then again, we can see ranges brought down by waves and high seas states to one or even one and half miles. This is some thing to ponder about and I think the Tactical Support Center coming next year to Rota may solve some questions.

The subject of CINCLANTFLEET, drives to mind a message which was re-addressed to Rota ASCAC and then routed to CTF-67. The subject was addressing Lajes use of that favorite acronym, CTU 84.2.3. The fellows down at Norfolk were making modifications to the plan which enabled prosecution outside the coast of Spain and Portugal. In other words, if the Soviets were sending down a carrier to the Mediterranean, this gives us an excellent opportunity for Rota to send a P-3 to get a picture of the incoming vessel. But wait, this apparently was not going to work out, because Lajes, would have to send a complete message to CINCLANTFLEET requesting that this be done. I can not believe this type of arrangement will work. For example:

a. Rota sends a top priority message for setting up CTU 84.2.3.

b. Lajes sends a duplicate (almost) message to CINCLANTFLEET.

c. CINCLANTFLEET will send a yes to Lajes request and it will be eighteen hours-plus two hours later by the time Rota gets the feedback.

I spend an hour trying to resolve this. Lajes had a meeting next week and the bone of contention was our hangup on the Achilles' heel. We got invited to the meeting and sent BOQ reservations as Captain Bradley was coming. The meeting was called by the Rota Officer in Charge and he presented as an overview the interchange of efforts that would be solved by the COMSIXFLEET borrowing that strip of water for an Inchop unit that was Mediterranean bound. The Commanding Officer of Lajes explained that the squadron in Rota was split between the two OPCONS. The only problem lies in getting CINCLANT-FLEET approval of a direct line so that CTU 84.2.3 is more effective and thereby more reactive to an immediate use of the area. This meeting was ended leading a few dots of the eyes, etc., needed for the agreement. Hopefully, this chain will be worked out.

With spring turning into summer, Jane had found Carney Park, which was a crater fashioned and designed for golf, football, baseball, and a swimming pool. The facility was about fifteen or twenty minutes from the house. Beth and Anne were playing softball while Mike was playing baseball. They went to practice about twice a week and then they played games with other teams. Beth, I think, played first base and Anne was a second stringer. Anne tried so hard to hit the ball, but when she struck out she cries. Sometimes, especially on weekends I worked with Mike. He got upset too, but what the hell, its all in the game.

COMSIXFLEET put out a message called National Week. Immediately this exercise reminded me of last December 1974.

Sharply stated, the exercise would involve both carrier task forces, all available aircraft aboard ships including the P-3C squadron and the VQ-2 squadron at Rota, Spain. Reading into the text I determined what were the good Blue guys and who were the infamous Orange aggregate. On the pedestial was the Blue Commander on down to the Orange Leaders. Admiral Williams was one of the leaders who planned, and took care of the Orange air evolutions including submarines, surface ships, VQ-2 Martime Surveillance, and lastly, the P-3C squadron in Sigonella, Sicily. Captain Bradley brought this message up about 9:30 a.m. and he appointed me as Chief Planner and Commander of the Orange Air Forces.

Within a week of the initial message, the numbers of aircraft were assigned to the Orange. I countered by sending a message to all participants and wanted them to attend with plans, unique tactics or unknow tricks of the trade to be discussed in two weeks. The clan met and I introduced myself and the rest of the men did the same. VQ-2 began by sending down several Air Intelligence Officers. They would man the OPCON twenty four hours a day. They would help me brief, debrief, or anything that I might need done. Airplane wise, VQ-2 will send 2 P-3's and four A-3's. The submarine force will have two SSN attack boats as their main force with two simulated SSBN subs. The destroyer force consists of three ships. We decided that they must stay near land but the area in which the carriers will be is the Ionian Sea. We were given communication frequencies and the arrangements were to be sent by message in two weeks. Admiral Williams was briefed, so I went to Sigonella, Sicily on a afternoon flight. It was hot on the runway but I had a LTjg meet me from VQ-2. We chatted about the weather and I asked him if we were set up. He acknowledged that they were ready for the Commissar. Right across the squadron spaces the trailer was set up and the VQ-2 came to attention when I walked in. We sat down and went throught our plans including the communications. Athough several of the Orange planes were coming to join our superior force, we broke for some Cokes. When we were back I reopened the door to the surprise attack to be held the morning of the third day. All in all, at least three or more variations of launching airplanes were discussed. Finally, I popped the question, how about a zipped lip takeoff to desolate the Blue carrier force? Everyone liked the idea, but can we make it happen?

The next morning we set parameters for the zip launch. All available officers were assigned to do certain things; a. Check with Air

Operations; b. Flight planning concurrence; c. Sending out a truck at the head of the airplanes and; d. I will launch the raid by firing a flare. By early afternoon we had a "go" for the launch with certain parameters yet worked out. I swing by and talked to Pete Baxter about the Orange new tactic. Pete thought it was an excellent idea.

The final day before the raid kept the intelligence force busy with messages about Blue aggression with respect to Orange aircraft. In the meantime we were setting up points equidistant surrounding the Blue force three hundred and sixty degees on slides to show at brieftime which is 0700 a.m. tomorrow. The Commanding Officer of VQ-2 stopped by and we chatted for a while. He asked if we had any questions and I told him no. If not, the Captain told me he will be taking off at five o'clock in the morning trying to find both carriers. His flight will consist of mainly North and South courses concentrating on the movements of Blue ships in the Ionian Sea.

At six fortyfive in the morning I had finished my review of the slides and I was just about ready to go to the briefing room. VQ-2 brought before me a hat which was given to me as a true "Commissar." Each officer under me wore a Orange badge which showed their allegiance to me. As we proceeded to the briefing room we noticed a carrier jet making an approach to the landing field. I had a bright idea and quickly called Navy Security. A seven o'clock I walked in to the brief, "ATTENTION," the Lieutenent said. The room was silent, and with my hat on the LTjg shot me a salute. With his characteristic Russian remarks, I saluted him. After taking their seats, I began the brief with the Orange prospective. The political, intelligence, and now the brief turned to tactics. I threw off my hat and we got to the first slide as everyone paid attention. It showed the routes of flight and where to launch the missiles (fighter aircraft). With the Bear aircraft simulated by the 7 P-3C, the 1 VQ-2 P-3, and 2 other A-3 aircraft give ten launch sites for the missiles. The fighters, which will be missiles, will follow the "BEAR" aircraft to the launch point and then simulate a missle inbound to the carrier assigned. With all of the assignments accepted, I asked if they were ready for a "zipped lip" launch?

The brief broke up and the pilots went to file at operations. I went hustling back to the trailer to see if the VQ-2 plane had intercepted both carriers. Back in the OPCON they had intercepted one carrier and the position was put on plastic board so the aviators can copy it down! In my view, the Navy Security Officer was right, this is Orange country and the two aviators were being held pending the attack for landing because of low fuel. Now we have the information for the second carrier. At last I make the final check list and I must get to the tower to make this superior takeoff to surprise the Blue forces.

In the top of the tower there planes turning and believe it or not, the sign holders are making there money out there by each plane writing down the position of the appropriate carrier. The first Bear (P-3C) pulls out of the line and the jets which follow the airplane fall in behind the Orion. One by one they fall in line, 20 aircraft and a pickup truck leading the pack. Back in the tower the gun is ready and then a UHF1 broadcasted, " A radio check." With only a minute left on the clock, this means that a green smoke light will launch the aircraft. Plane after plane lifted off after the flare went off. I said a prayer for the Orange Air as I knew our luck has changed for the best!

Flights of four A-7's and A-6's came to break over Sigonella airfield a hour and a half later. To meet these individuals were the Orange Elite. Fighter pilots were without a doubt, the happiest beings I have ever seen. The same was in evidence when we saw the P-3C pass on there way to its' line. After debriefing the crews we thought that we had eight kills or hits on the carriers (4 hits per carrier). We waited until we got the umpire reports which showed that the 2 simulated submarines launched significant damage to the fleet.

The next morning I was flown by helicopter North of Palermo, Sicily to meet a carrier for a debrief of the exercise. Many Admirals were there but, I believe I was the only Orange representative present. I listened to all of the Blue forces wth juices flowing, but then it was my turn. I introduced myself and gave a quick analysis of the account. The actual evolution of the gala attack was told and the intercepts were the keys which we needed. We launched twenty aircraft and made a surprise attack on the two battle groups. A question interupted me, "How did you get the aircraft off the ground?," an Admiral asked. We employed a "zipped lip" takeoff procedure, which works quite well. It was time to quit and I saw Admiral Train (COMSIXTHFLEET) nodding his agreement. National Week was a boost to me and indeed strengthened my idea of being the Chief Planner and doer of the non-friendly Air Forces. Through ploys, gambits, or unique tactics, that's how to disable a unified command.

The most fun that we had this summer was when Bob and Edna came to see us. We met them in Naples and got all of their bags. On the way to our house we stopped and had dinner. This was a happy occasion. Bob tried everything particularly after I suggested what not to eat. That week Jane took them around the city and they saw Pompeii and many other sites. We all left for Rome and stayed at the hotel near the Pope's house.

Another vacationing duo was my Mom and Dad. They took a scenic tour which they left the trip that got them to Rome. The next day they took a train to Naples where I met them late in the evening. The children and Jane were very excited to see my folks. On the following day my parents were going to Florence by train. Mom was upset that the kids had to go to school and I had to go to work. Jane drove them to the train and we were to meet them this weekend.

We spent most of the weekend seeing the sights of Pompei and staring in the crater of Vesuvio watching numerous particles of lava. We drove along the roads alongside the sea cliffs which were scenic. Mom brought a table that was shipped back home along with several pictures of Naples and its' surroudings.

The final trip was to Rome to visit and then after two days they depart for home. We toured the Vatican, numerous places, and then back to the hotel. Interestingly, it was Mikes birthday (six years old). We had a great dinner in the hotel. We had what Mike wanted-Pizza! In essence, we had bits and pieces of Italian food. I arranged with the waiter to bring a birthday cake (candles included) after I gave him the high sign. All of a sudden the cake is brought out with the candles abazing! Three waiters savy in Italian sang as Mike blew out the candles. The cake was good, but a least half the cake was left. Finally, I stood up and invitited four teeagers who had been watching the celebration. They accepted the cake and congratulated Mike, even kissing on the cheek by the girls. Mom and Dad left the next day with fond memories.

The departure of rockets, five inch and two point five inch varieties, set the stage for Bull Pup missiles. We sent a message over to Wing Eleven in Jacksonville to see about fake Bull Pup missiles. This generated a lot of noise and COMSIXFLEET wanted to fire these in the Mediterranean Sea. VP-45 won the toss and fired four missiles which got great pictures of the event. LCDR Pete Baxter came up from Sigonella in a VP-45 plane with a crew that was shopping crazy. Pete had several questions but I understood most of the discrepancies. It was Tuesday before Thanksgiving so I promised I would have the answer tomorrow. The next day, I got in early to fire out some messages. The phone rang and I recognized the voice, it was the CO of VP-8 in Rota, Spain. "Congratulations on early selection as Commanding officer of a squadron," he said. I almost fell out of my chair! My office door opened, and the Chief Petty Officer said that the Admiral wanted to see me. After many well wishes, I finally gave Pete Baxter the right answer in my view.

I had told Jane to met me and Peter, and go to the NATO Officers Club for lunch. At twelve o'clock she pulled up and we had an additional guest for lunch. Jane had no idea what was coming. But I told her as we were going to the officers club. She nearly wrecked the Datsun. When we got out of the car, she embraced me and told me she was mighty proud!

Christmas was coming and Jane prepared a list for Sears in early November. The Christmas party for the CTF-67/COMFAIRMED was at the Cave in downtown Naples. It was something to be seen! Pete and Diane Baxter came and stayed with us. The party was going great until the Admiral was interrupted by a phone call. Admiral Williams came and spoke to us using the microphone. He told us that the carrier John F. Kennedy (CV 67) was in a collision with the Belknap "CG 26." The party came to an end as all hospitals were receiving casualties and even dead sailors from the Belknap. We sent the girls home and went back to CTF-67 to assist.

Apparently the Belknap was acting as a plane guard on the evening of the twenty second of November 1975. East of Sicily when the carrier hit the cruiser, she sideswiped all of the superstructure causing massive fires. The CV 67 has minor damage, loss of avaition fuel, and some smoke blacken the side of the carrier. I understand that the carrier was painted early in the morning to cover the scorch marks of the fire to fool the Russians. Finally, the cruiser was towed back to Philadelphia Naval Shipyard for repair on the twentieth of December 1975.

The phone was an important part in the Brittingham villa. Impromptu events, such as staying late at work, meet me at the officers club for happy hour, or just call and if you need anything now is the time to communicate. The winter months brought in a new squadron from Jacksonville. The Skipper was a Naval Flight Officer and he was well-equipped for the job. LCDR Steve Grant, another NFO was his Operations Officer. I went down to brief the squadron on things to do and to stay on the straight and narrow. Numerous questions came up in this group. I made note of these inquiries and told the officers they would be answered. I also planned to ask our intelligence officer, but I am certain these questions would be intercepted via the Commanding Officer s guidance.

A new order came down from London to train the Iran P-3 pilots and navigators. This concept was sold to the Iranian Air force as a package deal. The pilots went to VP-30 to learn the system and fly the airplanes. We were told we had three weeks to prepare for these lectures.

The Iranians were sharp people, who know the P-3 systems and were to perform surveillance with the P3A airplane. I spent about four days with them and we had a party with the eight officers. I asked many questions, mainly how these officers were to establish a wing or something of that nature. We were given inroads to basic setup, command and control, and we gave them some rank structure so that they could pattern their Air Force. The Iranian group was armed with everything under the sun. I think the Iranian Air Force has moved to look for the P-3A, possibly the introduction of things such as Bull Pups!

In the latter part of February 1975, the staff concentrated on the new ASW prosecution policy. This was a delicate, but delinquent task that had everyone upset. After two days of discussion we drafted a message and the matter went to Sixth Fleet. Within two days, it was know as the new, prosecution policy for all areas of the Mediterranean Sea.

The number of Task Force Sixty Seven was rapidly reduced to twelve bodies. Admiral Charles Williams was one of the numbers including the aide which went from eighteen down to ten officers. I was a senior member drafting the operational order and I was busy as an Apache scout. The plan in theory was to assign Rota and Sigonella under the Sixty Seventh organization. The squadrons and the Tactical Support Centers would get together and decide what missions they are going to fly the next day. They would send it backchannel so the AIO and Operational Officer could review it. If it sat well with Sixty Seven, the Greens designing the missions would be forthcoming. Aboveboard, this idea may seem like a dumb thing to do. Almost always, a problem appears in the plan. Several of my workers were non-committal. Finally the controversy was settled and we forwarded our proposal up the chain of command.

The second National Week was scheduled this spring and I grabbed the Orange ring. We had a meeting which provided all of the Orange players with many ideas. The Blue force was to be in the

Tyrrhenian sea between Italy on the East coast, France on the North, Sardinia on the West and Sicily on the South. Two options came up first. We decided that the German made Italian aircraft in Sigonella would offer NATO chance to fly in National Week. Another choice is why not have the Air Force F-4C or G fly using their jets as missiles. The F-4 is ECM detector and can jam or use as a impetus to destroy the adversary. I drafted a message to Avianno Air Force Base requesting that they play in an Orange role. If they were interested, I would certainly come and brief them. The submarine force looked good, the VQ-2 had Air Intelligence Officers and briefs coming to Sigonella. The rest of the gang seemed pleased and went back to mobilize their plans. Three days later the Avianno Air Force sent a message, they wanted to participate. I called the Air Force and agreed that we would meet them next Wednesday. Two pilots and myself hopped into a S-2F and started flying to their airbase. We had a hell of a time flying up there because of the weather. After two hours we finally landed and a Major met me at the plane. At the hanger I was met by approximately twenty five people. I began my brief giving all the details. The Blue force, which the Air Force wanted no part of, listened very closely to detail. I suggested they rendezvous with the A-3 aircraft and lead them home to the nearest carrier. Well it was quiet; I thought I had my fly unzipped! The Colonel stood up and congratulated me and said they wanted the job. He appreciated the interest in their work which has worked beautifully. Next came lunch and the final hour and a half was spent working out communication plans and backups.

In the National Week three destroyers were given to the Orange. Three representatives visited our staff and they were excited. They had formed several schemes to move to another island where the ships would hide out North of Sicily. The Islands North of Sicily are known as Isole Eolie. This armada of islands, I believe there are five, is where the ships will hide until the Orange declares war on the Blue Force. These three ships will be incognito during the exercise. Finally, all was planned and checked. I flew down to Sigonella and the VQ-2 gang was there to meet me.

The first day of the National Week is usually hectic. The P-3C forces are supposed to find the carriers and more or less stand abreast of the carrier. After about an hour and a half the carrier transmitter on guard asks the P3 to identify. He said nothing, and about fifteen minutes later , two F-4s' accompany the P-3C offstation. The neatest thing was a Rota contingency which took off from Rota which was about three hours away. The squadron Operations Officer launched a P-3B and he did rig the carrier and returned to Rota. I think that was a complete surprise and well executed. The second day of the exercise was lousy weather. The low clouds and intermittent weather caused the first launch to be recalled. The next day we tried everything that didn't work the first day. Our Orange net was working and the Air Force was due to launch in an hour and a half. I finally called Avianno and got a roger which meant "all clear." The A-3 was sitting outside the western coasts of Italy when they held radar contact of twelve F-4Gs. I don't know what happened, but I caught the carriers fueling and the F-4G plowed the way for the Orange. When the noise settled we heard on the radio how the Blue carriers took the bulk of the Air Force F-4s. The Orange overall was remarkable on effectiveness and the attacks were powerful. The umpires were all confused and they said the A-3/F4 violated the airspace requirement. Anyway, the Orange still looked victorious.

I promised my family that I would go on leave for a week. We called several places in the Alps and made reservations. We left on Sunday, Easter day. We traveled to Northern Italy and made a stop near the hotel. We went to a restaurant and had pasta, pizza and several salads. Of course, we had wine which made the day. The next morning we go off at nine o'clock. We left Italy and entered Switzerland. The weather was hot and we had lunch in town. When we broke across the German line we never forgot the way the fields look. Hay was stacked, logs were cut and placed in piles, and the cows were busy chewing their curds.

Garmisch was a small town in Germany where the Army kept the town busy with tourist skiing or just plain vacation. We arrived at three o'clock. I went in and asked for lodging. About thirty minutes later we had a room. The facilities were nice and we roamed the town and we got back to supper as the doors opened. We dined on sour braten and numerous greens. The wine was good and enough said, I got a little drunk. The next day we took an excursion trip which included a house which had a monster house which was the hit of the day. Wednesday we left the Alps and proceeded east to Munich, Germany. This was quite a sight. The city was beautiful and the directions to the Army facility was easy to get to. We stopped at the hotel and I went in to confirm our reservations. We were booked and the gang helped me take the luggage in. We spent many hours touring Munich and bypassing numerous German prisoner of war camps which the children were apprehensive about which caused Jane and I to discuss these camps. Beth, Anne and Mike were strangely silent. It was as though they understood the immensity of the atrocity that had occurred at these camps. After I had reassured them of their safety, coupled with Jane's assurances, the kids returned to their jovial frames of mind.

The next morning it was snowing. Venice was the place we were headed. We headed South and once we got into Italy we turned to the left and headed straight for the famous city. It was raining when we got there. We parked in a garage and took a bag and rode in the boats to the hotel. After checking in, we hit the streets. What a beautiful city. The shopping was tremendous with shops all over the place. We had supper overlooking the waterway and then wandered back to the hotel. It was a shame that it had to rain, but I have to start heading back to Naples the next morning. Believe me sports fans that is the last day I can call my own.

The next exercise which comes to mind is the Command Exercise which is run by the Joint Chief of Staffs. With NATO being a viable command we play this religiously. The blackout starts in the Black Sea and soon it's throughout the Mediterranean. We launch the P-3C aircraft and they sight snorkeling submarines. The setting gets hostile and soon major forces come into the Mediterranean Sea. Immediately the secure phone starts ringing. The mining officer will check to see if a certain area is all right to mine if necessary. I walk down to my office (I'm the mining officer) and got the safe open. I looked and there was no number or slot available. I went back upstairs and called London. He was interested in mining a certain field in the Red Sea just before it became the Indian Ocean. This was a narrow opening to the ocean with at least 70 miles in diameter. The Soviet force, which was moving helter-skelter toward Egypt, told the whole story. I launched the P-3C squadron to Iran while a big Air Force plane moved the mines to Bandar Abbas, Iran. The planning of the men involved in the aircraft were kept to a minimum. The mines were late World War II vintage and should be dropped at the entrance or just prior to the Indian Ocean. The planes took off loaded like pregnant pigs. The mines were dropped at Bab el Mandeb, which is the strait that passes through Djibouti and Yemen along the Red Sea. The mines brought havoc with the Soviet Task Force. And waiting for this armada was the Navy's best carrier full of jets which capitalized a victory for the allies. When this was over I went home and to bed. The next day, I was called to the Admiral's office. Captain Bradley and I were ushered in. Admiral Williams stood up and congratulated me. He spoke of many Admirals' opinions and said there would be a message coming about my aggressive and unrelenting devotion to duty.

Jane had planned to go to the Soviet Union. Diane Baxter talked her into visiting that country even with the threat of incarceration for spying while you are there. Jane and Diane left Naples early Sunday afternoon. They stopped in Rome and got a four engine Russian jet airliner which took the group to Stalingrad. They changed planes for the final time and proceeded to Leningrad. There were few tourists but a plane full of Navy and other services' personnel. From the first day they entered the hotel room, they quietly looked around and found microphones monitoring their very presence. They went on tours the next day and found some black market Soviet Navy belts which they bought. On Wednesday after two nights of the Russian Ballet, the wives boarded a puddle jumper and headed back to Moscow.

Back in Naples, Italy, I was taking care of the children. I had to go to Rota, Spain on Monday and Capt. Bradley was going to be present at the CTU84.2.3 conference called by the Navy Lajes Sector Commander. We left by jet early Monday morning and we made it in good time. The Captain and I were seated in the meeting. The argument went smoothly and the agreement was signed, sealed and delivered. The only thing remaining was if the "players" really made the system work. We went to an additional meeting where I had the pleasure of meeting Bob Prehn. Bob had assumed command of VP-11, yet he had to fight like hell to survive. Commander Joe Kuckelkorn was Skipper when Bob was Executive Officer. There was, let's put it nicely, a degree of animosity generated between these two individuals. Bob shared with me all the events, but he assumed Command and the squadron has been "on a roll."

The plane landed in Naples about ten o'clock in the evening. The next morning I awoke with the phone ringing. Mike spent the night with some friend. The babysitter said he had a terrific earache. I knocked on the door about thirty minutes later. Mike was in bad shape; he was destined to visit the hospital. The results were a infected eardrum and sore tonsils. They took throat cultures and many prescriptions were written. After that deserved duty was accomplished, we hit the Navy exchange for some toys! I spend the rest of the week with the kids. We had meals via our grill just about every night and the girls practiced softball and Mike played baseball.

Sunday afternoon Jane and Diane came back from Russia. She looked tired but happy. The children greeted her and then she gave them some momentos of her trip. She gave me two Soviet Navy belts with a brass emblem depicting the Russian Star mounted on the head of an anchor. Jane went on about the details of the trip when the children went to sleep. Many stories are not well known, but you are interested in what your wife has just seen.

The fourth of July is the two hundred birthday celebration of our country. I was watching the Echo II about to come into the Mediterranean. Commander Prehn was about to unleash his troops to get contact. To slay the 'giant', one must know what to do with the entrance into the Mediterranean Sea. This is a channel separating Europe and Northwestern Africa and connecting the Atlantic Ocean with the Mediterranean Sea. It's significant crossroads location gives the straits both strategic and commercial importance. About thirty-six miles wide at the Western end and about eight miles wide at it's narrowest point. It is deepest in the East and shallow where it is 1050 feet.

The channel has great oceanographic prospective. The surface water moves Eastward from the Atlantic at a deep of 525 feet. Because of the denser more saline water, it flows Westward into the Atlantic Ocean. This phenomenon ventilates the Mediterranean and the more abundant surface event is favorable to fish life. An additional reason is that the sill shuts out the cold Atlantic which keeps the Mediterranean relatively warm, particularly the warm bottom depths.

Back at headquarters the calendar said 3 July and of course tomorrow is a holiday and I am the Command Duty Officer. VP-11 started their barriers early this morning and no contact as of yet. The covered phone rang about three o'clock and VP-11 has contact. The Tactical Support Officer said the contact was called after the crew debriefed. The P-3B was the aircraft that the squadron flew. Incidentally I knew what squadron I would get; I guessed the number. They have contact all night with various "closet point of approach."

The operational control was busy as I walked into CTF 67 on July the fourth. The duty officer briefed me and I went to get the intelligence brief. The VP-11 Extendex began outside in the Atlantic. Rota had initialized CTU 84.2.3 procedures and the Echo II was approaching the Straits. I looked very closely at the briefed sorties and the target was to break the straits about noon whereby, he proceeded into the Mediterranean. I worked in my office until noon and went home for lunch. I was hot so I stocked up on water and bought a case of Coca Cola and headed home. Everyone was hot and needed ice, but the Coke was the main seller. We were going to Carney Park picnic area for a feast and so were the rest of the Armed Forces to celebrate the second centennial. The Duty Officer back at CTF 67 knew I was supposed to call him at least every hour. We had a sequence where I would ask him if the rooster crowed. He would say yes, which would mean the contact, or the submarine is still in contact. That's good enough for me.

The middle of the afternoon we arrived at the park. The children went swimming and of course I was dressed in my khaki uniform. There was a massive crowd building at the massive dome of the crater. I checked every hour and the duty officer said all is well. I was worried about the submarine but at 5:00 p.m. the reply was what I expected. That night provided the most beautiful display of fireworks. It was so dry that the shooting rockets caught the rim of the trees on fire and it was rapidly put out. Aboveboard the crowd was large, and it took us nearly an hour to get home.

At the onset of summer the time went by fast and the orders were coming so I could start training before I became Executive Officer. The next thing I was involved in was Admiral Dick Hedges visit to Naples. Admiral Hedges is the new COMPATWINGSLANT boss who came from the West coast . He would be in Sigonella visiting the Jacksonville squadron and he was due to arrive in two weeks. Adm. Williams saw me and gave me his crew/boat to go to the Isle of Capri. Additionally I was going to have a party for the staff with Admiral Hedges and his wife Phillis as guests.

Admiral Hedges and his aide were met when the squadron plane landed at Naples. The CTF-67 staff briefed the admiral and the entire staff went to the officers club for lunch. That night Adm. Williams and wife hosted a buffet and Jane and I were invited. The next morning a party of eight left aboard the Navy cruiser for the Isle of Capri. We had the Hedges, the aide and wife, Jane and me of course, and Mrs. Williams. We had several Bloody Mary's and Jane became ill. Capri was beautiful. We had lunch and we spent some time shopping. The time was growing short because we had to be back at five o'clock. Jane had to get back to our house and get dinner ready. We spilt up and let the girls go on the hydrofoil. We arrived back at Naples at 5:00 p.m.

The Admiral enjoyed the trip and really showed an interest in me. The Chief who was in charge of the boat and his crew got a "Well Done," and I give him all that was left of the booze and beer.

I got to the house carrying ice and the other essentials. The party was supposed to start at seven o'clock and the children were really helping Jane. I went upstairs and did a quick change and then lit the barbecue. The first order of business was to fix pork ribs as appetizers and serve barbecue chicken as dinner. We had white wine which I got downtown for eighty cents and of course beer. Admiral Williams and Admiral Hedges arrived at seven fifteen and we had a grand time. My house overlooks the Tyrrhenian Sea. Sun was setting and the crowd of some twenty five were having a super outing. The party was great and competition excelled the level of wine that was poured freely. Admiral Hedges had to leave about 10:00 p.m. He gave Jane and I a compliment that I will never forget. The party continued until eleven o'clock and when the front door was closed; we gladly sat down in exhaustion.

The latter part of September would never be repeated again. For instance:

1) Commander Bob Prehn had received orders to NATO Commander of which Admiral Williams was head. Bob snagged a flight over to Naples to get a job check out. Mainly he wanted to find a house to rent. I met with him for two days and showed him around. He was due back the tenth of October with his wife and kids.

2) As Air Plans Officer I was head of all operations. With CTF-67 in a sour mood, I took over the vacant Captains ACOS (Assistant Chief of Staff) billet taking over added responsibilities which gave a more cohesive approach which outlined the increase in the theater capabilities by the Patrol squadrons in the Mediterranean. Also I was vitally interested in producing Tactical updates which I forwarded to COMPATWINGSLANT for consideration. It never gets dark enough when you go home to realize you have accomplished something.

3) I have expected the worst to come of this, but the Commander that became Captain (he rented my house)

called me and asked when I planned to come home! I told him I would be home before Christmas. The problem I have is where are my orders? I received a call at the end of September and this is what I was appraised of. The house had been empty for almost two months. The next door neighbors found that the furnace was out of fuel and it was time for the burner to be running. I was so pissed off I could not see straight. I called Don McKissock and told him to get the key to the house and assess the damage. In the meantime I wrote the bank and enclosed two months of mortgage payments. I appreciated all that they have done and mentioned that I would be home for Christmas.

4) Orders came the first part of October. I took the orders and had them processed. The orders finalized the dates for moving and the dates for moving out of the house and into a hotel across from the base complex. That night Jane and the children celebrated with dinner out.

In October we met Barbara and Bob Prehn with family. We looked and looked for a place to rent, but the Prehns rented a nice house almost to the fifteen mile marker North of Naples. We helped them move and then it was there turn to help us.

CTF-67 was not in a good mood about this time. Admiral Williams was going to be relived by Admiral McLaughlin. Another fly in the ointment was Mike Brittingham was leaving, and heavens to betsy, among other things, who was ordered in for AOCS for Plans? This required numerous heads to be placed in consultation and finally the decision was forthcoming. Captain Bradley called me in and said that Washington had orders replacing me in January 1977. He wondered if Bob Prehn could be moved over to my job. The light flashed a brief nanosecond and I was in favor of this brilliant analysis.

Bob was happy as I ferried him to Sigonella and Rota. We worked hard together to learn the tricks of the trade and finished all the things that I had running smoothly. With only one month left it was time to move out of the house that we rented. Bob and his family came over and the big decision was, what to do with the cats? The mother cat had five or six kittens in Mike's bedroom. He came downstairs and he said there was something in his bedroom. Jane and I went upstairs and found the mother cat and the kittens in the chest. Meanwhile, Bob and

I had decided to take the cat out to a farmhouse. We have really had a mess of cats and dogs near, around, or inside the house.

The last month was busy getting airline tickets, passports, shipping the car back home, and each of us getting one more real Italian dinner under our belts. The children were going to miss Naples. We were going to miss speaking the language and visiting Carney Park. Next came the packing and just how much they can carry. The next event was the good-by party of Commander Task Force Sixty Seven. The party was held in the NATO Officers Club. The invitees were Sigonella and Rota. The best and probably the worst missed was the men who kept the squadron and Tactical Support Centers running. Tonight was special because I believed this was the beginning of how to take control of a squadron. I have looked at various times, and at different conditions those factions which made the deciding influence on which parameters are made. The steps, these elements of fact or denial; are yet to be consummated without additional study. I am almost ready for the duties of the Executive Officer of VP-11.

Looking back over the past twenty two months, I have been a tired puppy dog. I have taken one week of leave and vacation when we went to Germany and Venice. Essentially, I have been in the thick and thin of things from the Plans Officer to Asst. Chief of Staff of Plans. I have embarked on any and all endeavors which made this job a Godspeed. The outpour from COMSIXFLEET about the firepower of the P-3 aircraft caused an uproar about the weapons that are no longer used by the Orion. The new awakening caused the first Bullpup firing in 1975 by VP-45. CTF-67 also put its new sword in its recommendations for the new ASW Prosecution Policy for the Sixth Fleet Maritime Patrol Aircraft. My experience in Command and Control, specifically National Week Exercises, clearly tells the story of how an innovation excels when the Orange Air depends on tenacity and fortitude against the Blue carriers. The work of VQ-2 intelligence and the conniving techniques that they put together equal the sum of a predetermined course of events. I will never forget when I led the first launch on the two Blue carriers!. All in all, this has been a great experience with a great shortfall in staff. I have helped the staff reduce, wrote a new CTF-67 Operational Order, wrote Atlantic and Mediterranean Bilateral Agreements which can correlate contact quicker in this situation. Finally, I am ready to come back to this deployment area as a Executive Officer of a squadron, where this is the toughest area to get LOFAR contact on any submarine.

Bob Prehn took us to the airport in Naples to begin the long trip home. We have incorporated the luggage so that I can carry two large suitcases and go back for more. Bob broke open the champagne and we drank to "Bona Napoli." We boarded the plane and we were off to Rome. We finally got all of our bags positioned from the Naples flight to the 747. There was a two hour delay in the flights so we had sweet buns, Cappuccino, and the children had Cokes. Finally, the airplane started loading passengers and we took off heading for the big USA.

The flight was fun part of the way. Two movies, several music stations, magazines, etc. were waiting for anxious customers. After about four hours I took a nap. I woke up with a start and I found my restless four asleep! I got up and went to the restroom and washed up and felt better. I found a stewardess who had a cup of coffee and ask when would we land. She contacted the pilot and relayed three and a half hours. I walked back to our seats and found Beth awake. I walked her to the restroom and then to get some milk.

New York City was a maze of small pin lights. The time was about eight o'clock when we started making our approach. After landing we taxied to the ramp. The customs were the next event. I had briefed my family on everything. The bags showed up and Mike let us know where they were. We all gathered around the luggage and Anne bless her heart, carried her fair share. The wait in front of the customs man was forever. He was a nice man who wanted all the bags opened. He wanted to know how much this and that. We picked up the pieces and walked out to the taxicabs. I got a taxi but first I wanted a room. The driver contacted a Holiday Inn that had a vacancy. I do not know how we made it across the globe, but we made the test and that Virginia Gentleman sure tasted good.

The next day we had to get the Newark Airport for a flight to Portland. Also on the list for today was to call the automobile facility in New Jersey about my Datsun. The transmission was not too clear with the car people, but I was told that the car had not arrived. With the baggage assembled, we got a taxi to the airport. I stood in line to see what flights would get us to Portland and then I called Don McKissock to see if he can meet us. We were all set to leave after lunch. The view was stupendous from the airplane and I kept looking for signs of snow. Snow was certainly covering the ground in the Northeastern part of the United States. In all actuality, the white stuff had not fallen but in the form of flurries. We will see a lot more come the latter part of December.

Nothing looked so good as the site of the kids embracing Don and Lee. It reminded me of our last visit with them. Beth, Anne, and Mike were really excited about everything including the farm, houses, and the blueberries growing in the back of their farm. The things were loaded in both cars because they could not carry all that luggage with one car. Don, Mike, Jr. and myself rode in Don's truck. We talked about everything including how Mike can play hockey the rest of the season. As we get closer to Brunswick, Don discussed the squadron deployment. Surely, he could talk all day but that did not budge him in the least. Brunswick was just like we left it. We crossed over the Androscoggin River into Topsham to our house. Then we turned left outside of Topsham and headed to the farm known as Maple View Farm, which is McKissock's farm. Lee drove right behind us and stopped in front of the farmhouse. We unloaded the truck and went inside. I hugged Lee because she was special to us. Don had taken off his coat and was making dry martinis. We drank for about an hour starting a fire in his brand new den. Mike was in charge of keeping logs on the fire. Dinner was super and by nine o'clock I was in bed.

The weekend was upon us and the next day we did grocery shopping for the McKissocks. In the afternoon, we had to go by the house. Don had the keys and we got there about two pm. The house looked okay, but when we went inside, I could not believe the mess. The floors and the house in general was in need of being cleaned up before the movers come. The upstairs bedrooms must have had many pictures up on the wall. It looks like they put toothpaste in the nail holes. This made a total of three rooms that needed to be painted. I looked out the kitchen window, which showed the backyard, and it resembled a garden which had been left since last summer to rot! Sunday we spent the whole day painting and cleaning up the plague that has invaded the house for the last year and half.

Monday, Jane went with the children and got them enrolled in class. In the meantime, I went to the housing officer. I gave them my orders and our household goods were here. Wednesday was the big day so I got all the paperwork ready and we should expect the movers at eight o'clock in the morning. Next we went to Sears. I have been advised by Jane to get some caulking materials and other necessities. Afterward, I went to the bank and the loan officer recognized me and we had a long chat. The mortgage was caught up and I did ask what if I decided to add on to the house. He gave me some pamphlets to look at.

The movers arrived at eight in the morning on Wednesday. The men were friendly and welcomed the coffee we had. It's amazing once you see the furniture again; it seems like the furniture was moved ten times already. It was cold outside but the movers did not mind the blustery weather. Jane went for sandwiches. At last the movers came in with the last item. We checked things out and we settled up and signed on the dotted line. As they pulled out I was tired and I knew Jane was also. The kids were home from school and were upstairs putting away their things. I was putting up the pictures in the living room and in the first floor hallway I put up a mirror on the wall.

On Thursday I got a call from the Housing Office that my car is ready in New Jersey. The man gave me the number, so I thought I would call them. The car had in fact arrived without any damage. I called VP-11 and asked if I can speak to the Executive Officer. He was not in but I spoke to the Duty Office. I was wondering if they had a local flight that could drop me off near the car at McGuire Air Force Base. Friday morning it was a cold day, but no snow. The airplane took off and we arrived at the Air Force facility about ten thirty. The transportation met me there and I met the man with my car at 11:30 a.m. It took about an hour to get the car and put gas in the tank. I cleared with the man and I headed for Maine. I turned on the radio and the weather was a mess. I finally got out of New York and things calmed down. Boston's weather was starting to come in with freezing rain. Now how could that happen. It was seven o'clock when I found a Howard Johnson's to stop for dinner. I called Jane and said that I was just North of Boston and I will be there around eleven or twelve o'clock.

I got back on the road and it was sleeting. The speed I was traveling began to fall as I entered New Hampshire. The sleet and freezing rain increased and I was greeted by cars skidding off the road and trucks throwing sand on the road. Speed was about forty-five miles an hour as I approached the main bridge at Portsmouth, New Hampshire near the state line of Maine. It was slick as hell, but I kept driving. The roads were covered with sand and had the sleet partially ploughed into slush. I got off and paid the toll and was twenty-five miles from the house. Finally I arrived at Brunswick and was relieved. As I passed over the river to Topsham I noticed the radio died. That puzzled me. I continued under the railroad underpass to the right turn that brought me into my subdivision. The lights were out as I continued to drive toward the driveway. After I turned into the driveway, the Datsun died.

Apparently the battery was dead, possibly the alternator. I got out of the car, locked it and opened the door to the house, and locked the door. I quickly fell asleep.

Tex's Getty service station had the Datsun in the morning. The car needed a new alternator. We went Christmas shopping for the first time after dinner. I bought a new television at Sears and Jane bought several gifts for her Aunts and Uncles. We got home about 9:15 p.m. and Mike helped hold open the door while I brought the TV set in. The next day I hooked up the cable outside on top of the garage roof.

Mom and Dad arrived over the holiday season. We had a difficult time meeting them. At first we were to meet them at four thirty in the afternoon at Portland Airport. Snow had all ready saturated the Maine area. The plane landed and we expected them to appear, but they were not on the airplane. I became worried and with the kids wondering where, why and what. I went to seek some help. Finally I got a clerk to query Boston about Mom and Dad. The only information that the clerk could find out was there was puddlejumper that was headed for Portland and should arrive in 45 minutes. Being two hours late could mean a late flight or whatever the delay may mean. Finally at 6:35 p.m. a small plane with two turboprop engines landed. Mother of God they were on this plane. The children were happy and boy were grandparents happy to see them.

It was a happy occasion to celebrate Christmas in Topsham with my parents. We had a tree decorated, and all the presents wrapped. Decorations were scattered throughout the house. Dad unpacked his suitcase to find a broken Virginia Gentleman with only the smell remaining. We laughed at that a hundred times. The snow fell the first four days that my folks were here. We went to the First Parish Church for Christmas Eve services presented by my favorite minister, John Wild. Christmas morning came quickly as the children wanted to go downstairs. The tree was overburdened with lights and candy canes with glowing red and white stripes. Mom and Dad left us several days after Christmas. This was the third or fourth day of snow showers that encompassed the Maine area.

The day after the New Year I went to work at Wingslant headquarters. I checked in at the front desk which issued a badge and I went upstairs to the Administrative Office. The Chief took all my orders and directed me to see the Chief of Staff Captain Dick Zeisel. I shook his hand gladly as I knew he had something to do with me getting command. We talked for twenty minutes, and I was very impressed with his topics of conversation. He told me the story of my deep selection as LCDR for Command. I was down to one other pilot in the Navy, but the Captain turned the tide. He was interested in CTF Sixty-Seven. I told him about the short-staffed status of it, but I think the system will work out. Captain Zeisel got down to brass tacks as he talked about what he wanted me to do in four weeks. The PATWINGSLANT Readiness Manual had been taking hits everyday and he wanted me to share my thoughts, changes to the qualifications exercises, and anything that must be addressed in this manual. With that said, he stood up and shook my hand and I departed. The room where my desk sat, took a small space in this room of computers and printers.

The major brunt of the readiness manual was to define, classify, and measure the productivity of a squadron. Specifically it gave the number of crews that you have; the number of Alpha, Bravo, etc. crews and what each crew's readiness is. The last portion of the manual is the exercise manual. Nuclear subs are just about all that we have in 1977 and beyond. I intend to revamp the qual system and try to sell the plan.

The next week I spent many hours changing different approaches to readiness interspersed with many comments interwoven by officers of this command. These officers are those visible of assuming flag rank which would surely give their comments careful consideration. Several squadrons came to Topsham to let the Admiral Dick Hedges hear their post deployment brief. I sat in on the brief that turned out to be very informative. After two weeks of experimentation I settled down and started to write my report.

I went home in the snow at the end of the week. The radio was on, so I listened to the weather forecast of more snow. For the last two weeks we have had snow rising above the cars. Currently, we have six inches with more coming. About a week later the snow was worse. I went downstairs and turned up the heat. Something fell by me and when I looked up, the ceiling was wet. The roof was pulling in water and it was flowing down like curtains along the walls of the house. I called Ray Riendeau, the builder to come over that day. He went upstairs and looked into Beth's closet. He removed the ceiling which yielded the attic. I got a ladder and we both went into the attic for a look. I was amazed by what I saw. The ice on the roof had worked under the shingles and was actually dripping down the walls. We stopped the majority of leaks at present, but Ray suggested that I climb a ladder and remove the ice and snow about two feet from the edge of the roof. He said he would bring a ladder later on in the day.

Saturday it was beautiful and cold as a hell. The ladder was a long ladder which was difficult to move in fifty inches of hard packed snow. Once I got the ladder on the roof I began my perilous climb up the ladder. The climb up the ladder could lead to a fall that I could not afford. On my left arm was a snow shovel and my right a small sharp ax. I began shifting the ladder and that takes me to the ice buildup approximately two or three inches thick. All in all, it took me about fifteen minutes to clear a path out two feet up the roof and the distance left and right was approximately four feet. After three hours of climbing up and down and moving the dam ladder, I was exhausted. At 4:00 p.m., the sun was setting and it still was below freezing, but I am finished with the front roof and tomorrow I have the back roof to look forward to.

Sunday after church, I had Beth change clothes and come out and watch me climb up the ladder. I put my boots on and we went outside, got the ladder, Beth on one end and I on the other. We carry the ladder around the house and there I raised it to the top of the roof. I told Beth what to do if she saw me fall. I started up the ladder with the snow shovel,the ax, and the ladder started moving. I stopped and tried to move the ladder but to no avail. Instead of snow shovel first, I took the ax and chopped near the ladder. The ice gave way and the ladder fell onto the roof. Then I started chopping on the left side of the ladder and the ladder was stabilized. I told Beth that I was all right and for her to go in. I do not know how I did the back of the roof but I was cold; just as cold as an ice man.

Finally I finished up my work on the Readiness Manual. The typist they gave me was sharp. I gave a short report of what I would do to the techniques and how I would correct the various readiness qualifications in the manual. There were few questions that I left unanswered. The time had come to pack up my bags and head for VP-30 Training Squadron. Jane and her siblings were not in favor of my departure. I took off the first Sunday in February to go to Jacksonville, Florida.

CHAPTER 11

NAVAL AIR STATION JACKSONVILLE, FL

Patrol Wing Eleven is situated in Jacksonville where it is responsible for six P3C squadrons. Additionally, it also has VP-30 there which trains people before they go to the squadron. We landed in the afternoon in warm weather. The Duty driver carried my luggage to the BOQ where I checked in. After filling out a form the driver took me even further down the road until we came upon nice quarters. I took my baggage to my room. Well it was not bad and I had a nice view of the St. Johns River. After putting away my gear, I went down to check the flight schedule. They had a new class beginning at 8:30 a.m. so I was about to go upstairs when I heard someone yell my name. It was Pete Baxter who was in the same class as me. We sat down and talked about who, how, and where the war has been going. Pete got orders right after I left Naples, Italy and left sometime in January. The class, as Pete understood it, was to meet at 8:30. I asked if I could ride with Pete because I was going to buy a used car.

Our introduction to VP-30 was led by their Commanding Officer, Captain Castle, who told those present that we were among the experts of antisubmarine warfare. Additionally, he said when we left VP-30 we would fit right in to your squadron. These were heady words I wrote that down as we started FAETULANT. The first subject that we had was nuclear weapons. This was a short course, yet the volume of information was intense. At the end of the course we had a period of study, questions concerning them, and finally the test. All of us passed. Then the P-3B made center stage when we went through the parameters of engines, turboprop propellers, generators, and the various busses that the systems generate power. The systems came back and stayed in the back of my mind.

VP-30 made me the coordinator for the flights going to Brunswick Friday and returning on Sunday. I generally went up every weekend so I was in my flight suit every Friday evening. The children were glad to see me. The news was not all glad as I gathered all of my tax documents and submitted them to the income tax people whom I would be hearing from shortly, according to them. After a month of riding with Pete Baxter, I found a used car priced at $800. I called to make arrangements to see the car. It was a green, four cylinder, Chevrolet station wagon. I looked over the car and decided I was interested, but wanted them to hold it until tomorrow. I told Pete about the car and he seemed excited about the idea. I bought and registered it in the state of Florida.

Jim Hagy surprised me in the Navy Exchange when I saw him. He told me to come down to the hanger and see him. Ron Martin from VP-49 was also here as the Operations Officer. One night Pete and I had an exam on the characteristics of the navigation inertial systems and we went to the Officers Club. About two hours later we went bar hopping. The second place we stopped had a terrific band. Finally I got this idea to call Jim and Judy. They arrived about an hour later. We were glad to see them as we were leaving in seven weeks for the squadron and Jim did not know which way he was headed for orders. Judy called Jane and the gang invited them down for Easter vacation. They decided to come down on Friday afternoon and leave Sunday afternoon. For some reason, we had a navigation dry swim to turn in on Monday morning. I met the airplane at the Jacksonville airport. We met Jim and kids at their house. I think that was the last time I saw the kids for two hours. Judy and Jim unloaded the car and who should show up but Ron and Jordan Martin. Talk, a trivial word, was vital to snatch all the gossip or rumors which reveals personal facts. Jim and I started the barbecue and continued drinking while we talked about killing submarines. It was after midnight when we got the children to bed. We agreed that at 6:00 a.m. we would get everybody up and head South for Orlando, Florida, i.e. Disney World.

At 5:30 a.m. it was get up or, well we were upon and praying for the coffee maker to finish making the coffee. I did not have the only headache among four adults. Finally everybody was ready, teeth brushed and we piled into Jim's station wagon, and off we went. The town of Orange Park was quiet at 7:00 a.m. on Saturday. Dunkin'

Donuts was the only shop open for our donuts and coffee. We got to Orlando in about two hours. We parked some distance from the park but the shuttle buses took you right to the front gate. Before leaving the kids, Beth and Alison were appointed leaders of the three. They were supposed to monitor the kids and maintain their whereabouts. Jane and I rode just about everything. We stopped and had a burger and fries with a Coke. We wandered all over the park. Jim and I sat in a rest area. About ten minutes later, I noticed a Dixieland Band playing, getting louder by the second. I turned my head and just to the left a New Orleans jazz band was rising up from the depths of the ground. I think the best ride that I had was around five o'clock that afternoon. Mike, Jr. really liked this ride, its a shame he did not notice that I was scared to death. After dinner we saw the rest of the amusement park. At 10:00 p.m. we saw the final finale, the big production of fireworks. After the loud booms we walked back to the cars. Just about everyone fell asleep on the way home. I talked to Jim and he nodded his head. I quit talking and I looked at Jim and he was fast asleep. The car was drifting to my side of the road, so I gripped the wheel and steered the car. I hit Jim on the side and he woke with a start. Jim thanked me and I asked if he wanted me to drive. He thought he could hack it.

It was at least 12:30 or 1:00 a.m. by the time we called "lights out!" I woke up at 8:00 a.m. and Beth wanted to know what we are going to eat for breakfast. Jane and the children were taking off around 4:00 p.m. in the afternoon. All of us said our good-byes and thanked them for a great visit. I sadly kissed Jane and the children good-by at the airport. I got back home close to 6:00 p.m. and I had to start on my dry swim. Believe me, I have not worked so hard before. At midnight I had a page to go, so I took a break for some Coor's Beer before I finished the dry swim. My lights went off at one thirty in the morning. Thank God my alarm went off and I think I woke up in the shower.

Today's lesson was advertised as navigation systems. We turned in our dry swim and mother of God, we had a two hundred and fifty question test recognizing the systems that FAETULANT taught us. I spent maybe two hours on the test. Finally, the instructor scored the test. At the end of the test, he said this was to familiarize the systems as we begin to fly.

The final readiness is the swim and parachute test. The swimming pool is a big facility. I did all that was asked by the instructors. I think the most exciting thing was climbing up a tall ladder, strapping on a parachute harness and jumping. The rubber bungee cord imitates jumping from the airplane and you are caught, which gives you time to unfasten the buckles on either right or left side and your slide from the top of the platform into entry to the water where you will release from the parachute. I was pleased with my performance.

April begins a phase of intensive flight and ground training at VP-30. Each preparation begins with fundamental relations to day-night navigation which includes keeping track of logs, systems and of course, celestial fixings. After we are tested with what heading (magnetic or true), true course, and what ground speed we are traveling, it is time for the navigation dry swim. Commander Dave Hilty, the C.O. of the VP-11 was standing outside the classroom when I went out for a ten minute break. I was surprised to hear he was looking for me and wanted to talk personally. Dave and I sat down in a vacant classroom. Candid and to the point, he asked me different things about the VP-30. Then he centered on the Executive Officer, Bart Bartolomei. Eventually, he told me Bart's wife was upset. This had caused CDR Hilty's wife to be concerned with me and my wife taking the reigns as XO. I responded that I too had heard through the grapevine that there was some animosity between both wives. As a matter of fact, the CO's wife was causing distress in the squadron. Dave and I agreed as the new prospective XO, I would lead the way with Jane by my side, to carry this squadron with the Commanding Officer and his wife as leaders of VP-11.

Tactics phase began on the 21st of April of 1977. Briefing the flight crew was my task and the mining flight was done in a simulator. Tactics 1 was a six hour flight which introduced a few sonobuoy patterns and if we were lucky, we tracked several merchants. Coupled with DIFAR, we located a merchant. Active sonobuoy ranging was done and we did quiet well. Back at the debriefing room, the instructor pilot had no qualms with me and was very complementary about getting into the alternative patterns. VP-30 has many Lieutenants as instructor Tactical Coordinators. Such men are needed to increase the flow of expertise to the fleet squadron in view of the Soviet submarine challenge. With my background in the VP Charlie world, I have not said a word about my deep selection as a prospective Commanding Officer. He was nice, kind, and was very impressed with my 'picking up the pieces'!

Navigation flight 2 took off on the twenty-six of April 1977. We all had a hand at preflighting, and we were headed to Bermuda. Basically, the track went out of Jacksonville and vectored to the

Northeast and eventually the track turned to the South and landed on the island. I have a two and a half hour navigation period during which I exercised the Loran system to get fixes. After the log exercise was complete, I shot the stars in order to get a true star fix. Star fixing, above all, worked out to perfection. We landed early in the middle of the night. We debriefed in the BOQ with a beer in hand. The logs were a bit ragged but they survived. Rain was the main weather that Bermuda had to offer. We went to a few night spots and we were back up to the officer's club. Slot machines were my favorite form of vice. I ventured on the nickel machines and you guessed it, I lost all two dollars worth of nickels. Horrendous weather set in the next day, or as a matter of fact, the day we were supposed to return to Jacksonville. Finally we left on the twenty ninth, a day later as the winds were up and down to thirty knots. Eight hours later we landed at JAX. Debriefed, I got home to the BOQ, showered, and fell asleep.

Flights and Weapon System Trainers are the tools used when tactics are designated and are practiced. Tactics flights were going quite smoothly so I swapped to the navigator and the student gave the brief. At debrief the instructor Tactical Coordinator came to me. He did not know I was designated as a XO/CO. He expressed his congratulation to me and wished me the best of luck. As a helpful comment, I told the instructor I was proud of being groomed as a prospective CO. NATOP's mean one thing, and that is the Bible of operations of all tactics, flying and when I reached the level of comparability, I'm ready for Mission Commander.

VP-30 was over for all practical purposes. The training was much better than the VP-30 of yesteryear! The well thought out program and instruction had risen to new heights. P-3B is a fine airplane and I was ready, although it's no P3C, I can manage its many changes to conquer antisubmarine warfare. Jacksonville has been a pleasure, but I have left my family in far away Maine. Still a weekend was not enough, but I would find there was something else I could do. Bravo Zulu and I left heading up to Norfolk for my next course prior to arriving at VP-11.

My car filled with gas and the station wagon packed with gear, I took off at 8:00 with two other cars. We were making good time but we signaled for a pit stop. After filling up again, one of our VP-10 guys decided to have his air conditioner looked at. We bid him ado and headed North. At two o'clock I signaled to turn in to McDonald's for a hamburger. I was so thirsty that the Coke wasn't enough. Back on the road I was starting to get tired. Down rolled the windows and I had made it to Virginia. I called Edna and Bob Givler and told them I would stay with them. At six o'clock I hit Richmond. I stopped on Broad Street and called Edna. Frankly, I had forgotten which way to their home. Right away she gave me directions and within fifteen minutes I was there. Their house was small but, wow the yard was beautiful, and a small garden was producing vegetables, and their flowers were beautiful. Bob looked well and was busy chatting about the many facets of Richmond. We spent Saturday shopping and called Jane and spoke to all my kids. Sunday I hugged and kissed Edna and I was enroute to N.A.S Norfolk, Va.

Finally I arrived at the Naval Amphibious Base located at Little Creek, Virginia. I was going to stay at the BOQ and the next morning I will check in at the school. Human Resource Management is the name of the course which all PCO/PXO candidates must attend. Thirty people were in attendance when I checked in. Many areas of attraction were dealt with during the week. Very quickly and succinctly we were dealing with organizational development and management, diplomacy, in particular, overseas and drug/ alcohol abuse was included in the five day course. All of the attendees gave remarks and comments which highlighted the responses of the group. Friday afternoon, we left with the thought that we were better prepared to meet the challenges to come.

I left Norfolk, Virginia just as the rush hour commenced. The main escape from Norfolk is the James River Tunnel on I-64. It was slow moving but I was on the way to Edna and Bob's house. At noon the next day, I was on the road to Baltimore, Maryland to spend the night with Frank, Jane's brother. I was gone the next day headed for Topsham, Maine. There were many cars on the road, including trucks which were "highballing" to their next stop. Brunswick, Maine was a welcome sight. It was nine at night when I pulled into the driveway. Mom looked good, everybody looked good, and my what it does to have you wanted at home.

CHAPTER 12

EXECUTIVE OFFICER VP-11

VP-11 was located on the North side of the field. This hanger was not tall enough to pull the P-3 inside the hanger. A device which fits in the nosewheel raises or elevates the nosewheel so the vertical stabilizer comes in to the hanger and the hanger door is closed. This causes concern when a simulated fire drill occurs in the hanger. I was met by Commander Bart Bartlomei. We had met before when we were on Wingslant staff. I sat down in the executive office and had a cup of coffee with Bart. He wanted to know how the last three months had been. I gave him a dose of VP-30 and I also included the Human Resources Management class at Norfolk, Va. CDR Hilty's Change of Command was due the 30 of June. I asked if there were any legal schools available as I had not had one. This was the one thing that Bart had taken care of. The next course started next week, and I was scheduled to go. A complete list of items was beginning to fill up one page of my note pad. These are things I should know about and keep track of. We then made the squadron tour and I met a lot of VP-11 officers. The Skipper was not in but I will meet with him tomorrow. Next on the list is the doctor, flight suits, and everything including money and flight pay.

Next morning an officer meeting gave me an opportunity to meet more officers. One of those officers impressed me greatly, Lieutenant Donna Brand the ASW Intelligence Officer. She was the first female officer onboard and she had great potential. By Friday, I had another office that I was working out of. I had contacted the band for the Change of Command and officially set up the basic program for the chain of command ceremony. My position was behind the microphone calling the various commands and keeping the ceremony moving. On stage was Commander Hilty and Bartolomei doing their thing along with a chaplain and Admiral Hedges as guest speaker. Immediately after the ceremony the coffee was available and the officers essentially get to the Officers Club for a cutting of the cake.

Dick Petrucci and I left for Newport, Rhode Island on Sunday. CDR Petrucci and I had been friends in VP-10 and in VP-30. We found out by chance we were going to a one week introduction of a lawyer's one week course called the Uniform Code of Military Justice. The courses got into various court cases, military versus civilian jurisdiction. Another thing which I must understand was the power of the CO. I could hold court on a young man, but what were my powers? Can I slice the man from E-5 to E-3? What sort of pay can I deny him? I'll know the answer to all of these questions in five days. Dick was going to be Commanding Officer of VP-26. In fact he is going to take the reins in two weeks.

The tension was building when I got back from Newport. The officer command dinner with full dress and several other parties were to be administered before the Change of Command. Commander Hilty performed admirably at the full dress dinner and the remarks were appreciable. The leaders of the hosting group did an amicable job and quite frankly they treated the heads appropriately with great amounts of wine. Finally after a half a day of dry runs, the podium, chairs and the color guard has been rehearsed to death. Officers and men, today is the moment we had waited for. I took my position which was right of the viewing stand. Fifteen minutes before the ceremony I made the announcements for those that were saluted onboard. This included the Admirals, Captains in Command and all the visiting Commanding Officers. The band was there and my God, were they fantastic! They played for the audience, the dignitaries and they finally played for the colors as they marched in from the side, at which point, I announced the playing of the National Anthem. The program started with the Invocation and lead quickly to the introduction of the guest speaker, the remarks by the distinguished speaker, and Commander Hilty his last remarks prior to the changing of the guard. The orders were read after a good-bye from the skipper to which read his orders. "I am ready to be relieved," he said. Commander Bart Bartolomei read his orders and takes the pin upon his breast. That is a device worn as a sign of status, that symbolizes he is now the Commanding Officer of VP-11.

With the new dynamic twosome beginning the move towards bigger and better things we move in one appropriate officer. Thusly, we sit down and plan out our action for the coming deployment. We had the department heads in attendance giving the ideas and lastly figures corresponding to maintenance, readiness, and reenlistment. Finally we decided to flesh out the Wing by contacting them to see if a particular event was planned before deployment. Noticeably we had been hit by the loss of manpower or the men leaving the squadron right after the last deployment. I recommended that each department head review the bidding on these particular milestones and make this a point of discussion next week. We broke up and the Commanding Officer said that this is a good idea. The rest of the week I started reviewing the squadron instructions and notices. It's amazing but I think I ripped up ten to eleven notices.

Mission Commander of a crew was noticeably impressive and I met with my crew. I spent many Weapons System Trainers with them and I must admit I had some rotten missions at first. About the last flight of the month of June 1977 we flew a flight Northwest of Bermuda. We were trying to find a merchant by other means. The Jezebel operators found a merchant but it was not the source of the contact. I asked for another contact and apparently the fault was not ours and gave us the qualification. After shuttling the quals, we found we were in Charlie status.

On Friday I had a hell of a toothache. I reported to the dentist and he found nothing but gave me a prescription for pain. The next night Jane and I went to a squadron lobster feast. The lobster had to be prepared at the park which had volleyball court set up, softball and Frisbee throwing. A fire was started and then seaweed, corn, potatoes and eventually lobster was put in the fire and cooked for about an hour. Beer was flowing and I couldn't notice that there were several sunshines on the telephone poles. Strangely the term forty appears underneath the sun. Well I think I will have another beer, as I met several new wives. One wife congratulated me and did not think I was that old. I realized that the sun was me because today was my fortieth birthday. Lobster was pleasing to the sense of taste and smell, Next it was CDR Bartolomei's duty to say goodbye and hello to the new officers. He got through all of this and he asked me to step front. I went up and he proclaimed that there were signs of an ancient proverb, they were shining through the baldness of my head. Everyone laughed and everyone lifted their cups and drank to my good health!

Monday was the first day of August and as usual we had quarters. CDR Bartolomei gave a few awards out to the men, but then he called me, front and center. I popped him a salute and Bart went on about having an XO as a Lieutenant Commander to which he read from Washington a directive which allowed me to wear the stripes until I was acknowledged to wear them. Out of the pack, Jane stepped forward and pinned on my hellacious Commander stripes. It was funny, but not as fast as I went to the exchange to buy some new bars. The department head meetings was held immediately after the quarters. Apparently the reports from the department heads were prompt and up to date. All the reports of men being late for deployment is down to a mere handful of replacements expected to report by the end of September. The skipper wanted to check out the deployment areas and he wanted to go on Monday the twenty-second of August. Operations would send the message and who were supposed to go. The skipper gave one from each department and have it in by Wednesday to the XO.

Early in the morning we left for Rota, Spain with about eighteen officers and Chief Petty officers. I went along to introduce each person whom I knew when I used to work in Command Task Force Sixty Seven. Along with us is one of Air Intelligence Officer Lt. Donna Brand. I escorted the Captain and Donna to a highly classified intelligence place which is eight or nine miles from the base in Rota. Commander Ed Stacy was the Tactical Support Center Director and acted as liaison when we deployed in October. Ed showed us the TSC and reviewed his plan of tactical action when it is agreed with by CTF-67.

Naples, Italy was anxious to see me and they were pleased when I was frocked as Commander! Captain Bradley was eager to meet Bart and he talked with him for about an hour. The majority of the time was spent in Commander Fleet Air Mediterranean where the maintenance and supply types met and reviewed the messages pertaining to engine and a great multitude of parts. All in all the meeting provided good note keeping by VP-11 and offered additional notes when we had a brief following the days events. The next day we departed Naples and flew to Rota, Spain where we picked up two Master Chief Petty Officers and we were back in the air again bound for Lajes, Azores. Lajes Air Force Base was about to be turned over to the Navy Air Base. All it took was a few details. We met the duty officers and went to the TSC. This was something new and the communication with Lajes/ Rota/CTF-84 made the joint operation a complete success. Out trip to Lajes lasted only four hours but we had all the bases covered. LE-1 took off for Brunswick, Maine at four and a half hours. The Chiefs briefed me about the certain areas that they were particularly uninterested in. I spent my time writing up the report. Administration will love this report being typed on Monday mornings. I put my head down at twenty thirty and I woke up with a start, "Set Condition FIVE."

The Antisubmarine Warfare Operational Readiness Inspection was the final test of our ability before deployment. The first was a brief on what was coming up. Lt. Brand gave us the most important bit of information that deals with Russian subs detecting airplanes and gives the kill ranges of the radar. Also she gave the other radar on the submarines which can mean a lot on initial detection. She last wrote down the various types of missiles (by name) for each Russian submarine (conventional or nuclear). Finally each crew was thrown to the "wolves." Crew one was the first crew to fly the Weapons System Trainer. They had contact on the submarine but this crew engaged and the sub got away. Crews did well and some did not. There were many mistakes and in fact one crew got shot down by a missile fired a mile and a half away.

We arrived at the WST about one o'clock. We got a brief which was a mission against a transiting submarine. The Wing 5 briefer gave the position of the Soviet Yankee submarine on a course of 210 at 10 knots. We were told to detect send a contact report and maintain contact unless otherwise directed. We were told what conditions we were in and the sound velocity profile was given to me to sort out the direct range. Amazingly enough, there was a convergence zone opportunity. We gathered all of our bags and event into the WST. My navigator is Lt.jg Eric Moorman, who is a budding Tactical Coordinator. I set about preflighting the ASA-16 and checking the inserts to the GTP-4, or the pilots visual display. Eric finished off the ASN-42, or the internal navigator and puts charts on the top of the Dead Reckoning Trace, which is what the navigator turns in, which is his plot/track of the whole three hours in the WST. The plane took off and we were on our way. After numerous conditions we set Condition Three and we descended for the first drop. The pattern that was called for was the

Walking Barrier. I was positioned 30 miles down course of the predicted target and I was dropping eight sonobuoys at ten miles apart. Soviet Yankee submarine would give me a range of 5 miles, so I expected a 50 percent probability. The ESM operator keeps low frequency intercepts. He reports them as low power search radar. Finally all eight sonobuoys were up, so I am heading to lay the next row. The final row was in, but the Jezebel operator screamed out contact on buoy five, which was in the center of the first row. I asked him if he had aural contact. "No sir," he replied. I contacted the pilot and told him to add power in order to mark on top 5 and head 030 for 30 miles and drop 3 buoys as there is an attempt to solve the convergence zone. The mark on top five was good at which I ordered, "SET CONDITION 2." P-3 B was moving right along when it reached 28 miles where began to slow down and when we did we dropped 3 sonobuoys 2 miles apart. The buoys in the center of the other buoys produced contact and yes, there was cavitation producing the submarine. Ordnance was busy loading Difar sonobuoys. We very quickly got down to one thousand feet and dropped two buoys. Difar produces a fix and with in minutes our Wing advisor told us to attack. Jezebel reported the submarine is gaining speed and is changing course. I guess gain the next fix which indicates that the Yankee submarines has turned and for some reason he is leaving the area. We mark on top the Difar buoy and return to the fix. The Sub was heading east at 12 knots. By now all important players are wanting for the all SSQ,-47, Active Ranging Sonobuoy. I entered a 4,000 yard pattern and after 2 buoys were dropped the Mad operator sealed its fate. "MAD MAN, MAD MAN, MAD MAN," "Set Condition One, pilot selecting master arm," I said. I knew I had that bastard; the master arm light came on and I selected station eight in the bomb bay. Station eight is the first MK-46 torpedo dropped from the bomb bay. The weapon is ready, the ordnance has loaded another sonobuoy and will drop a smoke whenever we get to madman. "Ten seconds, stand by, Mad Man, weapons away, smoke away, and remain in Mad pattern," I said. Aural told the story as the torpedo ran like hell and obliterated the submarine from existence. The bomb bay was closed and I told the navigator to record this drop position of the kill and send it with all other information. Weapon System Trainer was stopped at this time and the crew was excused to the debriefing room. I was happy as hell so I shook my operators hand and they too were happy. The pilots were overjoyed as they were congratulating the XO.

The debrief was complimentary and the flight was excellent. That called for a drink when I got home.

The initial debrief on the ASW ORE was held in the Wing TSC. We were qualified, so the wing said, but I was concerned about the ramifications that this would hamper the squadron. Commander Bartolomei thanked the observers and appreciated their service in grading as well as evaluating each crew in professional skill ability. Next and final on the list is the skippers brief which in essence simply tells the Admiral we are going on deployment. Our brief was during the middle of the week and 6 officers went to the COM-PATWINGSLANT building at Topsham, Maine. Admiral Hedges entered the room and Bart began. Every item was covered including readiness operation aspects, maintenance problems and finally reenlistment statistics. At the end of the brief, the admiral asked to see the crew readiness slide. Many questions were raised but the levels supported those listed and they would not change until after the deployment. Nothing more was said, so the meeting was dismissed and we went back to the squadron.

It was a mad house getting all my things ready and I had a minor accident, as I drove into the side of a car, throwing Anne forward on the automatic transmission. This frightened her. She cried as I got out of the car and swapped USAA cards with the other driver. The Air Force began landing C-141 planes as personnel were boarding with squadron maintenance and tons of other items.

VP-11 Deployment Naval Station Rota, Spain

Finally I left with a plane load to Rota, Spain. I told Jane that I would try to call her and pass the word to the wives. Talk about a plane load, we had the butcher, the baker and, for this plane, the executive officer to look after. I was met in Rota by the Commanding Officer of VP-10. Most of the crew was supposed to help move the bunks and make way for VP-11. I checked into the BOQ and took a substitute room. I rested only three hours and went back to the squadron. Pegasus was taking place in Rota as the scout airplanes landed that afternoon. Actually the VP-11 and VP-10 squadron crew's were relieving each other at Lajes, Azores.

At 9 a.m., the major jet Air Force planes had begun to land and unload the sailors and park up those that belonged to VP-10. Several truckers were parked to move and transport the men to the quarters.

Late that afternoon, the Skipper landed with the total of 7 crews here in Rota, with 5 Lajes. I briefed the Skipper on everything that happened and we assumed ready duty today. I was going on a flight the next day giving Bart a chance to move in. With all the bags arriving at the BOQ we carried them into CO's suite of rooms. Incidentally, they were ready for me to move. Well, what the hell, I have another half hour, I guess I got that done. These trips up and down the stairs made me tired. I stopped at a machine and bought a beer. That sure quenched my thirst.

At 6:00 a.m., I didn't have a good feeling. Shower, shave and into my flight suit, the Duty Driver said he could be there at 7:00. By 7:30, we were at the TSC for the brief. An officer conducted the brief which was described as an eight hour surveillance patrol, rigging and photographing all soviet block ships. Rota is big naval base. Submarines come in to get briefed on the Mediterranean Sea. These "boats"(commonly called vice submarines) are actual torpedo heavy attack or they are longer and heavier because they carry 16 missiles which are called "boomers." The flight will take off and check the area outside of Rota for an Elint which may have many antenna which she may try to get if a hostile submarine is in the area. Then the scheduled flight will fly through the Straits of Gibraltar and check where a ship or a combatant is tied up at these sites. We were warned we could not close with in 25 miles of Africa. The Eastern edge of our operational area is a North-South line throughout Sardinia. We were about to leave the TSC when Ed Stacy said hello. I shook his hand. He commented that he was getting ready to give the ready duty brief.

About 10:30, we took off on our patrol. We checked the nuclear sub port but to no avail. The passage through the straits were common but there was activity on the right. It was a big Soviet tanker tied up at an anchorage. We took several pictures but wondered what conventional sub was going to get this diesel fuel. We saw a lot of Russian force today. They know having a ball here really makes us work hard being at every second a second guess away from knowing that you exist. We were really flying here and in making great steps to gain submarine contact. On November 7th, we flew over to Naples. We got there about 10 o'clock and spent some time with the operation and the intelligence people. We discussed our problems with nuclear submarines and wondered if CTF-67 has anything in mind for us. The plans were laid out for a mini-detachment to Souda Bay, Crete in

March 1978. The detachment could be activated quickly depending on the activity of the Soviet forces. The Mobile Operational Van, I was responsible for, was right up my alley. The backup, although not necessarily, called the secondary system, becomes the main network which sets forth the tasking, contact reporting and sends a purpose of what the flight saw, did, or who it made contact with. Incidentally, I wrote down most of this verbage.

Jane and I talked Saturday night. I called her and was amazed she was home. I had three messages for her to pass on. Then I talked with her about the children finally I missed her. I could hardly wait, but I was coming home on the 5th of December on leave. Jane and the children were excited. Mike was playing hockey, Anne was studying hard and Beth was having fun in the eighth grade at high school.

The Commanding Officer and I met with Ed Stacy and planned out the rest of November. The Mediteranean Operations were at their peek. The carrier team just changed hands. The carrier task force was headed for operation in the western Mediterranean and they would need VP operations for the next 3 nights. The number of Soviet submarines totalled 6 within the Mediterranean. The Echo II is a straggler but now there are Charlie, Victor and an occasional whatever. The conventional subs are seeing the SS Tango class filtering into the Mediterranean Operations. Usually there are 2 nuclear and 4 conventional types. The nuclear is next to the carrier, however that's how you will plan the environment based on the requirements that you have to play the game. More lately, the Soviets have shown many armaments which are released in the Mediterranean. These are brilliant ships which advocate many new types of battle armor. They will be tough to suppress in actual war. But don't forget the Elint and the tremendous stress they put on the battle group commanders as they circumvent them to keep clear and out of their way.

On December 5th, 1977, I left Rota, Spain for Brunswick, Maine. A VP-44 plane came over to see the squadron and get a quick brief of what was going on. Can't remember how many chaps went with me but we all made the trip. The winds were gusting as we were limited by the ground speed as we slowly made Brunswick in 12 hours and 20 minutes. It was Christmas time and I spent time with my family. We went to the mall, to L.L. Bean and finally we started wrapping gifts for the Aunts and Uncles and of course the Grandparents of the children. On Saturday we bought a tree and took it home so we could decorate it

Sunday afternoon. Sunday we went to church at First Parish Church in
Brunswick. Mike was dressed in his hockey uniform and is scheduled
to practice after church. Rev. John H Wild was at the pulpit. He preach-
es a good sermon and we spoke with him after the service. It was a
sunny, cold, blustery day with temperatures in the teens. We stopped in
the driveway. Beth, Anne and the rest of us made it upstairs and we put
on our casual clothes. Jane made soup and it was good. The phone rang
and Jane answered it. Bart was on the phone so Jane gave the receiver
to me. "Hello Bart," I said. Bart said something and I did not understand his comment. I moved into the half bath and partially closed the
door. "We have lost an airplane. Everything is being done to tell the
other squadron members and I will contact you at the TSC in half an
hour." I came out of the bathroom and found Jane's arms around me to
console me. I got my hat and coat and off to the TSC.

On Sunday, December 11th, a VP-11 plane left Lajes on a surveillance flight destined for Rota, Spain. The crew was led by Lt. Jim
Ingles with CAC 6. This airplane was supposed to be swapped in Rota.
Several crew members were to go to Rota. The aircraft was due for
maintenance check.

LCDR Jim Radigan, the Officer in Charge of the Detachment,
along with the TSC launched a flight in the Southeastern corner of the
Lajes Operational Area. Apparently this flight was sent to check out the
ships in the area and there were no weather or rain squalls predicted in
the Canary Islands. Bart told me what had transpired at Rota after it
was reported a plane believed to be a squadron aircraft crashed with 18
people onboard. Apparently the specifics were unclear but the plane
crashed on the island called Hierro which was the Western island of the
chain of Canary Islands. LCDR Harry Zint plus four other Chief Petty
officers were flown down to the Canary Islands by a Rota aircraft. An
Air Force C-130 had been contacted and will fly to Rota in a few hours.
Tomorrow they will fly down to bring back the bodies of the aircrew.
Most important is to make sure that the wives, mothers, and fathers are
told. Bart did not have to tell me but he was sure that two wives should
be told. I told him that I had one Chief Petty Officer with me, and I
would enlist his help. He agreed and met me at the TSC. The Chief
knew the wives and he would call when he had given them the news. I
went home to put my blues on. All dressed up, I met the chaplain and
we proceeded to tell his NFO wife, Sharon Rowe.

We set out on the road to Lewiston, Maine. I can't remember the chaplain's name but he was nice. He asked me if I had any qualms about death. I had been in this circumstance before, as a CACO (Casualty Assistant Calls Officer) officer for a A-6 pilot. I was the messenger that spoke to the wife. After about twenty minutes of driving we pulled into a subdivision where Sharon Rowe lived. I got out and straightened my tie and walked up to the door with the minister. Someone came to the door and I announced myself and the chaplain, and we were let in. Three minutes later she came in the room. I stood up and immediately embraced her. She looked as though she had been crying for some time. I think she had known of the crash for possibly four hours. I quickly introduced the pastor. He remarked, "the loss of her husband was a terrible loss to mankind." The pastor then led us in prayer. I held Sharon's hand. Sharon and I went into the kitchen to talk and have a glass of iced tea. I told her of the events leading to the aircraft crash. She wanted to know more about the accident and I told her that CDR Bartolomei called me and told me about the airplane loss. There was an investigation underway, as we speak. Everybody is being notified and tomorrow morning you will be assigned a CACO that will identify and distribute your husbands belongings. I promised her that I will call if there were any other news on the crash. I empathized with her and we said a prayer before we left. I left without crying, but how many officers can do that when you are so close to the individual.

I told the pastor if there was any need, I will call. I called CDR Bartolomei and told him that two wives were told. Bart read me a list of items to check tomorrow. By the time he finished I hung up. We had discussed the need to keep me in Brunswick for an additional few days. By the time I arrived home I was worn out. Jane held me in her arms while I quickly touched on the days events. Sharon Rowe was courageous in every way, she displayed fortitude, beyond the call of duty. Bart wanted me to stay and act as a secondary post here in Brunswick. With that I went upstairs and changed my clothes. The children were not asleep so I hugged them and told them that plans are that I will stay with them for a while. Then I went downstairs and fixed myself a bourbon and water. I took my drink and sat down. There are so many things going through my mind. There was a knock on the front door. Jane opened the door and Marty and Shirley Martinsen came inside. I wasn't aware of who was at the door. Marty took charge and came into the den. I'm on my second drink but I really hugged him and started to cry. Marty went into the kitchen and fixed him a drink. What I think Marty did, was he made me talk about the crash. He wanted to know all about the details. Unfortunately not the elementary cold truth, but what I thought might have happened haunt this tragic occurrence.

It was cold at 7:00 a.m. when I got in the car. The TSC was busy and finally they had set up a desk for me. I got some pens and paper and rang up Rota. Bart was frantic cause the C-130 could not land in the Canary Islands to get the bodies. Apparently they need a C-130 which can land on a runway of four thousand feet. No doubt about the challenge, the plane had to get the remains back or the Spanish will burn their bodies. The second item deals with the Spanish Guard de Civil in the way it reported the crash. From them the Portuguese pass to the Lajes that one of their planes crashed. It is believed it is a Navy plane because their side numbers is the only visible thing remaining. But that's not the point, all of Spain is reading stories in the paper, as a result of the crash, there were bombs exploding. Case in point, the bodies were picked up by Spanish authorities, who found a document titled, "Naval Air Training and Operations Procedures Standardization." This paper had surmised, this was a bombing mission.

Admiral Hedges came by to question me. I told him what little I knew about the crash. He shared my grief, and told me to call if the situation required it. I started making phone calls and did not stop until 6:00 PM. I contacted the CACO office and told them I was the Executive Officer of the squadron. I would be assuming authority for the squadron. If there was any question, please call this number. They answered several of my questions, including the one about, they have notified all CACO's and they have seen four of the five wives. The next item on my list was Dover, Delaware. This is the US Air Force base where all the bodies will arrive in the USA. Air Force personnel were anxious to learn when the bodies will arrive. I told them the weather was overcast, and the earliest we could retrieve the remains would be tomorrow. I got home finally at 6:00 p.m. Supper was on the table. The newspaper caught my attention, with its lead front page story.

The next few days saw the accident scene turn into a beehive of activity. First was the retrieval of the bodies by a C-130. The details and wrapping up of the investigation had to be concluded. On Tuesday afternoon, I received many calls, asking for information. These came from families of the deceased. On Wednesday night, the bodies arrived at Dover Air Force Base.

Jane and I sat down and talked before I rejoined the squadron. My silent partner had meant a lot to me these last few days. I had been on one track, while she was on another. She had been acting as the commanding officer's wife. She had been trying to bolster the morale of the wives of the officers and enlisted men. I thank her profusely for her aid and understanding.

I left Friday with Jane crying, and the children kissing me. The flight was enroute to Lajes, Azores. It was to connect with a VP-11 airplane going to Rota. I slept most of the way, trying to gather myself and be ready for all the problems of the squadron. We arrived at Lajes late at night. I climbed down from the airplane and was vectored to a waiting VP-11. The crew was happy to see me and carried my gear aboard. We took off for Spain. It felt good to be in the airplane and around the men. The coffee was good, and it inspired me to say a prayer for the thirteen men, whom for reasons known only to God, had been called to their eternal glory.

We arrived at the Rota airport and taxied over to the VP-11 line. CDR Bartolomei was waiting and we hugged each other. Bart looked like hell. I picked up my suitcase and went up to the BOQ with him. He wanted to talk so I took my things into the room and joined him in the room adjoining his bedroom. We had a drink and he started at the beginning. This was a tragic crash site. Some details I should not hear to avoid repeating. The Canary Islands was where the accident happened. The plane crashed on the small island of Hierro. The reason why it took so long to get their bodies back, LDCR Zint did not know where the accident occurred until he landed in the Navy airplane from Rota. Furthermore, the next day LDCR Zint called and told Bart that the airplane crashed on the island of Hierro. LDCR Zint and his investigation team then departed to the island. Another factor in the crash was the scene of the accident. A rock ledge extending two hundred feet up was the end of the flight. Thirteen people in the airplane were smashed into the side of the rock along with burning fragments after the initial hit.

Bart continued with the officer complement in Rota. He had to order those pilots to go flying the next day. What if this happened to me? I ran over the many things that had happened to me in Brunswick. He was well satisfied with my work and we said a prayer that we both liked , the 23rd Psalm.

A week before Christmas the Merry Christmas airplane landed

and everybody got a gift. One of the VP squadrons sent an airplane full of gifts. Everybody got a gift from their wives. Donna Brand, our AIO officer, came to me and wanted to know if I had considered a Christmas Eve party. Well no, I confessed, but it sounds like a good idea. I put the word out and everyone pleased.

The Christmas party was held in a large room with a fireplace. The afternoon before the big event we hustled chairs, tables and made several trips to the liquor store. Ray Honey, the assistant operations officer, was sitting down resting about 4:30 PM. We were surveying the area with a can of beer in hand, when Ray said, "Where is the wood for the fireplace?" Frankly I thought that was taken care of. Then Ray wondered if the CO was going to use his car. I said go ahead and use the car but leave a note for him. An hour later here comes Ray and an Ensign in the CO's car which was heavy in the rear. I learned they unloaded twenty logs of oak wood out of the trunk in the dark. Thanks to the trickery of VP-11 the Navy Station Golf Course offered a major contribution to the Christmas festival.

Christmas was not a day of celebration, but of grieving for the loss of thirteen lives that I prayed for at church. I opened my presents and I shed a tear for the families I am separated from. Jane sounded good, and so did all of the kids. On the 27th of December I took a crew to Naples and saw CTF 67. Lt. Brand was with us. She stayed in a hotel down by the water. We had calamari, shrimp and wine for supper. When we got back we met the skipper's wife. I knew she was coming and I knew something was stirring. We arranged an event for the Officer's Club for New Years Eve celebration. Everyone was there including two flights from Lajes with the officers and enlisted onboard. It was a sad celebration to enter the New Year's. It was difficult to shake the loss of an aircrew and a plane. We had to get this loss behind us. Rise up VP-11, and let's strike back and go on with the spirit that we are going to get better.

The month of January was busy as Foxtrot was out at night coming and going through the Strait of Gibraltar. Another problem has been the Russian nuclear submarines. The Charlie class and the Victor class have found a manuever which at least I can't figure out. Every time we get up an inch we establish barriers outside the strait and monitor these sonobuoys for twenty-four hours. Then take a look at what you have and then comes the questions, how long should I continue the barriers? Ever time we did one thing the nuclear submarine was watching, laughing all the time.

On one flight of Foxtrots, we encountered the side number on the sail. We took these pictures and film to show the staff in Naples, Italy. They were very inquisitive about the submarines and we were glad that she was on her way home to Russia. I asked the question if we intended to go to Crete. "Yes, by all means," they replied. Look to go on the first of March. How in the hell are we going to fit in this equipment when we are supposed to redeploy back to Brunswick in the middle of March.

Also in January I took a flight to Lajes to see the other half of VP-

11. LDCR Jim Radigan, who was officer in charge of the detachment, met me at the airport. I had several medals, several citations and other at-a-boys. I told Jim that I needed Lajes, but first I want to see your men at quarters. An Enlisted man took my bags and I went to the

hanger. As I entered the hanger someone called "Attention." I acknowledged the salute of the Duty Officer when he said, "all present and accounted for." "Very well," I said. After I gave the men a parade rest, I told them that I was pleased to come over and see the Detachment. I summed up all of these operations and fantastic support from the maintenance division. Without further ado, I called the assembled group to attention and gave out the awards. I really feel super giving out these awards. Each person was happy and I was happy for them. I did not know how to do this but I told them to stand around me. I told them that the accident investigation was still going on in Rota. Again this will be over in Lajes next week. I went on about this and then I opened it up for questions. Several questions did come up and I answered them correctly with no regrets. My turn was over and the Maintenance Chief toured me through the shops. I had an excellent time meeting people and then Jim met me and we drove up to the BOQ. I told Jim let's go to dinner and leave the flying to someone else tonight!

In the morning I met with Captain Cook, the senior Navy Officer present. Captain Cook was Chief of Staff of COMFAIRWINGSLANT when I was stationed there. He was sad when he mentioned the crash. He talked about it and asked if I minded chatting with him. He closed the door and mentioned that he heard that Bart was going to be relieved. I pleaded not guilty, because this was the first time I had heard about this situation. Capt Cook was factual in that he had heard this report while he was in Brunswick, Maine. Anyway I decided to keep track of that most important item. I also met LCDR Stromberg, the Tactical Support Officer. Dave and I were in VP-49 together. I'll be a son of a bitch, the Executive Officer is Commander Joe Sullivan also of VP-49. Joe Sullivan was a tall lad that had been screened for CO/XO and was killing time here at Lajes.

That afternoon I thanked Jim Radigan for a good time. I told him to "keep the faith." As we went zooming down the runway, I thought of many possibilities that could bother a person. Jim Radigan will stay as Detachment Officer for the rest of deployment.

Once back in Rota, the CO wanted to talk to me. I closed the door and sat down. He told me in confidence that he was going to be relieved because of the accident. He admitted that they started too late and due to the circumstances he will remain Commanding Officer until relieved. He was pleased the Chief of Staff backed him all the way. It surprises me, but I'm sure that this backstabbing by certain individuals is commonplace in the world of the military.

February was a month that didn't exist. I got the sad results from briefings that happened in the CO's office. Lajes had really gone through a week of peek and probe. They questioned the Enlisted Club the night before the accident. The crew showed up around eight p.m. and started drinking alcohol. Some of he crew did not imbibe but drank soft drinks. The band or singer or whatever they saw perform, stayed lively until past midnight. All of the crew left after midnight and reportedly only about six remained. At 1:00 a.m., the remaining crew left and they were up at six o'clock in the morning. There is no reason to violate the twelve hour ruling before the individual goes flying. If this crew were to perform they should have stopped drinking at eight o'clock p.m.!

My thoughts had been elsewhere, but life must go on. I was working in my office when the doctor, a Lieutenant, wanted to see me. He asked me to see the doctor for a flight physical. I agree and went to the clinic next week. I stepped on the scales, got my blood pressure, and all the rudimentary tests that were necessary. The doctor was cooperative and inspected me and reviewed my test. "Do you have high blood pressure," he asked. "No, but what is my blood pressure?" My blood pressure was 135 over 90 which is high for the diastolic pressure. He asked me if I would return in a few days to get my pressure read, I agreed and for the next three days my pressure was below 125 over 85. Well, I guess that period from December 1977 to February 1978 was cause for my blood pressure change; I was a candidate for a likely incident.

The fifteenth of February we finally got our orders to Souda Bay, Crete. I was assigned not as officer in command but as an observer I had three flight crews to take over with me. We were packed when we find out that the supply or C-130 airplanes are unable for airlift. We had to make do as we launched a pilot trainer full of extra parts in case we had to use them. I took off in an airplane that was packed from stem to stern. We found a comfortable spot and stayed for five hours of flight. Souda Bay, Crete was a beautiful sight. It was located on an island which was scenic but one had to worry about the soldiers that were stationed on the island. The detachment at Souda Bay consists of everything including sonobuoys, torpedoes and God knows what else. The planes are usually on their auxiliary power unit (APU) while the crew is preflighting. If the APU is not operating, a power source is brought out to the airplane. Except that, an air compressor must be used to start the engine.

Crete, the biggest island of Greece, is situated on the Southside of the Aegean basin in the eastern Mediterranean. Crete is a long narrow island consisting of large rugged and now barren mountains with flat uplands with coastal plains that end with lowlands. A mild climate cultivates prosperous fruit and livestock farms. The mountains were full of timber which were harvested for shipping a long time ago. In Crete, one is always conscious of the sea. It flows into the Souda Bay where the Navy Facility was built.

The aircraft was stopped beside a hanger and shut down. Men came down the ladder to put in the locks and pens in the landing gear and cover other vents or valves that need covering. I don't know who the leader of the detachment was but he introduced me to a Lieutenant and showed me the BOQ and the eating facilities. The BOQ was nice and comfortable. We had a brief of the area at 1900 hours. Unfortunately, we did not have a AIO along to take up the slack of the brief debriefing. At the meeting at 7:00 we discussed the large area that we have to cover. Essentially we covered the entire area East to Israel. The Mediterranean Sea limits us twenty-five miles north of the African countries with borders on the Mediterranean. This was some concern of mine fourteen years ago. The Air Officer brought up several items and then the communication officer required about ten or fifteen minutes. I was on the schedule for tomorrow. Additionally we asked a few questions. The majority of them were answered. The brief tomorrow will be held in the White Whale or the Mobile OPCON van which was brought over by CDR Pete Smith.

The Mobile Van had not changed a bit. I think there are four enlisted men that are there to keep the van operational. An officer was there to brief us and repeat the warning areas which we must follow. I noticed the message board was set up and I asked if I could use it. "Of course, sir,: the Petty officer replied. The intelligence docket was what I was looking for. The submarine activity was very slim, with only a Foxtrot near Egypt. Nuclear subs were in the area, but where? A Victor and a Charlie have been unlocated for the better part of ten days. Normally the Soviet submarines usually work the eastern Med as the furthermost in their travels and once they are there, they start heading back home.

The flight today was very interesting. We developed a track which wound its way to the East. We encountered some Block ships and suddenly came upon a Elint. After several photo runs, we decided that we better head back. We got back and the van took our cameras to the photo lab.

Next day, I stayed on the ground and with the radioman, he handled the communication net while I gave him the message. With this system I could talk to the Rota TSC and eventually communicate with the Skipper. Some of the questions I was asking were where was the third crew, when do I get back to Rota. I got the answer to several things, but mainly our third crew arrives this afternoon. I paid a courtesy call to the Captain, who is head of Souda Bay Facility. I recognized the man and after he introduced himself , the lights came on! We talked for an hour and a half. As I walk out of the office I recognize that VP-11 aircraft had just landed. One flight was out on station and the second had a night flight. The third crew was happy to be here. They did not know how I was getting back.

The next couple of days passed quickly and the planes were holding up fine. The word came from the rest of the squadron that they were flying an Extendex in Lajes. Sounds like a nuclear submarine is entering the Strait of Gibraltar. The crew took me downtown and to eat at the restaurant. The fish were good including the shrimp and assorted relatives. Suddenly a plane landed in the Souda Bay and it was to take me home tomorrow. The next morning the detachment was breaking up. Two planes were to head back to Rota and the other plane was the last plane out. Remember the APU was the lifeblood of the airplane, well this problem hadn't happened thus far over deployment. We started engine #2 and it wound up to 100%. The number 1 started and engine 3 didn't start. After the engine four started the pilots contacted the second plane that was going our way. They had no problems starting their engines, but agreed to get situated so we could get right behind their engines three and four. Once this was complete, they went to 100% power on number three and four. Their wind began to buffet the wing structure, so we started engine number 3 and by doing she came online as planned.

VP-11 was certainly a wonderful sight to see. My clothes were filthy and needed washing. My desk really needed work after checking my in basket. Bart was concerned with our loading plans for our return home. Also we had done well in all respects except in the submarine world. Jane was anxious for me to get home. I told her I would be arriving on the 15th of March with the advanced party. She said that the CO's wife had given her the authority to meet with the Enlisted and Chief Petty Officer's wives. She had held several officer's wives coffee and luncheons.

VP-11 NAS Brunswick, ME

The days passed quickly and finally it was the day to depart. I had completed everything on my countdown list. We took off on a straight line to Brunswick, Maine. The plane was loaded with individuals that represented the whole structure of VP-11 that could be operated as a branch of that squadron as the initial advanced party. The crowd was large as we landed and taxied to our new hanger. The customs individuals were there and had all of their forms to fills out. Finally, the customs man left and I came down the ladder. It was pandemonium all around me. People were cheering and here comes Beth, Anne, and little Mike. Then Jane was in my arms. It was cold in Brunswick. I met many of my friends here and was glad to see the Commodore of Wing Five. Finally we left the plane and loaded the car. I had a present for each of the children. On the way home I was entertained with story after tale. Their smiles meant that I was missed yet I knew I had not been in their utmost thoughts for five months.

The hangar that we drew was facing West and was one of the smallest hangers. The hangar is divided in half with the other side being owned by VP-44. The bottom part of the hangar is wide for many maintenance shops necessary to run a squadron. The upper deck consists of the administrative, operational and other offices which run the squadron. My office is located to the right of the CO's office. We made a promise to do all of our assignments and only if we had primary hangups we would report our findings. Incidentally, we are to get a party for the officers in our Officer's Club. During the day we noticed a few more VP-11 airplanes. These aircraft are beginning the return of Lajes crews. The next day all of the planes returned home. The kids were overjoyed as they mobbed their dads in flight suits. CDR Bartolomei steps down the ladder and his wife and children were right there. I saluted and shook his hand and reported that everything is according to his wishes.

The next eleven days were rest and relaxation and fun with the kids. Mom and Dad have been in contact with us and agreed that they will come up to see me when I become Commanding Officer at the end of June. That is also true of Jane's parents. Jane and I have really not talked about this, but I want to have the whole squadron over after the ceremony. I have a lot to do before taking command. The number of thoughts concern me such as, where is our aggressive capability of ASW? I know the squadron has the ability to accomplish much more than it has shown to date. I must generate some pride of accomplishment, to excel, in each and every man under my command. We need to be some thing more than a lackadaisical and spiritless squadron, at the bottom of Fleet Air Wing Five.

In April, we tried to end the lingering frustration of the airplane crash by inviting the wives, Mother and Dads to come to Brunswick, Maine for a memorial of the crash. It was held at the NAS Brunswick Chapel, where we dedicated a graveyard stone in the honor of the thirteen men. Mostly all of the relatives were present. Each wife was given a momento that represents the depth of the loss of her mate.

In May the last duty of the Commanding Officer was made a part of the Naval Air Training and Operating Procedures Standardization (NATOPS). VP-30 is the coordinator, tester and has qualified people who conduct the flight and drills portions of the exam. As you may realize this word "NATOPS" has already come to the surface more than once in this book. Most, but not all people, believe that the word is found in the first book of the Bible, Genesis! The message stated that the test were to be given to all pilots and all others who are primary crew members. I took my book home and studied it after supper. I was in the CO's office when we were discussing who was to come to the Change of Command. After completing this I mentioned the NATOPS check coming up next week. Yes, he realized they were coming. I asked if he was going to take the exam. "No," he replied, he had other things to do. I knew I should be taking the quiz, but Bart was piling up work such as Captain's Mast, Change of Command, formal dinner for the Commanding Officer and the associated endeavors of me relieving him. The result of the disastrous debacle, VP-11 shook the heads of all VP East coast squadrons. The Ordnance men, Aviation Warfare (or Jezebel), two other primary flight crews, at least five pilots and three or four NFO's flunked the closed book exam. I should have taken the exam but I didn't because I acted as a second Tactical Coordinator on crew seven. This was a point blank approach to the accident which occurred the eleventh of December 1977. I was ashamed and just sat in my office. I know I could predict this but I tried to warn each division officer to get the word to his people. The next man to get the ax was Commander Bartolomei. The NATOPS team stayed and flew with certain crews. The VP-11 NATOPS team qualified and the whole thing was scheduled again in August. From this day on I sensed that the commanding officer was to sit in his office until the change of command.

The final party for the CO was in the Formal Dress Blues. I was moderator for the occasion. To set the record straight, we passed out pamphlets that describes how this function will evolve, but more importantly, I let it be known I wanted the affair to be jovial. We were going to frown on talk of the recent plane crash. This would not be the time or place to bring it up. To lighten up the crowd, I announced the ladies would have to ask me for permission to use the rest rooms. It was funny watching the young girls raising their hands to ask to go to the bathroom.

Sunday I went to church with the family. Mike, being alert wondered where the Chevrolet station wagon was. There was a sign that showed VP-10 making off with a proud horse of VP-11. I knew something was amiss but we went to church. Marty Martinsen joined VP-11 Monday. We had a meeting which detailed the change of command. The party after the ceremony was complete including food and drinks. A couple of rough edges were the color guard and various seating for the very distinguished guests. After we concluded the meeting I led CDR Martinsen around the hanger introducing him to all the officers and Chief Petty Officers. When I got back to the XO's office I found another part to the station wagon. I recognized the part and eventually I know some spies had the car because Jane had given the sneaky bastards the keys.

In looking through the messages I came across a Unitas message which meant action for us. Unitas is a joint naval operation which bonds together a patrol squadron, several ships which included a nuclear submarine and several destroyers headed by a flag ship. The task force there joins bonds with a South American country and exercises its naval units. VP-11 is to provide two airplanes commencing in July to the Eastern side of South America working around to the Western countries by October 1978. I immediately made a list of things that the detachment might consider, such as, name a detachment officer, what crew should attend Unitas and numerous movements of sonobuoys, etc. The Department heads got together and mapped out the meeting which the crews were based on site in early July, 1978.

The Change of Command was upon us. Bob and Edna Giviler as well as Mom and Dad were here. Both Anne and Mike were having a ball with their grandparents. Everybody got the jitters. The morning of the change of command I went in early. Men were all over the platform that we used for the speakers during the ceremony. Chairs were being set up and a sparkling clean aircraft (LE-1) was being towed into the hangar. My door was open and the Chief Petty Officer gave me my acceptance speech. I looked it over, and I was happy with it. The crowds of officers and enlisted started filling up the space between the outside of the hangar and the runway. When the men were ready I walked out, incidentally the squadron immediately came to attention. CDR Martinsen popped me a salute and reported," VP-11 all present and accounted for." Commander Bartolomei followed me and I reported to him. I followed him as he inspected the men. He stopped and shook hands and complimented certain sailors. Back at the podium the Captain said a few words but most of what he really said, was thanks for a job well done. He stepped back and said for me to wait a minute. I didn't know what was happening but around the corner came my freshly painted silver Vega, my Chevrolet station wagon. I walked over to the car and it was beautiful with Pegasus on the door and there are blocks inside the wagon which are marked VP-11 for parking. The men were laughing in the ranks, and I was a happy camper.

Commander Edward M. Brittingham, US Navy

CHAPTER 13

COMMANDING OFFICER
VP-11 NAS BRUNSWICK, ME

The promotion was what I had worked for. Captain Zeisel spoke since he got Bart and I in the positions we wanted. My family was seated up front where I could see them. I stood up and took the Command Pin and said, "I relieve you." I stepped up to the microphone and said the following:

"Distinguished guests, Officers and men of Patrol Squadron Eleven, sixteen years ago I joined the Navy. I was fortunate to be assigned to the antisubmarine warfare community. In my first patrol squadron I quickly realized the challenge of ASW. I decided that my goal was to assume command of a VP squadron as a Naval Flight Officer.

I am particularly happy to have my family, my friends in the civilian community, shipmates and their lovely wives to share in this special time in my life. I have been able to reach this goal with your guidance and support.

Commander Bartolomei, I wish you and your family fairwinds and following seas. To our new Executive officer, Commander Martinsen, Shirley and Tracy- again I want to say how pleased Jane and I are that the Navy has chosen us to work together as a team. To Jane, Beth, Anne and Mike I thank you from the bottom of my heart for your constant understanding and support, despite the winter deployments in Brunswick.

Officers and men of the Pegasus family! I am proud to be the new skipper of VP-11. I believe it is the best job in the United States Navy. Through God's help, professionalism, a positive attitude and pride

within ourselves, we will prove that we are the best. I challenge you
to promote Pegasus Power!"

I was a proud man as I shook hands with my Dad and hugged him,
too. Jane and all the children kissed me as well as Bob and Edna.
Dignitaries were fabulous and so were the many Pegasus fans who
gladly shook my hand and expressed hopes of turning this outfit
around. The officer's club was packed when I got there. Admiral
Hedges and his wife made known that I was expected to lead this
squadron to be the Navy's best. Jane and I cut the cake with Marty
holding the sword with my hand while Shirley was watching. We left
the officer's club, Marty and I went to the enlisted club. I discussed
with Marty two weeks ago what I wanted to do for the Petty Officers
and Chiefs. We decided to meet them over at the Enlisted club with the
beer tab been picked up by me! We had a hell of a time over there.
There must have been thirty or forty men present. Marty and I left
about an hour later and sped back home to get ready for the party at
home. Dad went with me a few days ago and we got some liquor
which I signed for. The cute girl who tends the bar at the O' club will
handle the bar in the den.

Looking back at the evenings celebration I can't think of an occasion when I have had so much fun. As I remembered, the officer's
wives brought different condiments as well as dishes and dessert. Dad
and Bob were funny. Dad always liked his liquor while Bob had trouble with alcohol and gave it up. Bob being a public affairs representative with Bell telephone he had no problems making friends. We closed
up the bar at eleven o'clock when the crowd started heading home.

We had fun throughout the weekend. All the grandparents went
with us to a local farm which had big, beautiful strawberries. Bob
picked at least two quarts. The next day we took our parents to church
and that afternoon we said good bye to Mom and Dad. Bob and Edna
were traveling by car so they left; it felt great to be alone.

I had quite a lot of thinking to do before tomorrow. VP-11 in its
entirety was to meet at the Enlisted club at nine o'clock in the morning. My XO and I and talked about what we wanted for our squadron.
Many good things came out of the discussion that suggested they
could capitalize in my talk with them. It is now my opportunity to be
the best squadron leader and to set achievable goals, for every man in
my command. We shall endeavor to set the standards, for all those
who will follow!

At nine o'clock Monday morning the Master Chief called the squadron to attention as I walked in followed by the Executive Officer. "At ease, take your seats," I said. I began my talk by thanking our men who had helped put on the change of command. And now I turned to the future of VP-11. "Tomorrow two crews begin to study NATOPS to get the best available score. Today, my first in command, let's set the record straight, we have got the lowest record of the six squadrons here in Brunswick! Let's build on this blemished record and a year from now let's be sure, we are a better prepared, highly trained, elite military unit, that can take great pride in knowing, we are the very best the Navy can offer. We concentrated on antisubmarine warfare. I know you are highly trained and highly skilled aircrewmen. Take the extra time to study, analyze the target and by God you will know what you are doing." And finally I told them that I was watching a VP-11 plane land in Rota, Spain. I noticed the Pegasus sitting on the tail. From this point I went into the mythical traits of this great horse. It's aerial ability and effectiveness indicative of VP-11. The only problem in achieving greatness is the size of Pegasus. Gentlemen, I propose that an artist or a group of men design a new and bigger Pegasus. The winner will be painted on all aircraft. I turned and saw Marty looking at me and nodding his head. This was my first day in the squadron as CO and many people commended me. I hoped I would earn their accolades.

Every Thursday at one o'clock there was the CO's meeting with the Commodore and his Chief of Staff. We met with the CO's and XO's and conduct business. We were brought up to speed on the calendar of events for next month. VP-26 will be leaving next month for Rota/Lajes. There are other important events which we need to know. After everyone had spoken, the Commodore gave his message plus a few "at-a-boys" to various artillery on the NAS Brunswick base. Finally he said that's about it, except he wanted to see me afterwards. He sat down after everyone had left when he mentioned, the NATOPS teams will be here in August. The Captain then stated he wanted to fly a flight with every crew, observing the preflight, briefs and infight emergencies during the flight. He stated the first flight will be flown on Monday. I started to speak but thought better of it. On the way back to the squadron I was angry. Marty felt the same way; I thought about it all night long and in the morning I called the Patrol Plane Commanders in the wardroom. The PPCs can sign for the plane but only they can determine or decide what situation is acceptable to land. I told them that the Commodore will be flying with each crew. He will attend the brief, preflight and attend all drills provided by the observers. The audience was quiet. "What's wrong with this," I asked. All of a sudden they erupted with forceful discord. I let them complain for about five minutes and then I spoke up. "I must be the guilty party. I recounted those days about two months ago when we destroyed the Blue Ribbon award. As your Commanding Officer I look to your expertise as PPCs and recognize your value. The Commodore is afraid you cannot carry out his ideals; I know you are able, and capable for all missions," I said. Everyone was quiet and understood my predicament. By then we all agreed to give the Commodore our cooperation. Monday began the long laborious crew check. Evidently, we succeeded and the PPCs were thankful.

Unitas XIX was going smoothly and Detachment Officer LCDR Jerry Nelson landed with crews back from South America. I scheduled a talk with him tomorrow. This conversation was one of pleasure. Jerry explained how difficult the logistics chain had to work. The airplanes performed without maintenance and led the scores for the number of kills of an attack submarine. I asked what if I came down and met the admiral on board his ship. Jerry's eyes raised and he said, "When are you coming skipper?" We looked at the calendar and the ship was in port the 18th of August. How about a message to go aboard the ship on the 18th of August and meet RADM Sagerholm, USCOMSOLANT. The message went out and immediately it was answered with a stipulation that supplies and other necessities were needed by the task force. I left the crew selection to the Executive Officer because I was going to South America. Well shiver me timbers, it's NATOPS week.

Monday morning a VP-30 plane from Jacksonville landed bringing the team. The officers met with Marty and me for coffee. The spaces had been taken care of at the Enlisted Club. The other spaces were passed out to the other evaluators. The officers were then carried to the BOQ for lodging. I have been studying for far too long. Marty said he was ready so of course a wager of one beer was awarded to the winner. The next morning all the PPCs, 2ps, 3ps and all sorts of PPTCS were gathered for the open and closed book exams. The open book did not seem so hard. I checked over the exam, particularly the three engine loiter. The closed book was nice. It covered the whole spectrum of the ASA-16 to the bailout drill. I turned in the test and

noticed Marty working away. I went back to the squadron to catch up
on paperwork. At 11:00, I received a call from the NATOPS TC. I got
a 3.9 on the open book and a 4.0 on the closed book. I thanked him
and wondered how the rest of the officers did. "All of the officers
passed with flying colors," replied the Tactical Coordinator. I thanked
him and went back to work. VP-11 had taken this test; every level and
every rank from ASW to flight engineers had passed their exams. By
late afternoon the crews were slated to fly on what date. By the time
all the schedules were out Marty and I treated each other at the club.

The second month in command was a highlight for me. Everything
is going my way we have to plan for future deployment. We planned
for a Administrative inspection, a Minex, and a deployment visit.
Looking at the commitments outlined, we could barely make the
deployment sites in November. Unitas XIX will end the last of October.
On the seventeenth of August myself plus eight of nine Pegasus took
off for South America. We stopped in Norfolk, Virginia to pick up eight
enlisted men destined for the surface group. Also, we had to fit a MAD
assembly that fits on the tail of the P-3B aircraft. The rest of it amounts
to bits and pieces of the needed aircraft, namely helicopters aboard the
surface ships. I briefed the new men including checking out with parachutes and the unsinkable May West. Finally we were headed to
Roosevelt Roads, Puerto Rico. We got there late at night and we made
arrangements at the Enlisted quarters,and the BOQ.

The next morning we were expecting to get a visa, an official go-
ahead to Brazil. After making several calls to the State department in
Washington, we took off for Dois De Julho, Brazil. We filed a VFR
(visual flight rules) route which was predicted all the way. Halfway
there we encountered a massive thunderstorm. Our radar was working
so we went around the storm, the rest of the trip was done by crossing
mountains streams and, more importantly, crossing the above with a
radio beacon. We landed about eleven o'clock at night. We got to the
hotel in time to see Jerry Nelson. We had a couple of beers and hit the
sack. The next morning Jerry, Lt Brand and myself rode out to see the
flag ship and the admiral. We were piped aboard his ship. The Petty
Officer took us to the Officer's wardroom. We got a cup of coffee and
met with the Operations officer. The Captain was sure glad to see us.
He wanted to know everything; how was the trip, the weather and by
the way did you bring the MAD head? I conversed with him about the
type of exercises they work with the Brazilian Navy. The crew hardly

knows what it is going to do until the exercise commences. The P-3B performance has been outstanding and the attack criteria is unbelievable. A Lieutenant entered the room and whispered to the Captain. He announced that we better hurry because the boss has many errands to run. We met Admiral Sagerholm, who normally resides in Puerto Rico. He was pleased by the alertness of the aircrews. I asked if there were anything I could do for him operationally and socially. The admiral smiling, said no. He really appreciated the supplies we carried down to his fleet. By this time he looked at his watch and stood up, whereby we stood up as it was time for the admiral to leave.

At Salvador we arrived with all our baggage. There seemed to be a problem. The PPC asked what to do with the exercise MK-44 torpedo. Apparently the torpedo was supposed to be carried by a plane that was here. If we leave it with the military forces here, we may never get it back. My response was I'll turn my head that way I will not see what was done there. So an ordnance man made the switch. We rolled down the runway and off to Rio De Janeiro. We have a full airplane with the mountainous gang moving further South to assist the airplane. Two hours out, the number four engine went to 110% and back to 70% fluctuation of revolutions thus we had to feather the engine. This happened moments before we started descending to the landing field. Immediately we strapped in and I reported Condition Five set. We landed with no problem and shut down next to a LE aircraft. The maintenance people jumped out of LE-9 and secured the airplane and began to check the engine for fod (foreign object damage) or part of a piece of metal in the strainers. Nothing was found so the engine was started and it worked "fine as wine." What if it didn't work right, or would we have enough fuel to get the plane back to Puerto Rico? Let's save that for Monday as our bus just arrived to take us to the hotel. The plane was then buttoned up and we left the airport.

Rio De Janeiro was filled with shadows as the sun had gone down behind the mountains. The street lights were popping on as we entered the downtown area. We finally stopped at the hotel which afforded us a view of the beach and area. We went up to our hotel rooms, showered and shaved. The officers showed up an hour later in short shirts and shorts. We roamed round from bar to bar. Finally we settled down and ate our dinners. After we had tied on the feed bag we were completely exhausted. I slept for 8 hours and awoke to the noise of ball playing. I went out to the porch and looked down on the water and sand. Many people were running or jogging in the sand. Later in the morning we had continental breakfast. We argued that swimming was in order. Myself and about five others went to the beach decked out in bathing suits. Donna had the tanning lotion and we helped ourselves. There is one thing we cannot overlook: bikinis. My God, they certainly do not have much covering their bodies. Another important item is that they forego with the top to get the whole back brown. This was great for an hour but I was starting to feel the sun's rays. We decided to return to the room and branch out to see more of the city. In fact we took a tour and saw a statue above the city. From that vantage point the island was visible out to twenty five miles away. We tried to take pictures but for some reason they didn't turn out. The night life was interesting but the night was short as we have to pack out tomorrow and head north to Puerto Rico.

The bus pulled up in front of the airplane and we got the gear off of the bus and onto the airplane. Both PPCs were over filing so I went aboard and talked to the flight engineers. Both felt that the number four engine was apparently going to be all right. Just how long it will run depends on how it will hold out. The coffee tasted good and the PPC climbed the ladder. To put the matter to rest, I asked what we should do about the engine; should it fail on take off, inflight failure or punch out the engine at the halfway point so we can reach our destination. The PPC deferred to me as I had the proverbial engine figured out. Finally we said good-bye to Jerry and wished them luck.

Five hours into the flight the engineer feathered engine number four. The engine performed well but you just can't take your eye off of the needles showing number four's performance. The plane landed with three engines at Roosevelt Roads. It was dark so we taxied and shut down and secured the airplane. We called Brunswick and told them the story. The Squadron Duty Officer will tell the XO what we had told him. The next morning the maintenance flight engineer dumped the strainers and found nothing foreign. Signals from Brunswick told us to hold where we are and there will be a plane to arrive this afternoon. We waited and waited and finally a plane landed. The PPCs had a conference and they decided to shift passengers, namely me and Lt. Brand to the plane from Brunswick. LE-9 took off and it was a test flight, I know it is night and the moon is out. Apparently one more flight is necessary as we launched and made it back to VP-11. Incidentally, LE-9 lost number four engine on the way back to Brunswick.

Cdr. Martinsen was more than happy that I was back. I spent the entire morning on what transpired since I was gone a week. The calendar was full of commitments through December 1978. Clearly, the road ahead was going to be tough, but what the hell, we are ready for them. The cancer that was starting to grow on the squadron was predicted by the six month crew chart. In January 1979 we had only eleven crews with bits and pieces of a twelfth crew. The hardest hit were the flight engineers. There were two engineers per crew, each one is training at VP-30 and continues training until he gets his aircrew wings as flight engineer. Inter alia, they are still deficient in certain crew members that show a definite shortfall in attaining twelve crews. I put the XO in charge of contacting the respective detailers. The other matters were taken care of by the respective department heads. Readiness was moving upward, and all was going well until Marty hit me with this one. Next week we were to move to hanger one! This is the big hanger approximately 200 yards down the right hand side of the road. The movers (VP-11) will move all of the maintenance gear and files, the operations personnel and admin. personnel will shoulder all the files including typewriter over to the new hanger which is occupied by the other side by Fleet Air Wing Five!! "All right Marty, what's next," I said.

I have neglected to tell you this story but it relates to the reenlistment of sailors to stay in the Navy. When I took over Command the enlistment Petty Officer transferred to another command. We had three volunteers for the job. The man that turned my head was a second mechanic working in maintenance. He had poise, a way with conversation and was knowledgeable about the various programs in the Navy. ASM2 Dave Bean went to the retention school and come back with nothing but new reenlistments. As a matter unrecorded in VP-11's history, I put on a QD-1 "poopie suit" and entered a MK-7 raft and enlisted a willing VP-11 sailor. Incidentally, I had several photographs of me in blues. What was so significant about these pictures is I wore my wife's wig. Now wait a minute, keep it clean. The photographer took one picture with the front view, the side view and with the cover off, the back view. I had these pictures posted in each shop regardless of whether its maintenance or whatever. They were posted all over the squadron.

After we got moved to the big hanger we began in earnest to think about mining. My philosophy towards mining has not changed in fourteen years. The mining concept through the years is the same old bugaboo. The source of fear above board is whether a P-3 airplane can deliver four mines without taking a missile hit or machine gun fire which knocks the plane to the ground. The minefield was off the coast of South Carolina. The specific mines were old but apparently there were plenty of them. Mines were dropped North and South on specific course lines. Each crew practices the runs in the WST. At least nine crews practiced the flights. AIO planned a flight which made a flight with no mines and made the navigator happy. The radar came on to find the radar aiming point. The Tactical Coordinator and the navigator teamed up and hit each box with the four mines given to each crew. The day before the minex we had six planes. The other three planes were in Equador playing Unitas with only three more weeks in the exercise. The morning of the exercise they got off at least five of the airplanes. The weather at the mining range was zero-zero. The VP-11 planes showed up but to no avail. Since the range was closed they returned for another try tomorrow. When the XO landed I talked to him about the flight. He said the flight was foggy as ever. The weather predicted for the next twenty-four hours remains the same. I wanted to do something for the squadron. I volunteered to preflight the six flight. Additionally I have a videocamera which I was going to film the start , taxi and take off of the airplanes. Halfway through the preflight a technician came in and removed the APS-80 radar to put in another plane. Finished with our preflight I went outside where I could see the airplanes lined up. I got the engine start and they all began to taxi. At precisely when the second hand hit zero, the first plane roared down the runway. Clearly it was a day of concern and I could not get started in anything. Praise God, the XO sent a message which broke out, "completed the Minex." The last plane had not landed, but the Duty Officer had told me that the airplane was struck by birds and they had been forced to land in NAS Jacksonville.

Presumably LCDR Don Rahn nursed his plane to Jacksonville and found the damage. A close encounter with a pelican caused the damage and in fact it was a miracle the crew made it back to the base. The pelican's final roost was the leading edge of the starboard wing of the Orion. That bird barely missed a relief air line or even a wiring handle that would have been disastrous. In summary, the total damage included a large dent on the nacelle, a popped cooling latch, and an impact hole. Landing at Jacksonville, the Aircraft Intermediate Maintenance Depot (AIMD) and Naval Air Rework Facility (NARF) are prime helpers in getting the plane operational in three days.

The Minex was a tremendous success. Out of twenty mines, I believe nineteen are in the box. The next morning at quarters I congratulated the crews which performed superior feats yesterday down at the mining range. Here I poked a little fun at the XO but he laughed as well.

Despite the flying and getting ready for something, Jane and I decided to have people over during the week. We know that twelve crews over one crew a night was a burden. Enter a calculus problem and the branch of differential and integral compromise that two crews are the obvious choice. We have a very good time at our house because the crews were themselves. The unpretentious crowd really know about life and being someone's friend means a great deal to me. The Administrative inspection came next. The Wing Five conducted the various inspection of the officers and the Chief Petty Officers. They inspected the officers that were in South America, which would be back in two weeks. Last but not least, a Command inspection was held and Commodore Osborn lead the review of officers and enlisted. I warned the Department Heads about being sharp. The Commodore looked for this but he never found a shabby uniform, shoes not polished, and I found sailors looking spotlessly clean. The Commodore was most happy with the results and was overwhelmed by the superior military expression of VP-11. Never holding back, the Commodore presented six medals and some reenlistments which almost stole the show. After the party from the Wing departed, I told the men that you are to be proud of yourself and Pegasus. You know, I am so nice you have the rest of the day off. That lead to a cheer, but the duty picked up by the watch and in ten minutes time there was nobody on the hanger deck.

LCDR Leigh Calloway and the two aircraft returned from South America. I chose Lee as the Detachment Officer for the second half of Unitas XIX. Lee did a bang up job in assisting airplanes and crew performing diligent ASW work. I remember that there was an airplane crash into the side of a mountain in Equador or Peru. I was in the Commodore meeting when I had a call from LCDR Calloway. I was pleased to know that it was not one of my airplanes. The XO and I welcomed them home and congratulations. Two days later the message was on the board giving credit which was well deserved by all hands. The professional and unselfish way in which our crews eliminated the threat of the nuclear submarine, clearly were appreciated by COMPATWINGSLANT and Fleet Air Wing Five.

With the winds blowing, the final event was the Fleet Air Wing Five Antisubmarine Warfare Operational Readiness Inspection. The squadron had a full officer brief and gave a brief summary of what the Wing was looking for. Tactics has been briefing crews on the same criteria which covers weapons, and various details of bad guy knocking down aircraft. I was excused from the operational exercise. As a matter of fact we could only provide eleven crews. Most of the aircrews did well, but one or two crews got hit when they fly to close to the target. In essence, I was pleased yet I was quite angry when an LCDR Wing observer told me about a certain crew. Afterwards, I told the XO to see the PPC and find out what went wrong with the crew. The result of the whole incident, was a mistake by the Wing observer not understanding what the problem was.

Department heads and the rest of us got together about ten days before we went to visit the deployment sites. The meeting was going on hell-bent for leather. As we surmised during a training presentation, we knew it would not help by rotating crews to meet individual squadrons going on deployment. In fact we have sixty days left before we deploy. All in all the list gained to twenty or thirty would be a reasonable guess relating to Eleven's shortage. From this colloidal substance, I gave the AIO the elements of the brief that I was going to give to the admiral. I had every reason to believe that in three weeks time nothing will dare to change its' present situation.

On the twenty seventh of November we take off to Lajes Naval Station and dropped off our Chief Petty Officer and then land in Rota, Spain. We went double-hatted the XO and I. We started by visiting with the Commanding officer of Rota, Spain. Then we went to the squadron occupying this important base. We paid a call while our Chiefs were checking on quarters, supplies, maintenance and other items. Later on in the afternoon we talked with Tactical Support Officer Commander Ed Stacy. He briefs us on many targets they have tracked over the last nine months. The analysis of AW's made numerous changes in the track Echo II, Charlie, Victor, and had just finished the conventional track which was revised. Ed told of many attempts to snare the intruder in the barrier outside the strait. There must be a practical way to stop this problem. He then switched to Foxtrot and Juliet's wander back and forth across the straits. Finally the Soviets had unleashed a very skilled fighting armada into the Mediterranean. We should have a ball here.

The next stop was Naples, Italy. I introduced Marty to Captain Bradley, Commander Bob Prehn, and several new bodies that I know in CTF-67. We talked about several things. We talked about Extendexs' outside the strait, conventional subs and Soviets making headlines with the super-ships in the Mediterranean (Sounds like CDR Ed Stacy!). Lunch was spent over at the NATO Officers Club where Mrs. Barbara Prehn met us for lunch. That night we went to several bars and wound up eating at the hotel. We flew back to Rota the next day and picked up out agents who needed support and maintenance contacts. The plane landed and took one passenger and were off to Lajes. Captain Rabuck has been in Lajes since the 27 June 1978. He became CO of Navy Air Facility, Lajes, plus several commands that are connected here. We met several friends who were related to the facilities of the base. Dave Stromberg was the TSC officer and he chatted with us for thirty minutes. He gave us several clues which are used in the Extendex missions both in the Atlantic but also into the Mediterranean Sea. The second mission gives Lajes the ability to exercise the CTU 84.2.3 link between Lajes and CTF-67. Strictly surveillance is normally only ten to fifteen percent of all tasking each month. The rest of the trip on the island was the review of sonobuoys, weapons (loading only) and additional engines and assorted propellers that we stocked ready for the asking. We flew home on the thirtieth of November.

Review of the data that the Air Intelligence Officer had accumulated for the Pre Deployment brief was refreshing but incomplete. Yes, and I was angry with the prognosis. Despite the many phonecons to Washington detailers, it looks like we are going with eleven crews plus this and that. We made numerous changes which will solidify our readiness and crew qualifications. Essentially this is our position as we drove over to present our findings at Wingslant. Admiral Hedges came into receive me and shook my hand. There were about 30 people present, mostly from the staff and from the Wing Five staff. I began my brief with Donna Brand manning the slide projector. I went through all the slides of administraton, operations and finally maintenance showing the separation of each base with Rota acting as the only base for maintenance work. Then came the big item and the slide designated "Deployment Lajes/ Rota 1979." On this pictorial were four or five "bullets." Each one of the other 'stoppers' caused concern with the audience. The first one was number of crews deployed. This viewgraph was replaced by the call made to the detailers starting in August 1978. This eventually turned into a shouting match with the Winglant Commander consulting with the Commodore about the needs of VP-11. Captain Oak Osborn agreed that he would do something for us and this would be approved by the Admiral. The brief was blown wide open by the questions which were asked and answered by my officers. I had made my point as the Commodore told me he would check with the assignment desk on when he could fill those billets. I must admit that I had shaken the building at Topsham, Maine. The checklist that means you are ready for deployment, certainly did not succeed after this show was over. I am sorry but others in command should have stepped in to resolve certain issues prior to deployment.

Forward Looking Infrared Radar (FLIR) was designed to be put aboard the P-3C aircraft. This FLIR was modified again and placed on the nose of the P3C. The FLIR is used at night and provides ranges out to five miles for a snorkel. The weather has its advantages and disadvantages. A low cloud layer at 1000 feet can be a hindrance to the detection range. Once a cloud is detected you must get under the cloud layer to maintain the range of the system. A message from Naval Station Rota, Spain said that all FLIR systems were down. We were info on this message. A meeting was called in my office about this system being used on deployment. That afternoon I was told that the system was in bad shape, no one helped the contractor with the systems and frankly we did not know whether that system would be available for use during our stay there. The bell rang and I told everyone that I wanted a message speeding up the fixing of the four FLIR sets immediately. Additionally I wanted the necessary back ups last years deployment could prove this was necessary to antisubmarine warfare. That message went out after touching base with COMPATWINGLANT and WING FIVE. Believe me, that message caused quick compliance and three days later WINGSLANT sent the plan to repair, fix, maintain the units at Rota. By the first of the year we were supposed to be sent a man to fix the first and remaining aircraft. I was pleased to know the remaining gear would be repaired on three aircraft.

There are many things that a Commanding Officer doesn't want to share with you. This time and place makes everyone wonder what happens to the Aviation Warfare rating? Case in point, a plastic binder similar to the VP Tacaid was produced for the Jezebel operators. During a recent check, one of the plastic binders was missing. It was missing for two weeks or more until I was told about the document. The document is classified beyond relief or secret noform. According to all the manuals, a message must be sent to the Navy Security Group. I checked with the Wing Five personnel and they said to send the message. Of course the Commodore was on a trip so we sent the message. At any rate, we should start all over again, and search with a fine tooth comb all safes in the immediate area.

Christmas was upon us; we started shopping and it had been snowing for several days. We had a beautiful tree and the house was decorated for Christmas. We attended many parties. We finally sat down in the den and lit a fire in the fireplace. It was nice and comfy especially if you have a small glass of Drambuie in your hand!

With all the divisons packing and moving equipment out on the pallets set down for packing on the C-141 aircraft. I can't figure out what squadron or what group these Air Force Planes fall under, but they sure do a hell of a job. The first aircrew left for Rota, Spain. We have sent some men to get the training and repair of the FLIR night vision device. Once the squadron is deployed, in Lajes each plane gets a new navigation system which adds a great load to the ASN-42 system which we have in the airplane. Soon the Air Force plane landed and the pallets of supplies were loaded. In one day we saw one half of our squadron leave. Marty left for Lajes and I imagine he will stay there about three weeks or so. We have many things to accomplish but we had better get on deployment.

VP-11 Deployment Naval Station Rota, Spain

I left on January 28, 1979 and it was the last of our nine airplanes. Jane and the children wished me the best and wanted me home as soon as possible. The P-3B rose into the air headed for Spain. We flew for eight and a half hours. It was light when we landed and the Master Chief was there to meet me. He welcomed me and said there were problems in the Bachelor Enlisted Quarters. Apparently the VP-26 enlisted had a field day with things like bed bunks, sheets, blankets, and numerous items. As it stands now, half of the men of VP-11 do not have a decent rooms in which to hang their hats. After checking into the BOQ, I filled up my room with gear. I changed to khakis and took my car over to the enlisted quarters. I saw what they were talking about. The BEQ was in horrible shape. I next went to see the

Commanding Officer of the base. I waited for a half an hour only to see him for five minutes. I told him that I was disappointed in the condition of the enlisted barracks. He was embarassed by my description of the broken-down, inhospitable and barren quarters that were offered to my men. Captain Hansen canceled the next meeting and made a series of phone calls. Fifteen minutes later we had verification of what I just alleged. I was pleased with this meeting. All of our men will be taken care of by 1800 hours!

Back at the Tactical Support Center I parked in the squadron CO parking space and walked over to see CDR Stacy, the head of the TSC. Ed Stacy was due to get command but that's coming later in the year. We discussed what was going on today wth regard to VP-11. SIXFLEET was running carrier operations in the Western Mediterrean Sea. Something that I did not know, was the first flight by LCDR George Conner PPC, detected a Charlie Class submarine. Ed led me into the room where pertinent AQA-7 gram analysis is being conducted. The reason that the tapes are played over is that you can dip below the detection range and can hold a target at least by five decibels below the AQA-7. The Charlie submarine was shadowing the carrier group. The P-3B was putting in a lofar pattern and detected the sub which yielded a closest point approach on one buoy. The crew extended a lofar mini-barrier ahead of the submarine. Immediately the minibarrier got contact on one buoy. The sub appeared to change depth and all of a sudden it was gone. We talked about all the exercises that were coming up in February 1979. Finally I went over to the squadron to set up my office. The Administration/Personal officers were set up and running. The safe, which held a secret document, was turned over to me by the communications officer. The first message was released by me which states that VP-11 is in control at the time to CTF-67 and info COMSIXFLEET.

After lunch at the Officers Club, I took a two hour nap. Down at the hangar just about all personnel were in the working spaces. I borrowed a set of ear protectors and walked out on the line where two men were putting on the Forward Looking Infrared Radar (FLIR). One of the men was a company representative who shook my hand. He thanked me for stirring up the pot! This airplane was the last one to be configured for FLIR. I told both men that I was glad that we had four pieces of gear that worked. No, I was wrong, they had five FLIR's that worked.

At 5:00 p.m., I showed up at the BEQ. The people were working on fixing the problem. The Master Chief was still hot around the collar, but the building was taking shape. The station reps were there and a load of sheets and beds arrived as we watched. Apparently, the finalization of everything is due tomorrow, Saturday. By the time I got the car, a Petty Officer said that the Commanding Officer of the base wanted to see me. It was five thirty and the secretary told me to go in. He wanted an update of the situation based on what I had told him this morning. I went through the episode step by step until the situation was starting to take shape. He asked me a question, had I called the Wing Commodore and complained about the problem? No, I had not called because I knew that someone else was at fault.

My phone was ringing when I got back to the BOQ. It was Marty reporting that the enlisted and officers' rooms were nearly destroyed by rampaging men of the Navy. Marty reported that he called the Wing and reported the damage. Marty was happy with the move and he wanted me to review all of the officers fitness reports on the fourteenth of February. I told Marty that we had some success (submarine) and we were looking to get more.

Monday morning was a cloudy, rainy day. The station reserved the theater for us. The station introduced us to Spain, it's habits and it's customs. We had the attention of everyone and then the Commanding Officer of the Rota Naval Station shows up. He spoke on many subjects. His lecture on drugs and other narcotics and the Spanish outlook, made men listen or they paid the consequence. I walked the Captain out and he said, "By the way, Captain Osborn is coming this afternoon!."

Captain Osborn arrived at Rota, Spain late Monday night. I met him and Dick Petrucci when they got off the plane. They went to the BOQ and retired that evening. The next morning they toured the BEQ and went over to see the Captain of the Naval Station. I got a call requesting me to meet with them in my office. About fifteen minutes later Captain Osborn came in along with six officers. Once they got inside, the door was closed. Captain Osborn indicated that this was something that was going to stop. They toured Lajes yesterday and saw much of the damage that the previous squadron had inflicted. I feel relieved when the mess in Rota had been rectified. Clearly, I know that drunkenness breeds aggressive behavior; unbecoming of an Enlisted man or Officer in the Navy.

This squadron was busy starting in February. The first thing that happened was a FLIR sighting of a Foxtrot alongside a tanker. We started conducting carrier operations and on the fifth of February I went to Naples. We were intending to fly on the Foxtrots before they came through the straits. This would mean advanced information on the target and thereby we could initiate CTU 84.2.3 operations. Of course, the only detection that works is when the submarine can snorkel and he does it at night. The answer is FLIR, which appears as if we are flying in the daytime. The theory caught quite a few off guard, but wait until we have pictures of the wily Foxtrot.

CDR Stacy met me coming down the airplane in Rota. He said he had permission to lay a barrier for the Victor nuclear submarine that was detected off and on from Iceland. In the TSC we looked at the display and where it supposedly was regained. That fix was twenty four hours old and the barrier should be in place at eight o'clock in the morning. In three minutes a message went to Lajes and a simular message from me requesting barrier operations for the new intruder. At ten o'clock at night the Duty Officer called and said all arrangements have been made. I could not sleep. I got up at five thirty in the morning. LCDR Ray Honey met me at the TSC. The offgoing ready duty is the first flight out and all other flights have been rescheduled for the barrier flights. I wish I was a pilot not a Tactical Coordinator!

At eight o'clock at night we did not have contact. A CTF-67 message was sent indicating that the Extendex will be termimated at eight o'clock tomorrow. That did not set well with me. I sat down and did some figuring. I know dam well the the Victor was watching his VHF monitoring those frequencies of the sonobuoys.

On the fourteenth of February I took off to Lajes Naval Facility. I really missed Marty and I went to get him! All joking aside, I went to debrief the officers on the fitness reports. The weather was rotten with wind reaching gusts to sixty or seventy miles per hour. On the first night I spent time reviewing seven fitness reports. My idea of reviewing a fitness report is showing and explaining what data goes into the first section of the report. Then I go on to tell what factors are used in the specific aspects of performance and in the warfare specialty skills that are viable in this report. The pluses and minuses that characterizes the individual, clearly enables me to rank and give a clear, succinct picture of an individual. The next day I finished the thirty officers. They, by and large, appreciated the time and the effort that I spend on each of them.

With just a month gone in the deployment I was trying to figure out what was going on with respect to finding submarines. We had failed miserably in setting up the barriers outside the straits. In fact, CTF 67 has entered in a stop at twenty-four hours of no contact. Let's set the record straight: we have two or three positive Foxtrot with signal numbers courtesy of forward infrared systems and our Charlie nuclear sub picked up by sonobuoy. That reminded me of a recent message which I received earlier in the morning. I yelled at the Administration Chief to get the message board right away. In five minutes time he presented the message board and I found what could be the key for further prosecution. The apparent fix was a Foxtrot which was heading to the Mediterranean and the estimated position which would be twenty four hours by eight o'clock the next morning. I opened my left desk drawer and pulled out a blue notepad. I began writing a message and before long I called Ed Stacy to tell him that I wanted to see him. The navigation office was down the hallway. I grabbed a chart that covered the Atlantic Ocean and out to 018 degrees West. The latitude blanketed the area West of the straits and went up a latitude of forty-six degrees. I plotted the estimated fix of the Foxtrot which was headed south at six knots. Based on my plotting the submarine would be in CTU84.2.3 area by dark tomorrow night. Ed still had not showed, so I grabbed my message pad and went over to see him. Ed was busy with one of his officers so I asked the watch officer if he could call up the Foxtrot that should be entering the Mediterannean within five or six days. He entered in two buttons and "presto-chango" the track was displayed from Norway into the Strait of Gibraltar. I had the Petty Officer of the watch downscale and enter the track from forty three degrees North all the way to thirty six North and 006 degrees West. Intricate and exact, I used the arrow range markers to enter the initial position. This would be our initial fix position that we would use for FLIR detection.

Cdr. Stacy finally finished his discussion with his officer and he knew what plans I have been plotting. He sat down and listened. He went over all reports of intelligence and agreed the best deal reckoning position is the one for VP-11 to prosecute at night. The tactics could wait but lets get the ball rolling. My spelling when he reviewed my message, was atrocious! We then worked on CTU84.2.3 message and now we waited. It happened like 'gangbusters' and in four hours we were granted permission of the Atlantic area.

The next morning we had a morning officers meeting. After the speakers were though, I stood up and announced that we were commencing a Foxtrot chase and if our plans gain contact, and track it each night until we escort it through the Straits of Gibraltar. Additionally we can figure out what's wrong or what's right with this prosecution. I want to hold this contact until I am tired of being on top or we set a new record of contact time. I went on to say that I will lead the Foxtrot into the Mediterranean Sea.

At 5:00 p.m., the first airplane took off. The estimated position was a forty one fifty North, thirteen degrees West. The crew was to remain passive an hour before onstation. At onstation they will begin a FLIR search at five hundred feet working up the reverse of the submarine course with tracks employing ten mile track spacing. The distance is fourteen to twelve west and continues up to the previous fix. I was camped out in the TSC. It became ten o'clock and no news was heard from the first airplane onstation. At ten thirty the crew found the snorkel, a Foxtrot submarine, 180 at 5 knots. Yes, I was happy and now the long hard road begins. The next evening Donna Brand showed the picture of the snorkel to the maintenance night shift. Many of the Petty Officers were excited. I was there answering any questions they had. Night prosecution flight number two found him. The target had adjusted his course as he continued to enter the Mediterranean. Flight number three had difficulty gaining contact because of the fog in the area. Finally both crews had him on FLIR. The final flight depended on night flight four. The plane took off when it was dark. The plane searched and could not find the submarine. Finally, the second sortie got contact. The submarine was at 36 05 North and 007 West. He pulled the plug and the next flight will be my flight to welcome him to the Mediterranean. Just to keep my record clean, LCDR Honey will be on the flight to back up what mistakes I may make!

We were off at five o'clock sharp and we made it to onstation at 6:00 p.m. We started heading West searching for eye contact and a half hour later we concentrated on the FLIR. At nine o'clock the Foxtrot came up and started snorkeling. The FLIR operator was having a big celebration. I drafted up the communications report and told the communicator to send it. We dropped a Lofar sonobuoy to show the Jezebel operator what the grams look like. Twenty minutes later the radio operator still had not gotten through to the TSC. I went to the cockpit and told them that we had not gotten a roger for the contact report. We climbed up to twenty thousand feet and the only way we got through was to call the Squadron Duty Officer. I told him we were sweet when we made contact. He rogered that remark! At ten o'clock the moon came out so we climbed up to four thousand feet and maintained our flexibility to return and employ active tactics. I already loaded the active sonobuoy and smoke in the retro. I must add that we changed the man monitoring the FLIR scope. We change about every forty minutes or when the man gets tired. Finally at eleven thirty we heard a covered message which announces the arrival of Ray Honey and crew. I gave him the position which had FLIR and other outstanding information. I passed to him that he be as covert as possible as the Foxtrot is going to dive as soon as the sun comes up. Ray rogered all and said see you later. We retired to the West and climbed to twenty thousand feet and headed home.

At 6:00 a.m. I was awakened by the phone. The duty officer said that there had been some problems with the onstation aircraft. I could not venture a guess of what happened. I got up, showered , shaved and got dressed and into the TSC thirty five minutes later. Unbeknownst to me or to anyone else, a French carrier barged in a 4000 yard active sonobuoy pattern and lost the amazing Foxtrot submarine. As soon as light commenced from the East the submarine pulled the plug. Ray Honey was right there with active prosecution, MAD and over the horizon comes the French carrier interfacing without permission. I

must admit that after five nights of prosecution this information leaked into NATO after it had been readdressed to the appropriate allies! The prosecution lasted over seventy-five or better hours. We prosecuted one more day and then gave the prosecution to the P-3C squadron out of Sigonella, Sicily. They had their eyes on the target when they detected him on their first flight.

Let's turn the tables on Lajes. CDR Marty Martinsen had been working on the reserve liaisons which permits reserve squadrons to spend two weeks active duty at Lajes Naval Facility. Captain Rabuck had been fully appraised of the squadrons and they have been doing a bang-up job. VP-11 has been worked into all Extendexes concerning particularly the Yankee class nuclear submarines. This submarine spends about sixty days on a mission from port to port. As it comes around Norway it takes a track of two hundred degrees true and comes into the North Atlantic Ocean. Once it gets to the volcano position which stretches from Iceland, Lajes and through the Atlantic, the submarine enters the Lajes prosecution area. VP-11 ready duty is usually the first aircraft airborne to lay a set of barriers with hopes of making a detection. The Extendex really shifts to high gear when initial contact is gained. The reserve aircraft are interjected and produces excellent contact and tracking. The Yankee SSBN (had sixteen missiles pointed at the continental United States) goes onstation and slows to four or five to eight knots. The target comes to one eight zero and goes for a certain period comes to two seven zero for a short period and from there, heads home for a sixty day period.

On the twenty eighth of March I went on a patrol to Lajes, to pick up the XO. I spent some time with my troops. Marty was glad to be leaving. He has made quite an impression with the VP-11 and the deploying reserve. The next day we took off and we were Rota bound. We rigged several ships when we got a call from the TSC in Rota, Spain. They requested that we assist a destroyer and helicopter who had contact in the strait. We had two more hours of fuel onboard, so we headed through the Strait of Gibraltar. Radar picked up about four targets about thirty five miles ahead. The pilots started to communicating with the destroyer. The helicopter had contact but lost contact. After we had gotten the gist of the data we laid a pattern with two miles spacing. This did not work and soon the destroyer that was pinging soon became detected by the sonobuoys. Soon our two hours of fuel were gone and we checked out with the destroyers.

Donna Brand brought me some intelligence that indicated that the Foxtrot we had so much luck keeping track of, is headed back home. Tonight's flight will be against that particular submarine. That night the wires were humming as the airplane got contact on the Foxtrot. After review of the pictures, Donna Brand showed us the marking on the sail. It was a match. We sent out a perfect match of the Foxtrot, but certain members of CTF 67 did not believe this was the case. I became infuriated with these imbeciles and the next morning Lt. Brand and I went to Naples to clear this incident. I got all of the intelligence nits, the Captain and showed them the FLIR film tapes of the incoming and outgoing Foxtrot. Without a doubt, we had the Foxtrot permanent number fifteen on the sail. With that finally lodged in everyone's mind, we left Naples knowing that we had done what we were supposed to do.

At eight o'clock in the morning the TSC provides me with a morning brief. The ready duty sits right behind me as I ask them if they have any questions or comments. I have found this brings out the questions. The last item that CDR Stacy brought up was Echo II contact that was headed South, presumably headed to the Mediterranean. It looks like Lajes is good to fly on this contact. The submarine is in position for CTU 84.2.3 operations in twenty four hours. "I think we should fly, don't you, CDR Martinsen?," I said. With that subject getting warmer we discussed the ready duty and started a message to Lajes. Lajes has programmed six flights and they were going to switch submarines and go Yankee hunting. Lajes launched the request and included COM-SIXFLEET as info. CINCLANTFLEET was asked to approve CTU 84.2.3 operations. The flight was barely in side of the operational boundary. The Echo II was picked up on the third barrier. He was tracked for an hour and a half. The aircraft left station and there was a six hour delay in one event. The second airplane started laying sonobuoys and finally gained contact. One hour after contact the plane laid a minibarrier and waited for contact. The contact came but then it faded away. I think if this would have happen to me, I would ring sonobuoys around the last fix or the center of the minibarrier. Contact was never regained on the Echo II. We wanted to try a standing barrier West of the straits. But this paltry gang in Naples refused this request.

A major point in my life had been talking to my wife every weekend. She told me the good, the bad and even the incidental news of the squadron wives. Jane dealt with women. All kinds and that made a difference in my life. She told me of old problems that are resolved and new ones that are on the horizon. One problem hit me the hardest, she had to have surgery. She told me of her female problems and she would go under the knife next week. Her Mother and step Father will be with her in Brunswick, Maine. I told Marty about this and wondered if I could get back for the operation. Before I knew it, Marty had me flown to Lajes and away I went to Brunswick. I got to the hospital and Jane was coming out of the operating room. The doctor was there and he said she was all right. That night I spent with my children and with Bob and Edna. The next morning I was at the hospital bright and early. I spent most of the day with Jane and I was back on the plane headed to Rota, Spain.

In the third week of April I was concerned about the airplane turboprop engines that we have been replacing. During the deployment we had countless engine changes due to propeller feathering problems, o-ring seal deficiencies, fluctuation of revolution per minute (110%-90%), engine hydraulic fluid change and myriad other problems that continued to pull both aircraft and readiness down to a new level. With a Rota/Lajes split the major maintenance facility is where the CO is positioned. I must say that I had the best and hardest working maintenance division that I have ever known. We weren't strong but in April we made many replacements of men and Chiefs and we turned around the up status of the Pegasus airplane. I looked back over the accumulation of Allison turboprop problems and most amplify the wrongs of the timeframe:

1. We did not have the additional knowledge of these peculiar problems with engines.

2. The hydraulic fluid was not standardized and all the engines were made to change to a new modern fluid. In other words, we had a P-3B model so we changed to the new fluid. I am not sure about this but I think we shifted back to the old hydraulic fluid.

3. The P-3 community banded together to get more turbine blades in stock. Lockheed, the builder of the airplane, was short of blades as well. So back in 1978 through 1979 there was a shortage whereby cannibalizing the old turbines was the only way to keep enough turbine blades in the fleet.

One of my finest experiences came when we reached out and touched the Spanish P-3 antisubmarine force. LCDR Ray Honey gets the credit for having the Commanding Officers down and soon we played the conventional submarine. We got permission of the Spanish P-3 to fly during the daylight hours. Yes, they got a snorkel or a periscope just inside the straits and it obviously was a Foxtrot sub. We made several trips up to their officers club. We played soccer with them but no doubt you know how that turned out.

Talking about engine failure, I was reminded of Lajes having unbelievable problems. Lt. Andy Scontras was Plane Commander who was having success in nuclear submarine hunting. Andy, known about town as an accomplished Greek pilot aficionado, was well liked and well thought of.

Andy was launched with his crew on a Yankee SSBN and made initial contact. He was tracking the submarine when one of the mysterious consequences described previously struck one of his engines. He feathered it and decided that he would return with three engines. He left onstation about an hour early and tried to gain radio contact with Lajes. The next thing that happened was the second engine had similar overspeed problems that Andy encountered an hour ago. Let's set the stage for what will happen at Lajes Naval Facility. With two engines turning, everybody was strapped in a Condition Five, and the plane landed successfully. Every crew member waited for Lt. Scontras and he came down the ladder of the airplane first and kissed the ground! I read the message first and sent him a personal message, giving him credit for his flying skill. He did not know it but I recommended that he receive a medal for his emergency management accomplishment.

May is only forty days away from the Change of Command. The program has been selected by Commodore Osborn: introducing the guest speaker, remarks by Captain Leo V. Rabuck, and other details to be worked out. Donna Brand was in charge, so off to the printers. We made another trip to the Western coast of England. The facility acts as an early warning station which gives a heads up on important targets such as submarines. We left at seven o'clock in the morning. We were nearly there when the number 3 engine started giving "bouncers." The rpm ranged from 90% moving right back to 100% engine revolutions per minute. The PPC chose to shut number 3 down and check the engine on the deck. The airfield was spacious. The British and

American counterpart began briefing the procedures they used to predict the intelligence for us. We spend the afternoon asking questions and at two o'clock we were at the airplane. The Plane Captain and the PPC said the engine did not need an engine change. The pump and strainer of number three engine was free of engine particles which indicates engine breakup. Finally we got back to Rota but I was right, another dam engine change!

Hot, humid and muggy was the weather in Rota. In fact, I had decided to wait for rain rather than walk the mosquito-infested golf course. We, the XO, and several others, used to exercise the "white ball" but were eaten alive! Saturday night Jane called and said she was not coming to the Change of Command! She told Shirley that the surgery she had last month was still sore and painful. I asked her to reconsider but was turned down. I had anticipated her position when I last saw her doctor.

Saturday night at the Officers' Club Marty and I had a beautiful dinner with wine. Marty and I have become friends. The things that we kept secret beyond were aboveboard when we were talking behind closed doors. We sensed each other's problems, that assisted open discussions about which way to turn. If we had fifty conversations, then I guess we had over one hundred answers. One thing that amazed me was in May he complained of chest pains. I recommended that he go see the doctor ASAP! Marty told me about his dad who died early of a massive heart attack in his late 40's. Marty is my trusted right hand man.

The Monday message board told of VP-11 deploying to Souda Bay in five days. Marty had a gang of five which represented the major department heads. Ray Honey went through the needs and wherefores of the detachment. He nominated three crews and then each department chimed in on certain parameters. Lt. Bill Ford was my Maintenance Officer. He gave his list of Chief Petty Officers he was sending. Finally the Communications gave their pitch, with two men to fill this detachment. With that said, in 20 minutes the appropriate messages were sent. Lt. Donna Brand could not go but sent her Petty Officer who was building a current file of intelligence. I wanted to see this information before the planes left. With the crew chosen and the planes ready, the Detachment Officer, I believe, was LCDR Don Rahn. I gave him names of the personnel who were there last year. In my view I could see big happenings in Souda Bay and Don reinforced those ideas.

Commander Glenn T. "Marty" Martinsen

Saturday I saw the three planes take off and that left us with two aircraft. As if we were going to have a quiet few days in Rota, Ed Stacy was waiting in my office. Lajes was working an Echo II which was transiting south, presumably taking a left at the strait and entering the Mediterranean Sea. Ed and I sent a message info CTF 67 giving our two or three crews ample time to prosecute the nuclear sub. The next night three consecutive crews both held contact and it was Rota's turn to draw blood. CTU 84.2.3 was established and our plane took off. They gained contact and held contact throughout onstation. They were happy and they felt that tracking the sub was elementary. But the submarine was getting further south and the water was getting more conducive to shorter ranges. The second crew out was onstation and the maximum range of the target was two or three miles away. No contact was their message when they came onstation. Eventually they lost contact about two hours before, so the Tactical Coordinator went down the course line 30 miles and started a barrier. Two hours later, bingo, he started printing on a sonobuoy. This led to a series of Difar sonobuoys which established a course. Perilous fixing continued for about an hour. Difar was placed about five miles down the track and then the crew waited. Nothing happened, no sound and the predominate harmonics was silenced by a drastic reduction of speed or a check of her aft which requires clearing of her baffles. That was the last time this crew saw the Echo II!.

Meanwhile, back at Souda Bay, Crete, the detachment was flying patrols off of Egypt. The intelligence which I saw had good locating data on a Charlie nuclear submarine. Apparently it was sited near a docking facility near the city of Cairo, Egypt. The British Nimrod was flying that day and with little strain we had contact on the Charlie. The Nimrod came over and had contact as well. The only problem was that the Charlie was headed into one of the danger zones that we are aware of in our briefing book.

VP-11 was together again as the Change of Command was only four weeks away. On our backs was a new task force fielded by the Soviets. Kiev and other modern surface ships were headed down to enter the Strait of Gibraltar. I have an idea. I invited VQ-2 (a Fleet Air Reconnaissance squadron) to participate. The first launch was VQ-2 with at least two planes with gear that could intercept this ominous task force. They would raise us by covered voice and we would intercept them without radar. We could utilize electronic warfare, visual, LLLTV (FLIR), but don't use radar! Down the runway went a Pegasus airplane. One hour later the VQ-2 made contact with the Soviet fleet and the contact was reported to the VP-11 aircraft. The airplane was amazed at the armada they saw. The Kiev was laden with firepower. All of the accompanying ships were exuding power. When the airplane returned, the pictures went to the Photography Lab. Lt. Brand was overwhelmed with the task force. She had made arrangements for a station helicopter to take pictures as the force proceeded through the Strait of Gibraltar.

LCDR George Conner was first to volunteer for an airshow that was put together by the Rota Naval Base. George, our NATOPS officer, participated with the maneuvers that the P-3 could do. One engine feathered to two engines feathered on opposite sides were performed. I witnessed the impressive performance. It showed the pride and professionalism we had in our plane, the P-3B Orion.

My final trip to Lajes was my last visit as Commanding Officer of VP-11. I met the men at quarters and told them of what had been going

Captain Oakley Ernest Osborn, USN

on in Rota. I gave out reenlistments, advancements in rate, and finally I called Lt. Andy Scontras, front and enter. This was the first time that I had seen Andy since he landed with two engines out. I don't know whether or not I had a medal to give him, but I read a wonderful citation about his efforts to get the crew and the airplane back on the ground. When finished I walked over to him, shook his hand, and embraced him. I told him the medal was coming, and I wanted to be there when he received the award. Deployments are tough. I would like to relate to you what an aircraft looks like denuded from all four engines. LE-4 was the plane and she was just about void of all workable parts. All the Chiefs that were with me used the term "Lunch Bar" as she sat there on the line. That term is embedded in my mind. The Chiefs promised they and their men would start mounting engines on LE-4. Would it be ready for my Change of Command? "We'll see, said one Chief!"

Getting ready to relieve Command is a big deal. John Morgan Evans has checked in as the new prospective Executive Officer. Bob

Prehn has agreed to come over from Naples and be a guest speaker at the Commanding Officer formal dinner. Commander Parol Wing FIVE, my boss, had wanted Captain Osborn to offer the introduction of the guest speaker, Captain Leo V. Rabuck. As of yet, no word from Naples on who was coming in the Admiral's place. Marty Martinsen assumed the position as guest speaker of the formal affair. I sat down with many bottles of wine, sherry and Bob Prehn at my side. As you would expect the evening turned into a drunkex with many VP-11 officers doings "landings on the carrier." Naval Station Rota the morning after was no better than before. A bloody Mary was what took the edge off and the rest of the day was filled with Cokes and ice water.

It was the night before the Change of Command. Commodore Osborn arrived and was checking into the BOQ. Tomorrow, as expected, Captain Rabuck would arrive in the morning, as well as Captain John T. McNalley, the Chief of Staff of CTF 67. Unfortunately, CTF 67, Rear Admiral Callaghan, would not attend the event. Shirley, Marty's wife, arrived by commercial jet two days before. I worked on my speech well into the night.

Without a doubt, the hanger looked superb for a Change of Command. Dressed to the hilt in whites, swords, and medals, I walked to the platform along with Commander Martinsen. At attention we watched the representatives who were brought aboard by the Chief Bosun Mate's whistle. Another surprise, Admiral Semalea, head of Spanish forces, was accompanied by Capt. Hanson, the Commander of Rota Naval Station. Who chose the band picked a winner. First the National Anthem of Spain and then the National Anthem of the United States of America was played. After the invocation, the audience and the members on the podium sat down.

Captain Oakley Osborn, Commander Patrol Wing Five, was the next speaker to be introduced. I honored him as having a distinctive career in Anti-Submarine Warfare. He was in charge of six Patrol Squadrons, each manned with 300 enlisted and 60 officers. With that said, I welcomed him to the platform. Commodore Osborn addressed all of the titles that were present and stated that it was an excellent day for a Change of Command. Captain Osborn began by stating that two weeks ago he no plans to attend this function. One morning as he was shaving, he knew he must come to Rota. VP-11, in his view, had earned tremendous respect for its' work and professionalism while on

Captain Leo V. Rabuck

deployment. The support in Lajes and Rota, the VQ-2 and the work with the Spanish P-3's, and the BEQ indicated that VP-11 are good residents of Rota. In looking over the year that you had Command, I see the passing of NATOPS, superb Unitas detachment, and this deployment. VP-11 will be counted with the best. And then he turned to me and said, "Commander Brittingham, you have every right to step down today with a warm feeling." Then he introduced Captain Rabuck, Commander, U.S. Naval Forces, Azores.

Captain Rabuck took the platform. I had great respect for the man. I remember in VP-10 dreading my detailer being Rabuck. He said he had been impressed with my deep sense of dedication and responsibility to the mission of Anti-Submarine Warfare. Results count. People perform the functions which man aircrews and the systems that keep them flying. Finally, he spoke of me as having the highest regard for both men and women in my command. Captain Rabuck concluded by remarking Pegasus Power is "the creation of your Commanding Officer."

Not listed on the program was Captain John J. McNally, sitting in for Commander Task Force Sixty-Seven. Captain McNally had two points to make. The Spanish allies and their excellence of anti-submarines was coupled with VP-11's accomplishments, and made a first class exchange of superior forces. Lastly, he talked about the ASW Hook'em Award. Yes, I knew we had won the award. Captain McNally read a part of the message which gives VP-11 the award for April 1979. Incidentally, this message was signed by Vice Admiral James D. Watkins, COMSIXFLEET. Many good thoughts went into the planning and conception of the tracking of the Foxtrot.

After accepting the Hook'em Award, I was called to give my remarks and orders. I started out by remembering a year before we had said we would promote Pegasus Power. Pegasus was a special vision I had for my squadron. It reflected our singular effort to become the best at our task. It was our distinguished insignia. We cared for our personnel. We achieved superior readiness. I was very proud of our reenlistment record. This had been my finest hour.

My one negative thought today is that my partner in marriage is not here today to share this experience with me. Jane Brittingham is not here in person, but she is with me in spirit. For myself and on her behalf, I thank all of you and your wives, whom you have cooperated during these periods of assignment away from our homes.

In conclusion, this past year has been one of great satisfaction due in total to the performance and growth, of our personnel. I shall always remember your unselfish dedication to duty. Your untiring effort to excel has brought Pegasus Power to the forefront. Now I gladly relinquish command to a very highly qualified Commander, Marty Martinsen.

As we take off, headed to Lajes, I said goodbye, to VP-11. Sixteen years had expired. That was the time it took for me to gain command of a patrol squadron. Now I look to the future with anticipation fully expecting good things to happen.

ADDENDUM

Naval Air Station Pensacola, Florida became the first facility to accept and train Naval Aviation Officers on July 1, 1960. These officers found their place in many aircraft. When I became Ensign on 8 February 1963, I became destined to fit into antisubmarine warfare including the Lockheed airplane SP-2E and my first squadron, VP-10.

VP-10 was beset with small problems during my first deployment. With Commander Keith Sharer's guidance and plethora of ASW training, I wrote a letter requesting assignment as a regular Navy officer. Clearly this would lead to my idea of being a respected Navy Flight Officer.

My fitness reports showed personal traits that were desirable when new tactics and procedures were developed or improved. Case in point was the improved manual plotter which I modified into a more workable tool. I was presented the Navy Achievement Medal. As the sailors were headed to P3C schools in January 1969, the officers were sent to Burbank, California for training in the new computerized airplane. I led a group of seven NFO's to Lockheed for five weeks of training in the P3C. The CP-901 computer was called a lot of names, but we learned and catalogued computer language, and preflighted all of the systems that made up the entire electronic network.

I learned recently (1997), that in 1969 the computer system was just catching on. For example, let's take the Tactical Coordinators Multipurpose Display and tray (IP914/ASA 70). The ASA 70 display is the heartbeat of the antisubmarine warfare system. Starting with the trackball, which is located in the center of the table with the TACCO's keyboard immediately to the right, there are three Matrix Select switches when pressed, change to indicate a Matrix Readout. Let's take TACCO "B" Matrix Select and depress transforming it to the Matrix Readout Label. So, for example, lets' experiment with Geo Nav or Geo Navigation. We can now Read LAT LONG, INSERT LAT

LONG, set up a FLIGHT PLAN FTP (fly-to-point), set up a Data Link GRID POSITION, and finally a GRID REF POINT. We are in the technology of today. Windows 95 is our answer to getting any problem solved quickly and accurately. The concepts introduced in the P3C matrix select switches are now in the Menu selections in Windows 95.

In the early seventies I reached my peak as a Mission Commander and Tactical Coordinator in the P3C. I was in a position of naval high regard in 1971. I was on a streak of twenty or more submarines flying at home or on deployment. From 1972 through 1974 my job was helping all squadrons develop and publish tactical documents, readiness evaluations, and trying to untie the bonds of pilot phobia. Indubitably in November 1975 the command list came over the communication lines—I have been deep selected for command.

Captain Dick Zeisel was the man who promoted me. I can't say how many NFO's were selects but in Brunswick I was the second selectee. So the Navy will choose its leaders from its very best. Pilot or Navy Flight Officer demands both airmanship and other characteristics that would elevate this individual to the position of command in a squadron.

On July 31, 1997, I drove up to New Haven, Connecticut where I spent the night in the Quality Inn. The next morning I ended my trip to the Northeast by marking on top McDonalds for a lobster roll, french fries, and a large Diet Coke in Brunswick, Maine. Patrol Squadron Eleven was supposed to be disestablished a year ago. The remainder of the squadron dropped to three people: Commanding Officer CDR David A. Williams, Officer in Charge LCDR David A. Falk, and Command Master Chief, AOCM (AW/NAC) Gerald P. White. All of the former Commanding Officers were sent an invitation and were informed of a "happy hour" at Bath, Maines' Museum at 5:00 p.m. On Friday afternoon, I met with LCDR David Falk. He gave me a notice which stated events for both Friday and Saturday. On Friday at 5:00 p.m., all would gather for a "happy hour" at Bath, ME's Museum. Then on Saturday, August 2nd, would come to the disestablishment ceremony.

Bath, Maine is no stranger to the United States Navy Shipbuilding regime. Bath Ships had been building Frigates, Cruisers, and produced two DDG-51 Arleigh Burke superpower vessels this past year. With the Navy falling by the wayside this year and still eroding next year, we have a skeleton Naval Force, few but the best SSN/SSBN submarines, and twelve carriers with barely enough supporting ships!

The museum was crowded at 5:00 p.m.! I met all of VP-11 from the skipper when Pearl Harbor was bombed to CDR D. H. Wiss who brought VP-11 back to Brunswick, Maine in May 1952. We had beer, wine, and all of the drinks started at a reasonable price. I met many people to include RADM John R. Ryan, who flew over from Naples, Italy. It was a pleasure to shake his hand once again. Admiral Ryan was supposed to speak at the gathering on Saturday. I joined the Admiral and CAPT Richard Brooks and his lovely wife for dinner later that evening.

On August 2, I saw the program for the Disestablishment of Command and the Fleet Air Reconnaissance Squadron VQ-11 Establishment of Command. "Proud Pegasus" is the term that I created or used in my tour throughout my command. It was displayed on the cover of the announcement during 1978 and 1979. That gave me a sense of pride. Regrettably, the commanding officer turnout was less than desired! Commander R. F. Falkenstein, Commander John Morgan Evans, RADM Ryan, and the last skipper, Commander David Williams, were the principals of the ten or so CO's that showed up. To my right in the distinguished seating I had Commander Don McKissock sitting by my side. As you know, he was my friend since 1972.

The program features the arrival of the official party and then the Parading of The Colors followed by the National Anthem. The Invocation was presented by LCDR Tim Lantz and CDR David Williams gave his remarks about the VP-11 disestablishment. CDR Williams went back to the earlier days of Naval Aviation in 1924. LCDR Falk and Command Master Chief AOCM Gerald White hauled down the flag pennant. Next came Captain Richard Brooks who introduced RADM Ryan. Admiral Ryan spoke very briefly as CDR Williams had apparently stolen some of his lines! Finally a new squadron was going to be established as a command, VQ-11 Bandits.

At Naval Air Station Brunswick, Maine there is a site which remains in memory of those who were on deployment that fateful day of December 11, 1977. On August 4, 1997, I paid a visit to the Naval Air Station Chapel. The church looked the same. I went to the office where I met RP1 Maria Murphy. I introduced myself and wondered if I could see the memorial that was put there in April 1978 when we returned from deployment. Petty Officer Murphy and I went outside into the garden that surrounded the church. We checked several markers, and then saw the bronze memorial. It listed the names of those gallant men who went down with the airplane on the island of Hierro, in the Canary Islands. The memory of that disaster brought tears to my eyes. It was neccessary that I explain to Ms. Murphy my relationship to those men.

It was this time in my life when GOD became, and remains, the Supreme Being I knew him to be. I know those thirteen who died in the crash now enjoy everlasting life, in the garden of Eden, where the love of GOD abounds, and all are safe and secure for evermore.

Grave Stone marker for lost crew and plane

GLOSSARY

Active sonobuoys—SSQ-15 or SSQ-47's are the active sonobuoys which give you active pinging for thirty minutes.

ADF—Automatic Direction Finding

Alfa Pattern—a 2000 yard circle with four active buoys.

Ambient Noise—the noise of the sea itself.

APA-69—Direction Finder Group which covers 50-10,750 megacycles in the SP-2E.

APN-70—Loran installed in the P-2 and in the follow on P-3.

APS-20—the SP-2E/H radar system.

APS-80—the P-3 radar which has two systems which provides 360 coverage.

APS 115—P3C has two advanced radar sets.

APS 122—Doppler system for the P-2 and the initial P-3.

APS 153—P-3A&B doppler systems.

APS 187—P3C doppler system.

ARR 72—Sonobuoy receiver system in the P-3.

ASA-13 & 47—the navigation computer system in the SP-2E, SP-2H, and the P-3A/B aircraft.

ASA 16 -Tactical Coordinator Display in the older aircraft and including the P-3 airplane.

ASA 64/71—mark and recognize sub signals in the P3C.

ASA 66—Pilots computerized display and a visual screen readout that assist's the P3C pilots.

ASA-70—the Tactical Coordinators multipurpose display and tray.

ASN-37—altitude heading reference system.

ASN-42—inertial system which provides all systems to operate in the P-3A/B systems.

ASN 84—two inertial systems provide computerized performance in the early P3C systems.

ASQ 114 or CP 901—the computer that runs the P3C.

ASW—antisubmarine warfare.

AVQ-2—SP-2E searchlight is a high intensity carbon arc device.

Baffles—the sonar-blind area to the rear of a ship or submarine.

Bathometer—monitors the BT sonobuoy and prints out the water temperatures to 1000 feet below the surface of the water.

B-5 Driftmeter—to determine the drift angle and ground speed in knots or in miles per hour.

Bermuda Current—a warm current which starts at the tip of Florida and runs all the way to Iceland.

Blades—blades form an arm of a propeller which equates noise and movement.

broadside—with one side forward/sideways or parallel to the sonobuoy.

BT sonobuoy—SSQ-36.

Bullpup—missile used against surface ships.

C-130 Lockheed Airplane—a four engine turboprop which is usually a cargo plane.

Cavitation—the formation of tiny air bubbles around rapidly revolving propeller blades when the depth is to shallow for speed. As these bubbles collapse, this makes the ship or sub easier to detect.

CODAR—Correlation, Detection, and Recording.

CODAR PLANT—a standard plant of 2 sonobuoys at a spacing of 350 feet.

COMARSURVRECFORCESIXTHFLT—Commander   Maritime Surveillance Reconnaissance Force, U.S. Sixth Fleet. (CTF-67)

Convergence Zone—30—35 nautical miles in temperate to tropical zones and 25—30 miles in cold latitudes.

CPA—closes' point of approach.

CW Homing System—in the SP-2E THE #1 Needle of The Bearing Distance Heading Indicator homes to a sonobuoy selected.

Data Link—provides computer to computer exchange of tactical data between aircraft and other units.

Deep Sound Channels—permit transmission of low frequency sound at a great distance.

DELTIC—Delayed Time Compression.

detection threshold—a ratio in decibel units of the signal power in the receiver bandwidths to the noise power, in a 1 Hertz band, required for detection at some preassigned level of correctness of the detection decision.

DIFAR—Directional Frequency, Analysis, and Recording.

DIFAR bearing—a true bearing from the sonobuoy to the contact.

ELINT—Intelligence collected by electronic means.

engine—a machine for converting energy into mechanical motion.

engine rpm—engine revolutions per minute.

ESM—Electronic Support Measures.

F-4—one of the finest attack-fighter aircraft that flew on the carriers of the U.S. Navy in 1965 circa.

FFAR—Folded-Fin Aerial Rocket

FLIR—Forward Looking Infra-red Radar

FRS—Fleet Replacement Squadron (VP-30)

Ground Approach Radar—pilots depend on radar to enable them to land when bad weather makes landings difficult.

HVAR—High Velocity Airborne Rocket

Intevalometer—stores and weapons may be dropped when this device is set with numbers and accurate spacing.

isothermal—water that is marked by equality of temperature.

JP-4—kerosene-like fluid which is used to fuel jet engines.

jet engines—Westinghouse turbojet on the SP-2E aircraft.

Julie—a charge is dropped on a Julie buoy, the charge ignites and a echo is measured on the Julie recorder. In other words, Julie means a passive buoy goes active!

Labrador Current—a cold body of water which is concentrated along the Newfoundland coast stretching to Greenland.

LAMPS—Light Airborne Multipurpose System (helicopter)

Lofar—Low Frequency and Recording

MAD—Magnetic Anomaly Detector

MC—Mission Commander

MF1—compass system

ML1—fluxgate magnetic compass

MK-44—early torpedo carried by the P-2 and P-3 aircraft

MK-46—lightweight ASW torpedo carried by P-3 Orions

MK-54—a depth bomb that was carried in World War II to counter the enemy submarine on the surface

Mobile Operation Control Van—a van which acts as a rapidly deployable operational control center.

NFO—Naval Flight Officer

Nimrod—a British antisubmarine warfare aircraft

Operational Controlled Brief—a brief for an ASW or surveillance mission

OTPI—On Top Position Indicator, as in selecting a channel on the indicator and the needle swings indicates "mark on top"

P-2—a early land-based maritime patrol and ASW aircraft, which became known as the SP-2E and SP-2H aircraft.

P-3 Orion—long-range land-based maritime patrol and ASW aircraft operated by the U. S. Navy

PRF—pulse repetion frequency

propeller—a device fitted with blades that is used to propel a motor-boat, a ship, submarine, or an airplane.

PT-396—a self-contained dead reckoning plotter installed on the navigators table in the

SP-2E/H and in the P-3A/B aircraft

rockets—2.75" folding fin or 5.0" rockets

RPM—revolutions per minute

snorkel—used by a conventional sub to draw air from the surface of the water while remaining submerged

SOFAR—sound fixing and ranging

sonobuoy—an air-dropped buoy which designed to detect submarines and transmit their data back to the aircraft source level—the intensity of the noise radiated to a distance by an underwater source

special weapons—refers to the B 57 weapon in the P-3 aircraft

SS—diesel-electric submarine

SSK—diesel-electric attack submarine

SSBN—nuclear powered ballistic missile submarine

SSN—nuclear powered attack submarine

SUS—sound underwater signal

Tacan Approach—using the approach headings and radials, follow the flight path to a successful Tacan landing .

target strength—refers to the echo returned by a underwater target

TSC—Tactical Support Center

Ultra High Frequency—UHF

velocity profile—the variation of sound velocity with depth or the velocity depth function

Very High Frequency—VHF

VOR/ ILS—VHF Omnidirectional Radio/ Instrument Landing System

VP—Patrol Squadron

VQ—Fleet Air Reconnaissance Squadron

REFERENCES

Enclopedia Americana 1991, Grolier Inc.,
    Internationational Headquarters, Danbury, CT
"Hughes to Produce FLIR Systems for Navy P-3 Aircraft,"
    Hughes Aircraft.
Jane Fighting Ships
Lockheed Aircraft since 1913, Lockheed Aeronautical Systems Co.,
    Marietta, GA.
Naval Air Training &Procedures Standardization
    (NAVAIR 01 SP-2E)
Naval Air Training & Procedures Standardization
    (NAVAIR 01 75PAA-1.1)
Naval Air Training & Procedures Standardization
    (NAVAIR 01 75PAC-1.1)
Pejepscot Historical Society, Brunswick, ME.
Principles of Underwater Sound for Engineers.
    Robert J. Urick, Urick, 1985.
"Silencing Undersea Sound Monitor Opposed,"
    Richmond Times-Dispatch, June 23, 1984.
The New Encyclopedia Americana, 1991 Grolier.
The New Encyclopedia Britannica, 1987, Robert P. Gwinn, Chicago.
The World Book Encyclopedia, 1966 Edition, Chicago.
World Air Power Journal, Lockheed Aeronautical Systems Company,
    Marietta, GA.